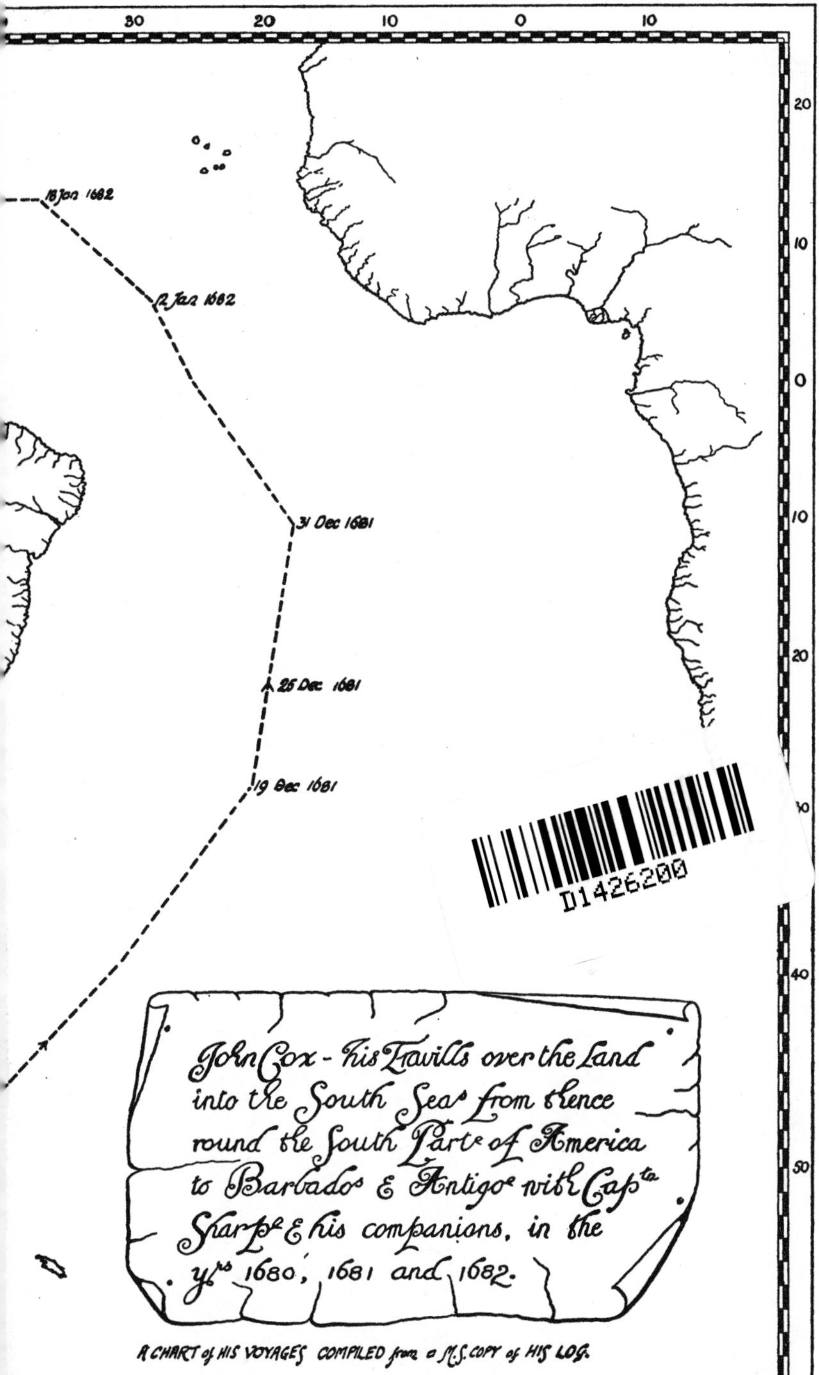

30
20
10
0
10
20
10
0
10
20
30
40
50
18 Jan 1682
12 Jan 1682
31 Dec 1681
25 Dec 1681
19 Dec 1681
John Cox - his Travills over the Land into the South Seas from thence round the South Parte of America to Barbados & Antigoe with Captn Sharpe & his companions, in the yrs 1680, 1681 and 1682.
A CHART of HIS VOYAGES COMPILED from a M.S. COPY of HIS LOG.

The History of
PIRACY

CAPTAIN AVERY AND HIS CREW TAKING ONE OF THE GREAT MOGUL'S SHIPS

The History of Piracy

PHILIP GOSSE

DOVER PUBLICATIONS, INC.
Mineola, New York

Bibliographical Note

This Dover edition, first published in 2007, is an unabridged republication of the work originally published in 1932 by Longmans, Green and Co., New York. The map entitled "John Cox—his Travels, etc.," has been moved from the endleaf to the frontleaf for this edition.

Library of Congress Cataloging-in-Publication Data

Gosse, Philip, 1879–1959.
The history of piracy / Philip Gosse.
p. cm.
Originally published: London ; New York : Longmans, Green, 1932.
ISBN-13: 978-0-486-46183-0
ISBN-10: 0-486-46183-1
1. Pirates. I. Title.

G535.G58 2007
910.4'5—dc22

2007008613

Manufactured in the United States of America
Dover Publications, Inc., 31 East 2nd Street, Mineola, N.Y. 11501

To

IRENE GOSSE

FOREWORD

To write a complete history of piracy from its earliest days would be an impossible undertaking. It would begin to resemble a maritime history of the world. What the following pages attempt to do is to show what conditions, geographical and social, preceded the rise of piracy, to trace its periodical rises and declines, its forms and fortunes, to depict the more outstanding members of the profession and finally to show how national organisation, backed by the steamship and the telegraph, brought it to an end.

The material required for such a record as that contained in this book compels the author to cast his net far and wide and in many of the by-waters of history and literature. There have been but two or three books written which have attempted to deal with the subject as a whole, and these contained many gaps which could only be filled by research into all sorts of unlikely sources. Who for example would have thought to find important pirate material in a life of St. Vincent de Paul, the "patron saint of practical philanthropists ?"

Even so it has been found impossible in certain periods to acquire that amount and quality of detail without which no book can be more than a synopsis, and it is for this reason that the chapter on Classical Piracy has, with some reluctance, been reduced to an appendix. The outline exists, the detail that gives life is unfortunately lost for ever.

One great difficulty which confronts the pirate historian is the diffidence shown by his heroes in recording their own deeds. The successful pirate, unlike the successful man in almost any other profession, did not crave notoriety, for obvious reasons, and it is doubtful whether even the most indefatigable of journalists, had they existed in their modern form, could have overcome this modesty. The pirate who escaped the gallows preferred retirement into obscurity with his fortune, and very few were ever induced, either by the need for money or the craving for renown, to write an autobiography.

Another difficulty has been to decide who was or was not a pirate. Usually this point is easily settled, but there are borderline cases which defy definition. Webster defines a pirate as "a robber on the high seas, one who by open violence takes the property of another on the high seas, especially one who makes it his business to cruise for robbery or plunder; a freebooter on the seas; also one who steals in a harbour." By this definition it is hard to determine for instance whether Francis Drake was a pirate or no. A sixteenth century Spaniard would have answered with a vigorous affirmative, and even the most patriotic Englishman must admit that the early voyages of the Elizabethan hero to America were simple piracy, though in most of his voyages Drake held openly or by implication a commission from the Crown. Yet so did other notorious seamen who called themselves privateers, even if their commission bore the seals of states which had not yet been born or which did not know of the holders' existence. In general privateers of this sort must be excluded from the strict category of pirates save when they exceeded the terms of their very liberal commissions.

It is impossible to acknowledge all of the help and suggestions I have received in the writing of this book. My thanks are due to Mr. Oskar Lundberg of Upsala who brought to my notice several Norse pirates; to Mr. L. C. Vrijman of The Hague, a profound student of the subject, who allowed me full use of much material relating to the Dutch pirates and buccaneers which was new to me; to Mr. Basil Lubbock for permission to reprint parts of the hitherto unpublished Journal of Edward Barlow describing the activities of Captain Kidd in the Red Sea and Indian Ocean; and to Commander John Creswell, R.N., for the labour he took in tracking out the "Voyage of Captain Bartholomew Sharp in the Pacific" from the original journal of Captain John Cox, one of Sharp's companions — this is the first reliable map showing the wanderings of the buccaneers on what is perhaps the most exciting of all such voyages.

I wish also to thank Mr. G. E. Manwaring and other members of the staff of the London Library who have rendered me invaluable help; Miss Olivia Hawkshaw for translating several Norwegian and Swedish books; Mr. Frank Maggs for his untiring search for rare or out-of-the-way books and manuscripts concerned with piracy; the editor of *The Times* for permission to reprint certain valuable extracts; and Messrs. Dulau & Company for permission to use material out of "The Pirates' Who's Who."

Last but far from least I must acknowledge my great indebtedness to Mr. Milton Waldman for reading the manuscript and making many valuable suggestions and corrections.

P. G.

CONTENTS

Book I: The Barbary Corsairs

Book II: The Pirates of the North

Book III: The Pirates of the West

Book IV: The Pirates of the East

Epilogue

LIST OF ILLUSTRATIONS

MAPS

The History of PIRACY

THE HISTORY OF PIRACY

BOOK I

THE BARBARY CORSAIRS

CHAPTER I

PIRATES IN GENERAL

PIRACY, like murder, is one of the earliest of recorded human activities. The references to it coincide with the earliest references to travel and trade; it may be assumed that very shortly after men began the transport of goods from one point to another various enterprising individuals arose who saw profit in intercepting these goods on the way.

Trade follows the flag, and robbery whether by land or sea follows trade. "As surely as spiders abound where there are nooks and crannies," wrote Captain the Hon. Henry Keppel, the great hunter of Oriental pirates in the nineteenth century, "so have pirates sprung up wherever there is a nest of islands offering creeks and shallows, headlands, rocks and reefs — facilities in short for lurking, for surprise, for attack, for escape."

In all the seas of the world and in all times piracy has passed through certain well-defined cycles. First a few individuals from amongst the inhabitants of the poorer coastal lands would band together in isolated groups owning one or but a very few vessels apiece and attack only the weakest of merchantmen. They possessed the status of outlaws whom every law abiding man was willing and eager to kill at sight. Next would come the period of organisation, when the big pirates either swallowed up the little pirates or drove them out of business. These great organisations moved on such a scale that no group of trading ships, even the most heavily armed, was safe from their attack. Of this sort was the era of the Barbary corsairs, of Morgan and his buccaneers, of the wild West Country seamen early in Elizabeth's reign — pirates against whom competition was hopeless and authority powerless.

Then came the stage when the pirate organisation, having virtually reached the status of an independent state, was in a position to make a mutually useful alliance with another state against its enemies. What had been piracy then for a time became war, and in that war the vessels of both sides were pirates to the other and subject to the same treatment. In these times rose such men as the terrible Kheyr-ed-din, better known as Barbarossa, who carried the Crescent into the strongest ports of the Mediterranean and counted a victory over the Imperial fleet of Spain as all in the day's work; the sailor geniuses of Cornwall and Devon who, during one short and dazzling era, wrote the annals of piracy in poetry instead of prose; and Lemarck's Sea Beggars and Condé's Rochellois, who made war on Church and State in the name of liberty and the Reformation.

In the end the victory of one side would as a rule break up the naval organisation of the other, as Don John of Austria raked and burned the fleets of Islam in the narrows of Lepanto. The component parts of the defeated side would be again reduced to the position of outlaw bands, until the victorious power was strong enough to send them scurrying back once more to the status of furtive footpads of the sea whence they had arisen.

Piracy at its greatest moments becomes a major part of history itself but even in its lesser phases there is a fascination that is peculiarly its own, apart even from the spell that crime can exercise on the imagination. For it is crime of a very special sort, demanding of its followers much more than boldness, cunning or skill in the use of arms.

The master pirate had to be able to handle his ship (in the beginning often an unseaworthy one until he could steal a better) in tempests and in fights, make his way disabled to sheltering harbours, control his unruly ruffians through disease and discontent, employ the arts of the diplomat to provide himself with a safe market on shore for his stolen wares. Men like these are rare, and few of the respectable professions can show more masterful personalities than those to be met at the top of the pirate tree. Apart even from the semi-legal adventurers like Drake, Morgan and Barbarossa the pirates' Hall of Fame contains many a remarkable hero who in life was quite properly regarded as a criminal beyond hope of salvation.

They were a queer lot — in their oddities perhaps even more than in their abilities lies the secret of their fascination. As far as salvation goes it is astounding to find how many of them carried through their most desperate acts in the belief that they were laying by a credit for the after life. It was regard for his soul that inspired Captain Roberts, who always wore in action "a rich damask waistcoat and breeches, a gold chain round his neck with a large diamond cross dangling from it," to enforce a strict temperance on board his ship and a due respect for the sanctity of womanhood. It was this same concern for his soul that urged Captain Daniel to steal a priest for the celebration of Mass on board his vessel and to shoot one of the crew for making an obscene remark in the course of it. And probably no more fervent Utopian has ever existed than Captain Misson, who founded, fifty years before the French Revolution, amidst torrents of exalted oratory, a pirate republic dedicated to Liberty, Equality and Fraternity. The captive whose conscience refused to allow his escape from the owner to whom he had been sold because it would be cheating a man who had paid good money for him, the Quaker shipmaster who declined to use force against the Barbary corsairs and in the end prevailed against them nevertheless, are perhaps nearer in spirit to such pirates than were Blackbeard and Kidd.

The history of piracy is therefore not a mere grim chronicle of the triumph of law; it is more than a series of romantic yarns about gold, fighting and adventure. It has its amusing side as well, strange lore, ludicrous happenings, the bizarre in human nature. We follow Captain Bartholomew Sharp in the most amazing of all pirate voyages and listen to one of his captives, a Spanish gentleman, whiling away the monotony of the quarter deck with stories of how a priest went ashore in Peru while ten thousand Indians stood gazing at him, and before them all laid his Cross gently on the backs of two roaring lions who "instantly fell down and worshipped it," whereupon two tigers followed them and did the same. We share the terrors of Ludolph of Cucham, who in 1350 wrote a catalogue of the dangers which might be experienced at sea from "sea monsters" and especially the sea swine, an animal which will rise up near the ship and beg—"if the sailors give it bread it departs but if it will not depart it may be terrified and put to flight by the sight of a man's angry and terrible face." If the sailor is frightened he must not show it: "he must look at it boldly and severely and must not let it see he is afraid, otherwise it will not depart but will bite and tear his ship." And though one must be distressed at the stories of Christian sufferings in captivity, one can also delight in the opportunity which the experience gave good St. Vincent de Paul of studying the alchemy which stood him in such good stead afterwards, and sympathise with the complaint of "Sir" Jeffery Hudson, Charles I's pugnacious dwarf, that hard labour in captivity had increased his height from one foot six to three foot six.

Nor is there humour lacking in a notable pirate kidnapping which occurred in the Ægean Sea in 78 B.C., an event which, had it turned out a trifle differently, might have changed the whole history of the world.

In that year a certain young Roman gentleman of exalted family connections, having been banished from Italy by the dictator Sulla because of his adherence to the dictator's exiled rival Marius, was travelling by sea to Rhodes. Being a young man full of ambition and having nothing else to do while Rome was forbidden him, he had decided to improve his time by perfecting himself in an art in which his masters had told him he was deficient: elocution. To this end he had entered himself at the school of Apollonius Molo, the famous teacher of oratory.

While the ship was sailing past the island of Pharmacusa, off the rocky coast of Caria, several long low craft were suddenly seen coming out towards her. The merchantman was a slow sailor and with the breeze dropping any hope of escape from the pirate boats, propelled by the long sweeps and strong arms of slaves, was out of the question. Dropping her little auxiliary sail she waited for the sharp-beaked craft to slip alongside and in a short while her decks were crowded with swarthy ruffians.

Looking round at the groups of frightened passengers the pirate chief was at once struck by a young aristocrat, exquisitely dressed in the latest fashion of Rome, who sat reading, surrounded by his attendants and slaves. Striding up to him the pirate demanded who he might be, but the young man, after one disdainful glance, turned back to his book. The infuriated pirate then turned to one of the young man's companions, his physician Cinna, who informed him of the captive's name, which was Caius Julius Cæsar.

The question of ransom was at once opened. The pirate wanted to know how much Cæsar was willing to pay to gain his own freedom and that of his servants. As the Roman did not even take the trouble to answer, the captain turned to his second-in-command and asked him what he considered the party worth. This expert looked them over and gave it as his opinion that ten talents would be a reasonable sum.

The captain, irritated at the young aristocrat's superior airs, snapped, "Then I'll double it ! — twenty talents is my price."

At this Cæsar spoke for the first time. With a lift of his eyebrows he remarked, "Twenty ? If you knew your business you'd realize I'm worth at least fifty."

The pirate chief was staggered. It was something quite out of his experience to find a prisoner who considered himself so important that he would volunteer to pay nearly twelve thousand instead of three thousand pounds in ransom. However he took the extraordinary young exquisite at his word and bundled him off into the boats with the other captives, to wait in the pirates' stronghold for the return of the messengers sent to collect the ransom.

Cæsar and his party were installed in some huts in a village occupied by the pirates. The young Roman occupied himself principally with daily physical exercise, running, jumping and throwing large stones, at times in competition with his captors. In his less strenuous hours he wrote poems or composed orations. In the evenings he would often join the pirates round their fire and experiment on them with his verses or his oratory. It is recorded that the pirates entertained an extremely low opinion of these compositions and said so with indelicate candour — either their taste in such matters was low or else Cæsar's verse, now lost, did not attain the literary standard of his maturer prose.

It was a strange life for the spoiled dandy whom Sulla had described as "the boy in petticoats." He sounds like a character in an Oscar Wilde essay who very successfully rose to the demands of life amongst Albanian brigands. All the witnesses agree that under his precious affectations he was utterly fearless. Not only, like a true Roman patrician, did he despise his captors for their uncouth manners and want of education but bluntly charged them with these deficiencies to their faces. And he thoroughly enjoyed himself in telling them what would happen to the whole gang if they ever fell into his hands in the future, solemnly promising that he would crucify the lot. The pirates, more amused at his effeminacy than angry at his threats, held him in a kind of condescending respect and thought the promise of a general crucifixion an excellent joke. Once at night when, according to their custom, they were sitting round their fire far into the night, drinking and indulging in various unmusical noises, their perplexing captive sent a servant in to the captain to desire him to keep his men quiet as they disturbed his sleep. The request was honoured: the chief told his crew to pipe down.

At last after thirty-eight days the messengers returned to say that the ransom of fifty talents had been deposited with the legate Valerius Torquatus, and Cæsar with his companions were put on board a ship and sent to Miletus. It had taken an unexpectedly long time to collect so large a sum of money, because after Sulla had banished Cæsar he had confiscated all his property and that of his wife Cornelia. In the circumstances it might have been better for the young man to have diminished his self importance somewhat.

On his arrival at Miletus the ransom was paid over to the

pirates, who at once departed, and Cæsar went on shore to carry out the plan he had determined upon. From Valerius he borrowed four war galleys and five hundred soldiers, and at once set out for Pharmacusa. Arriving there late the same evening he found the whole pirate crew, as he had expected, celebrating their luck in an orgy of eating and drinking. Taken completely by surprise they were unable to resist and surrendered, only a few managing to escape. Cæsar captured some three hundred and fifty of them and had the satisfaction of getting back his fifty talents intact. Putting his late hosts on board his galleys, he had all the pirate ships sunk in deep water and then set sail for Pergamum, where Junius, the Prætor of the province of Asia Minor, had his headquarters.

Arrived at Pergamum Cæsar clapped his prisoners into a well-guarded fortress and went to interview the Prætor. He found that official, who was the only authority with power to inflict capital punishment, away on duty. Following and overtaking him Cæsar explained briefly to the Prætor what had happened; he had in safe custody at Pergamum the whole pirate gang with their booty, and asked for a letter to be given him authorising the deputy governor at Pergamum to execute the pirates or at least their chiefs.

But Junius did not take kindly to the idea. He disliked this imperative young man who rushed in to upset so unexpectedly the tranquillity of the prætorian round and took it so easily for granted that he had but to order and the Governor-General of all Asia Minor would instantly obey. There were other considerations as well. The system whereby his merchants paid tribute to the pirates for immunity had the sanctity of an old custom which worked, on the whole, not too badly. If Junius did as Cæsar wanted, the pirates' successors, being strangers, would most likely prove even more extortionate than Cæsar's captives. It was, in addition, an understood thing that officials like the Prætor, stationed far from Rome on the outposts of the Empire, were there not only to serve the state but to turn a profitable penny against the day when they should retire to civil life at home. The pirate gang was rich and might reasonably be expected to make a proper acknowledgment to the Governor if he exercised his prerogative of clemency and turned them loose.

However it would have taken too long a time to explain these complicated affairs of state to a young man, one for whom, moreover, Junius entertained such a strong dislike that amiable conversation was difficult. He promised Cæsar to go into the whole matter after his return to Pergamum and later inform him of his decision.

Cæsar quite understood. He bowed himself out of the Prætor's presence and by forced rides achieved the return journey to Pergamum in a day. Without more ado, on his own authority (probably the new situation in Rome was unknown to the provincials) he ordered the pirates to be executed in the prison, reserving the thirty principals for the fate he had promised them. When they were led before him in irons he reminded them of that promise, but added that out of gratitude for the friendliness they had shown him he would grant them a last favour: before being crucified each of them should have his throat cut first.

Thereupon Cæsar resumed his journey to Rhodes and in due time enrolled himself in Apollonius Molo's excellent school of oratory.

Of course it would be absurd to pretend that all pirates were either heroic or good humoured, or that their practical extinction has not been to the benefit of mankind. Their virtues are more easily appreciated when they are dead than while they are alive, and most of them, all but the greatest, were small blackguards who preferred attacking women to men and cheating to fighting. Sixteen hundred years after Cæsar's ransom, another illustrious captive who fell into their hands received such brutal treatment that the world was nearly robbed of one of its greatest literary geniuses, Miguel de Cervantes. Countless thousands of other less conspicuous folk were sent to rot in the galleys, or had their throats cut for a few sheep or a few pence. But pirates were men after all (though, as will appear, they were sometimes women) and like men in general exhibit an infinite variety of what we call human nature. The history of pirates may be a history of bad men, but it is a history of men nevertheless.

CHAPTER II

THE BARBAROSSAS

The first great era of modern piracy originated at some vague time in the Middle Ages, reached its climax in the sixteenth and seventeenth centuries and was only effectively halted by concerted international effort about a hundred years ago. Its centre was the Western Mediterranean, its agents the inhabitants of the Barbary coast, which extended from the frontiers of Egypt to the Pillars of Hercules. The name "Barbary" was derived from the tribal name of Berbers.

The practice of piracy dwindled after the fall of Rome and became a comparatively unimportant factor in the life of the Mediterranean peoples for the fundamental reason that during nearly a thousand years there was very little maritime trade to prey upon. Presently, when the Crusades, followed by Venetian and Genoese enterprise, began to revive the ancient glories of the Eastern commerce, the familiar temptation was renewed, and dusky men in turbans and long robes flitted in oared boats from coast to island in the path of the gorgeous high-decked galleys of the princely Italian cities. The threat of the outlaws was not yet very formidable: no great power had yet risen to protect them, and the combined vigilance of the Mediterranean states was for several centuries able to keep them in check. If it had been otherwise one wonders how long the Renaissance would have been postponed, or even whether it would have flowered at all. The Turks had not yet taken Constantinople and spread their dominion over North Africa. Venice, Genoa, France and Moorish Spain were strong enough in conjunction with the Knights Hospitallers of St. John of Jerusalem, heirs of the Crusades and hereditary enemies of Mahomet, to protect their ships against the isolated bands of the "skimmers of the sea."

The most determined of the early efforts to suppress the Barbary corsairs occurred in 1390 when the Genoese, aroused by a sequence of losses at sea, raised "a great number of lords, knights and gentlemen of France and England" and set out to attack them in their lair at Metredia on the Tunisian coast.

The English contingent was commanded by Henry of Lancaster, afterwards King Henry IV. The brunt of the landing was borne by his longbowmen, whose vigorous fire, as at Crécy and Poitiers, broke the enemy's resistance along the shore and drove him into his fortress. The invaders then settled down to carry out one of the long and tedious sieges which are characteristic of mediæval warfare. The Christian forces, lacking in efficient artillery and inadequate in number for an assault, sat down to wait outside the city. But disease wasted them even more quickly than hunger decimated the defenders; after two months a peace was patched up and the Europeans sailed for home. Though the pirates had not been exterminated they were for some time, as usual after these punitive expeditions, intimidated into more restrained operations.

But in 1492, that year of years in modern history, the situation changed abruptly. Spain under Ferdinand and Isabella wrested control of the Iberian Peninsula from the Moors and sent them scurrying back across the Straits of Gibralter after over seven hundred years of residence in Europe. The effect on the social and political life of North Africa was of course instant and profound. Into a country barely able to support a few poor tradesmen, farmers and merchants, were suddenly thrown several hundred thousand proud, civilised and warlike people with no available employment, a large measure of ambition and a passionate itch for revenge.

It was revenge for their wrongs at least as much as the desire to compensate themselves for their lost property that incited the Moors into an unrelenting hostility against Spain which ultimately became part of a Holy War between their co-religionists and Western Christendom. At the very beginning the exiles possessed certain advantages in their raids on the rapidly expanding commerce of the infant Spanish Empire. They knew the language, they were familiar with Spanish trading habits, they possessed unlimited sources of information in the persons of their compatriots left behind in Spain. Instead of an ally of the powers policing the Mediterranean they were now an enemy, and the federation was by that much weakened while the enemy became at a stroke immeasurably stronger.

At the date of their expulsion the sea was an unfamiliar medium to the Moslems, and navigation an art they had yet to learn. A large proportion of them felt a superstitious horror of deep water, much in the manner of most of the ancient Greeks. There is a story that after the conquest of Egypt by the Arabs, the great Caliph Omar wrote to his general in command to ask what the sea, of which he had heard so much, was like. The military man in reply described it as "a huge beast which silly folk ride like worms on logs." The Caliph thereupon at once issued a general order that no Moslem should venture a voyage on this dangerous element without express permission.

The whole character of Mediterranean piracy changed almost in a night after the expulsion. The new race of corsairs built bigger and faster vessels, supplementing oar with sail. They developed the organisation aboard ship, augmenting the captives available for the galleys with the fruits of raids on their neighbours in the interior, and putting only trained fighting men into the boarding parties. Appreciating the fact that piracy was a branch of business as well as of navigation they perfected a comprehensive system whereby, through payment of percentages (usually ten per cent of the booty) to the native rulers along the coast, they ensured protection for themselves and an outlet for their captures: the sheik, in consideration of his interest, undertook to protect his associates from their enemies and to provide an open market for their wares at the termination of each voyage.

In 1504 occurred the first raid on the grand scale under the new dispensation, one that stirred Christendom into almost as deep an alarm as the advance of the Turk up the valley of the Danube.

Pope Julius II had despatched two of his biggest war galleys,

A FIGHT BETWEEN TUSCAN GALLEYS AND BARBARY CORSAIRS

heavily armed, to carry a consignment of valuables from Genoa to Civita Vecchia. The leading vessel, several miles ahead and out of sight of the other, was passing the island of Elba when she sighted a galliot, but suspecting nothing continued slowly and steadily on her course. The captain, Paolo Victor, had in fact no reason to anticipate the presence of pirates in his vicinity. The Barbary corsairs had not appeared in these waters for many years and in any event were accustomed to attack only smaller vessels. But suddenly the galliot drew alongside and the Italian saw that her deck was a mass of moving turbans. Without a hail, even before the galley had time to stand to, a shower of arrows and shot was poured on to her crowded decks and a moment later the Moors were swarming over her sides, led by a thickset figure with a fiery beard. In a few moments the great galley was a prisoner and the surviving members of the crew were being pushed and prodded like cattle into the hold.

The red-bearded captain then put into execution the second part of his programme, which was no less than the seizure of the second Papal galley. Some of his officers objected to the second venture, as too dangerous in the circumstances: the task of holding the prize already won seemed sufficient without attempting another. Their chief silenced them with an imperious gesture; he had already devised a plan whereby the first victory was to serve the second. He ordered the prisoners to be stripped of their clothes, which were then assumed by his own men, whom he distributed in conspicuous positions on board the galley, taking in tow his own galliot to make it appear to the newcomers as if the Papal ship had taken a prize.

The simple ruse was effective. The two vessels drew together, the crew of the second crowded to the side to find out what had been going on; another hail of arrows and shot, a boarding party, and in a few minutes the Christian sailors were chained to the oars of their own ship in place of the released Moorish slaves. Within two hours of the original encounter the galliot and her victims were headed for Tunis.

This was the first appearance of Arouj, the earlier of the two brothers Barbarossa, on a stage where he and his family were to be the most distinguished actors for a long generation. He was the son of a Greek Christian potter by the name of Jacob who had settled in Mitylene after its conquest by the Turk. While still a youth Arouj had voluntarily turned Mohammedan, enlisted on board a Turkish pirate vessel and soon obtained command in the Ægean. In person "he was not very tall of stature but extremely well set and robust. His hair and beard were perfectly red; his eyes sparkling and live, his nose aquiline or Roman and his complexion between brown and fair."

It was not, however, as a Turkish vassal that Arouj turned up so unexpectedly in the Western Mediterranean, but as an independent rover. Barely had he been let loose in the Ægean when he persuaded his crew to repudiate their allegiance to the Grand Porte and join him in a career which would enable them to dispense with both vexatious authority and profit-grabbing capitalists in Constantinople.

However some sort of backing was necessary, a port in a storm and an accessible market, if not capital. Arouj sailed for Tunis and concluded a suitable arrangement with the local Bey, who undertook to supply these requirements in return for twenty per cent of the plunder, later reduced to ten after the freebooters were strong enough to dictate their own terms.

Arouj's sensational exploits, culminating in the capture of the Papal galleys, attracted to him all the adventurers of the southern and eastern shores of the Mediterranean as well as a large number of renegades from the different countries. His appeal was as strong as that of Drake to the youth of Devon and Cornwall in the second half of the same century. Imitators also sprang up and soon the Mediterranean was infested from end to end with companies of freebooters from the Barbary ports. The insurance rates became prohibitive and business in certain lines was all but strangled. Ferdinand of Spain, now the acknowledged leader of Christendom and, as head of the greatest maritime power in the world, the worst sufferer, shouldered the responsibility of repressing the former masters and present enemies of Spain. At the head of a strong fleet he blockaded the coast and within two years, 1509–1510, reduced Oran, Bougie and Algiers, at that time the three principal strongholds of the corsairs. On the conclusion of peace the Algerians undertook to pay the Catholic King a yearly tribute as an earnest of future good behaviour, a guarantee which Ferdinand reinforced with a powerful fortress he constructed on the island of Peñon opposite their harbour.

While Ferdinand lived the pirates were held in some sort of check, and two attempts to retake Bougie, in 1512 and 1515, were beaten off; in the former action Arouj lost an arm, shattered by a shot from an arquebus. But after the death of the Spanish king in 1516, the Algerians revolted and invited Salim-ed-Teumi, an Arab from Blidah, to become their ruler. Salim accepted and shortly afterwards instituted a blockade of the fort of Peñon.

Finding his own resources insufficient Salim sent an embassy to Arouj, who had two years before taken Jijil from the Genoese, to come to his assistance. Arouj accepted and at once marched to Algiers at the head of five thousand men, while his brother, the terrible Kheyr-ed-din, who was soon to succeed and surpass him, followed with the fleet. On his arrival Arouj, perhaps impressed with the difficulties of a divided sovereignty, strangled Salim with his own hands and became master of the place, nominally as the vassal of the Sultan of Turkey.

The tiny Spanish garrison at Peñon still held on and against it the pirate chief could make no headway. On the other hand Spain could not manage to relieve it. An armada sent in 1517 by the Regent, Cardinal Ximenes, under the command of Don Diego de Vera, was defeated, seven thousand Spanish veterans being routed by the Moors, and the fleet wrecked by a storm. It was not until 1529 that the fortress fell.

Meantime Arouj Barbarossa was consolidating his position. Shortly all of what is now Algeria was included in his kingdom and he began to overflow into the neighbouring provinces of Tunis and Tilimsan. The Algerians soon found his rule even stricter than his predecessor's and in 1518 again revolted, calling in the Spaniards to help them. The Emperor Charles V, alarmed at the growing power of the corsair chief, was only too willing and sent a force of ten thousand picked veterans to overwhelm him. Arouj was surprised at Tilimsan while at the head of a force numbering only fifteen hundred. Seizing his treasure he made a bolt for Algiers, the Spaniards, under the Marquis of Comares, Governor of Oran, in close pursuit. The chase grew too hot — Arouj, hoping to distract his enemy, scattered gold and jewels behind him, like Atalanta's suitor, in the hope of causing a distraction. The implacable Spaniard looked and pushed on, catching the Moslems as they were crossing the Rio Salado. Arouj himself got safely across, but seeing that his rearguard was caught, without hesitation recrossed the river and threw himself into the fight. Practically the whole of the fleeing army was killed and with it the one-armed commander with the fiery red beard.

It is as rare for genius to repeat itself in pirate families as in those devoted to the more sedentary arts. Arouj was a genius in his line, the first of a mighty Islamic breed. But his younger brother, baptised Khizr, known to Mohammedans as Kheyr-ed-din, and to Christians after his brother's death as Barbarossa also, was an even greater than he. With Arouj's daring and warlike ability he combined a statesmanlike prudence which raised him beyond the rank of bandit chief to the highest posts in Islam.

It may be interpolated here that the repetition of Mohammedan names is unavoidable. The reason for the repeated use of Barbarossa is obvious. But often a man is known by no other name than his familiar title. Thus all the corsair chiefs were termed *Reis,* which means merely captain; no less than three outstanding figures during the following century bore the name of Murad; hence Murad Reis is as likely to appear in the annals of the Barbary pirates as Captain Jones in the roster of the Royal Navy.

In appearance Kheyr-ed-din was even more striking than his brother. "His stature was advantageous, his Mien portly and majestick; well proportioned and robust; very hairy with a beard extremely Bushy; his Brows and Eyelashes remarkably long and thick; before his Hair turned grey and hoary it was a bright Auburn. . ."

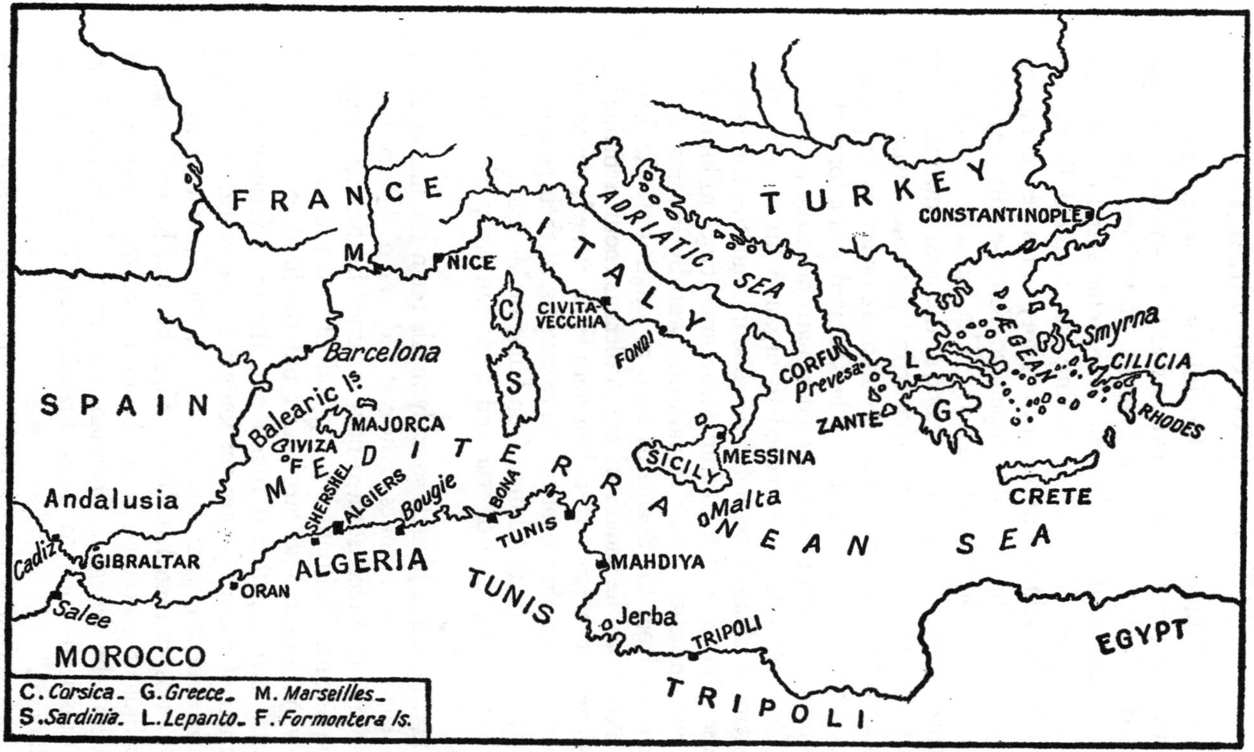

MEDITERRANEAN SEA—ANCIENT PIRACY AND BARBARY CORSAIRS

Kheyr-ed-din's first step after inheriting his brother's name and estates was to send an embassy to Constantinople to make formal offer to the Grand Seignior of his new province of Algiers and to declare himself the humble vassal of the Ottoman Empire. The Sultan, having just acquired Egypt, was delighted to add this important territory to his new dominion, and in accepting the offer appointed Kheyr-ed-din Beglerbeg or Governor-General of Algiers. The harassed corsair thus secured himself the support of one of the most powerful rulers on earth, while retaining sufficient independence owing to his distance from Constantinople to do more or less as he pleased. The first substantial advantage he acquired was a force of two thousand janissaries from the bodyguard of his new suzerain.

The new viceroy proceeded to organise his territory by a system of alliances with his neighbours and the conquest of those who were of most immediate importance to him. One by one the coast towns so painfully won by Ferdinand were retrieved from the Spaniards until at length only the fortress of Peñon, at the mouth of the Algiers harbour, remained in his enemies' hands. In the meantime he routed one Spanish force after another, bent on the reconquest of their possessions, in 1519 driving off Admiral Don Hugo de Moncada, who with a fleet of fifty men of war and a veteran army had tried to take Algiers.

Having made himself so early in his reign the master of all the coast for many miles to the east and west of Algiers, Kheyr-ed-din with a reconstituted navy resumed his brother's aggression against Christian shipping and Christian towns. He was now no longer a solitary leader but the head of a group of fleets, having gathered round him the most formidable collection of master pirates yet known in the world: Dragut, a Mohammedan from Rhodes; Sinan, the "Jew of Smyrna," who was suspected of black magic because he could take a reading of a position at sea by means of the crossbow; and Aydin, the renegade Christian, known to the Spaniards as "Drub-devil" but to both French and Turks as "Drub-Spaniard."

Each spring as the weather became settled these gentlemen

set out from Algiers and swarmed over the western Mediterranean, their favourite hunting grounds being the fairways off the coast of Spain and the Balearic Islands, although occasionally they would even venture through the Straits of Gibralter to intercept a Spanish treasure ship returning from the Americas to Cadiz.

The practice became so settled that it grew monotonous unless varied by some particularly spectacular raid or even more spectacular collision with an avenging Spanish flotilla. In 1529 Drub-devil started out on one of the routine expeditions to the Balearic Islands. After the usual captures, including several ships and a host of slaves, news reached him that at Oliva, a small port on the Valencia coast, there were many "Moriscos," Moorish slaves who were willing to pay handsomely for an opportunity of escape from Spain.

Arriving off Oliva that night Drub-devil embarked two hundred families of Moriscos and sailed away to the island of Formentara. Scarcely had the corsair disappeared when General Portundo, with eight Spanish galleys, appeared off the coast, heard the news and started off in pursuit in the direction of the Balearics. Drub-devil, finding his ships unworkable by reason of the crowd of refugees on board, landed them on Formentara and prepared for the unequal contest.

The Spanish ships drew close, but to the amazement of the Algerians passed by without firing a shot. The Spanish commander had paused to negotiate for a reward of ten thousand ducats from the owners of the Moriscos if he returned them intact, and was afraid of drowning them if he launched a broadside of his heavy artillery against their present custodians. The corsairs, construing his hesitation as cowardice, thereupon took the offensive and "rowing with the utmost fury they swooped upon them like eagles and had surrounded the eight galleys before the amazed Spaniards knew what they were about." In a short time General Portundo was dead, seven galleys had surrendered and the other was scurrying for safety to Iviza, a few miles away.

The corsairs then reembarked the two hundred families, who had been anxiously watching the battle from the shore, and after freeing several hundred Mussulman slaves from the rowing benches of the captured galleys and replacing them with the crews, rowed back to a triumphant reception in Algiers.

In the same year Kheyr-ed-din finally reduced the troublesome fortress on the island of Peñon. Time and again the Algerian ruler had flung his growing resources against this stronghold without success. Its possession was almost vital: owing to its situation no ship could enter or leave the harbour without permission of the Spaniards; consequently, all the corsair ships had to be beached outside, an undertaking involving great difficulty.

The attack this time was launched with unprecedented violence and determination. After a heavy bombardment which continued uninterrupted for sixteen days and nights, a storming party of twelve hundred advanced and overwhelmed the remnant of the defenders, all of whom were compelled to surrender. The courageous governor of the castle, Don Martin de Vargas, was, in spite of his wounds, bastinadoed to death in the presence of the arch-pirate. The latter then had the fort razed and began the construction of the great mole which still shelters the harbour of Algiers, an enormous task which took the toil of thousands of Christian slaves two years to finish.

The disaster for Spain was not yet complete. Fourteen days after the fall of Peñon nine transports loaded with troops and ammunition for the reinforcement of the garrison appeared. Dumbfounded by the disappearance of the fort the squadron was cautiously reconnoitring when out darted the pirates in their long-oared galliots and seized the whole convoy, out of which they obtained twenty-seven hundred prisoners and great stores of ammunition, guns and provisions.

Barbarossa himself, though ordinarily at the centre of his great and growing web, occasionally took to sea. In 1534, having constructed a fleet of sixty-one galleys after his own design, he sallied forth to attack Christianity in its very centre. Sailing direct through the Straits of Messina he appeared before Reggio ere the inhabitants were aware of his presence and carried away all the ships in the harbour as well as hundreds

ESCAPE OF THE LOVELY LADY JULIA DE GONZAGA

of Christian slaves. The very next day he stormed and destroyed the castle of St. Lucida, taking eight hundred prisoners, and then cruised north, plundering and raiding indiscriminately.

Stories that he heard on his progress of the lovely Julia Gonzaga, Duchess of Trajetto and Countess of Fondi, next tempted him to an exploit of a somewhat different character. The young widow was the most famous beauty in Italy; no fewer than two hundred and eight Italian poets had written verses in her honour and the device emblazoned on her shield was the Flower of Love. It occurred to the corsair that she would make an excellent token of his devotion to his new lord, Suleyman the Magnificent.

The lady was at Fondi. Thither the pirate travelled, swiftly and by night. But the fame of his presence preceded him and the lady had just time to leap from her bed and gallop off on horseback dressed in the flimsiest of night garments and accompanied by one male attendant. She managed to escape, and afterwards condemned the attendant to death because, she alleged, he had been unduly familiar during that desperate nocturnal ride. Kheyr-ed-din, annoyed at the escape of his sultan's fair prize, gave over the town of Fondi to a terrible four hours' punishment at the hands of his men.

The real object of his cruise had not yet been disclosed. While the courts of Europe continued to hear of his plunderings and burnings along both shores of Italy and of the great shiploads of spoils he was despatching regularly to Constantinople, he suddenly turned south, dashed swiftly across the Mediterranean, entered the harbour of Tunis, bombarded the city and in a single day captured it. Hassan the Sultan, Spain's protégé, fled, and with him departed the balance of power from the inland ocean. Not only was Spain's foothold in North Africa nearly broken, but her tenure of Sicily threatened by the isolation of the island from both east and west.

This was not to be endured. Charles V promptly assembled a huge fleet, numbering more than six hundred vessels, at Barcelona under the command of Andrea Doria, greatest of all Spanish admirals though by birth a Genoese. In May 1535 the fleet departed for Tunis. The army on board consisted of Italians and Germans as well as Spaniards; on the way the expedition was joined by a squadron of "the Religion," Knights of the Order of St. John, from Malta. Like most of these voyages of chastisement the racial composition of the forces resembled the musters of the Crusades.

After a short intensive bombardment a breach was made in the walls of the Goletta, the fortress guarding the entrance to the harbour of Tunis, and the Chevalier Cossier led the Knights of St. John through the breach and planted the banner of the Order within the fortress. After fierce hand to hand fighting, during which Sinan the Jew led three desperate counter attacks, the Moors were at last driven out.

Barbarossa placed himself at the head of an army of ten thousand and advanced to meet the Christian army in its march on the city. But his troops broke and ran, and Kheyr-ed-din with his two generals Sinan and Drub-devil fled to Bona, a port some miles away, where the corsair commander had with his usual foresight stationed his fleet.

In the meantime thousands of Christian slaves broke out of the citadel and joined their rescuers in sacking and plundering the city. For three days the Emperor gave the town over to a carnival of murder and looting, until finally the Christian soldiers and the Christian slaves turned on one another and fought over the spoils. Even the Catholic chroniclers speak with shame of the affair, for the victims were not pirates in any sense but the innocent inhabitants of Tunis, who a year before had been the friends of Spain and accepted Kheyr-ed-din's authority under compulsion.

The Emperor then made a treaty with the deposed Sultan, whereby he continued to hold the Goletta and to receive an annual tribute, with the promise that all piracy should cease. By August Charles had left Tunis, assigning to Doria the task of catching Kheyr-ed-din dead or alive. The Emperor returned home the hero of Europe, the crusader and knight errant who had vanquished the scourge of Christendom; and countless presses and studios worked overtime to immortalize him and his exploit.

But even while the poets sang and the painters painted, Barbarossa was on his way again. On his arrival at Bona he had at once collected his twenty-seven galliots and as soon as they were ready stood out for Minorca.

In three days he arrived off Port Mahon, his squadron flying Spanish colours. The islanders, who had already heard rumours of the Emperor's success at Tunis, thought that the ships were part of the returning armada and prepared to receive them in triumph. Guns from the fort fired a salute of welcome — the answer to their blank charge was a well-directed rain of ball and arrow. The city and the wharf, where lay a great Portuguese ship with a rich cargo, were swept clean, and Barbarossa sailed for Constantinople to offer Suleyman six thousand captives as a mitigation of his offence in losing Tunis. The Sultan was graciously pleased to accept the explanation in this form and appointed the Beglerbeg of Algiers High-Admiral of all the Ottoman fleets.

The following two years saw both Doria and Barbarossa at sea, each inflicting great damage but without making contact with each other. In 1537 the Spanish admiral defeated an Ottoman force and carried twelve Turkish galleys off to Messina. The Algerian retaliated by laying waste the Apulian coast. While so engaged he learnt that Venice had joined the Holy War against Islam. He thereupon sailed to Corfu, then a Venetian possession, and landed twenty-five thousand men and thirty cannon within three miles of the castle. Four days later he was reinforced by twenty-five warships. The largest gun in the world was brought into action for the first time, a fifty pounder which fired nineteen times in three days, a thing to marvel at. The monster's accuracy was not worthy of its size, however, as she only planted her mark five times on the fortress in the course of a month's siege. The resistance proved too strong and on September 17th Suleyman called off the attack with the remark that a thousand such castles were not worth the life of one of his brave men. Kheyr-ed-din protested but obeyed, and finished the season with a dash up the Adriatic, killing and burning as he went, and retreating with thousands of captives, amongst whom were some of the noblest of the Venetian families. The inventory of his spoils includes four hundred thousand pieces of gold, a thousand girls and fifteen hundred boys. As a present for his Imperial master he sent two hundred boys dressed in scarlet, each bearing a gold and silver bowl, two hundred more with rolls of fine cloth, and thirty to offer the Sultan thirty well stuffed purses.

In the summer of 1538 he was off again when word reached him that the enemy was cruising in the Adriatic. Doria's fleet, now augmented from the navies of Venice and the Pope, was the most formidable ever sent out in pursuit of the corsairs. Kheyr-ed-din, sweeping his eye over his own hundred and fifty ships of the line, decided to risk action. Abandoning a profitable cruise in the neighbourhood of Crete, he moved off for the Ionian Sea. He located the enemy in the Bay of Preveza on the Albanian coast.

The two greatest sea powers, the two greatest sea fighters, were at last face to face. With Doria were eighty Venetian, thirty-six Papal and thirty Spanish galleys, totalling with fifty sailing galleons nearly two hundred ships of war, carrying some sixty thousand men and two thousand five hundred guns. Kheyr-ed-din had under him the cream of Islam's sea forces and the incomparable lieutenants he himself had trained, Dragut, Sinan and Murad, the last of whom was to succeed him as the thorn in the side of Christendom after another battle had been fought with another result thirty-three years later in the near-by Gulf of Lepanto.

It was on September 25th that the two fleets came in sight of each other. Neither commander wanted to begin the fight but to manœuvre, waiting for the wind and to see what the other would do. Doria appears to have lost his old dash. Though outnumbering the enemy he clung to the harbour until he had lost his original advantage. His timidity may have been due to age or, as some have hinted, the hatred of the old Genoese for his city's ancient enemy Venice, on whose behalf he was largely fighting. Not until the 28th, when every external advantage favoured the Turks, did he lead his fleet out of harbour. A terrific running battle ensued in which the Christians were beaten and as the wind rose to a gale they fled, leaving numbers of their countrymen in the enemy's hands. The flag of Suleyman the Magnificent now floated supreme over all the waters of the Mediterranean.

It was three years before Christian Europe had sufficiently recovered itself to attempt revenge. This time it was determined to root out the pirates from their central lair, Algiers, and Doria was again entrusted with the command. With him were the old allies, although nearly every Christian country was to some extent represented by volunteers. The English contingent contained Sir Henry Knevet, the ambassador of Henry VIII to the Spanish court, and "his familiar friend Sir Thomas Challoner, by birth a Londoner, by study a Cantabridgian, by Education a courtier and by religion a devout and true Catholic," who was one day to succeed Knevet as minister to the same court from the Protestant daughter of Henry VIII. Amongst the Spaniards was Cortez, the future conqueror of Peru, of whom Morgan * rather incredibly reports that "he lost out of a napkin tied round his middle two most precious vessels made out of entire emeralds valued at three hundred thousand ducats."

Barbarossa himself was not in Algiers at the time; he returned to it but once after his appointment as High Admiral of the Turkish fleet. His deputy was a Sardinian renegade, Hassan, who had been kidnapped by pirates from his native island while still a small boy and sold to a master who "took a singular liking to him on account of his promising aspect and uncommon vivacity and soon caused him to be castrated."

The armada, consisting of five hundred ships manned by twelve thousand sailors (a far larger expedition than that which sailed under Medina Sidonia to punish England in 1588 for somewhat similar offences) sailed for Algiers on the 19th October 1541. Doria objected to a venture so late in the season, when storms were to be expected in Northern Africa. Charles overruled him: it may be that Preveza had diminished the Emperor's confidence in his admiral, or that he considered the lateness of the season would ensure the presence of the corsair navy at Algiers. In any event Charles was so confident

* "History of Algiers," 1731.

of the invincibility of his armada that he even took some Spanish ladies with him to witness the victory and applaud the victors. The Emperor himself sailed in Doria's flagship, and the land forces were under the command of the Duke of Alva, the greatest soldier of the sixteenth century.

Doria's forebodings were soon realised. On arrival at Algiers a gale rose which prevented any communication with the shore for three days, and even after it subsided the landing of the troops was dangerous and difficult, most of the soldiers having to wade up to their necks in the sea.

Once on shore the Spanish army had no trouble in advancing on and surrounding the city, for Hassan had but few reliable troops. A sharp bombardment of the walls from the heavy cannon began and the Spanish infantry was drawn up ready to rush the breach and storm the citadel. The victory seemed as good as won when suddenly another gale arose accompanied by a tropical cloudburst. The Spaniards had been in such a hurry to take Algiers that they had not even waited for their tents or stores to be landed and were without adequate clothing. All that night they stood knee deep in mud, stung by the rain and frozen by the cold wind. Daylight found them a hungry, shivering, dispirited rabble, unable even to fire a shot since their powder was wet.

Suddenly the Turks made a sortie and flung themselves on the Christians, who began to waver and would have broken into panic which could only have resulted in a massacre had not the Knights of Malta with cool courage covered the retreat.

In the meantime the gale had increased and many ships were driven on shore and wrecked. Doria stood out to sea with the rest of his fleet; after the storm had subsided sufficiently he brought it back into the Bay of Temendefust and with great difficulty the exhausted troops were reembarked. So crowded was the depleted fleet that all the horses had to be thrown overboard to make room for the men.

On November 2nd the fleet at last got away, just as another violent storm broke which scattered it. Several Spanish vessels were wrecked on the Algerian coast and their crews made captives. The rest beat against the storm for three weeks before the remnant of the once splendid armada reached haven in Spain.

It had been an overwhelming disaster. Three hundred officers and eight thousand soldiers had died of wounds or drowning. The slave-barracks, the bagnios, of Algiers were so overstocked with slaves that it was commonly said that a Christian was scarcely fair exchange for an onion. Not even glory was saved out of the wreck, except perhaps to the company of the Knights of Malta; the spot where they made their gallant stand is to this day known to the Algerians as the "Grave of the Knights." The defeat at Algiers was the severest blow that Spanish chivalry sustained before 1588; but from the former at least it was temporarily to recover.

An event which shortly took place moved the suppression of the pirates even further into the future than the successive Turkish victories at Preveza and Algiers. Francis I, King of France, called in the Moslems to help him to a favourable settlement of his disputes with the Emperor Charles, an alliance which many of his own subjects decried as impious. During the two centuries when the corsair terror was at its highest it was Christian differences that enabled it to wax. The resources of Western Europe, the growth of its national power, the quality of its armies and navies, would probably at any time have enabled it to keep the Mediterranean reasonably clear had this desirable end not been constantly frustrated by the dissensions amongst the Christian nations themselves. Had Western Europe set out with one purpose, under one great leader, as did the Romans in 67 B.C., they would have achieved what Rome did under Pompey. Louis XIV's mot, uttered in the next century, that if there had not been any Algiers he would have had to create one, indicates, though to a lesser extent, the policy of the sixteenth. The Turks not only recruited many if not most of their greatest corsairs, like the two Barbarossas, Sinan and later Murad Reis, from amongst Christian peoples, but the latter were constantly giving them encouragement by these alliances against their own kind.

In 1543 Francis concluded his first alliance with Suleyman, and Kheyr-ed-din was despatched to Marseilles. On the way he collected a few prizes but was apparently meaning to attend strictly to his commission when the Governor of Reggio in the Straits of Messina imprudently fired one shot at the fleet "as if in defiance, which so exasperated the choleric Captain Pasha that though he had no such design he immediately landed twelve thousand troops and battered the town so much in earnest that he soon got entrance." *

As usual Kheyr-ed-din took quantities of captives but this time he too was taken captive. Amongst his prisoners was the daughter of the Governor, a charming girl of eighteen, with whom the great corsair so fell in love that in spite of his age, which tradition puts at ninety years, he married her and gave her her parents' freedom as a wedding present.

The early days of the honeymoon were spent at Civita Vecchia, the town at which long ago the two Papal galleys from Genoa had never arrived, and where the bride now had her first experience of a large-scale, pirate raid.

Kheyr-ed-din then proceeded to his triumphant reception at Marseilles. The French admiral's flag, the banner of Our Lady, was lowered in Barbarossa's honour and the Crescent run up in its place, a spectacle which the Marseillais must have witnessed with no great feeling of pride.

The ceremonies over, the corsair found time hanging heavy on his hands and sailed over to Nice, then in the Dukedom of Savoy, where he passed an unprofitable few days owing to the sturdy defence put up by Paolo Simeoni, a Knight of Malta who had once been Kheyr-ed-din's captive. He then took up his station off Toulon, where he and his merry men proved to be most expensive and unsatisfactory guests to their French allies. Amongst the hundreds of galley slaves in his ships were many Frenchmen, whom his allies begged him to release. He not only declined, although they were dying like flies of a plague, but replaced the dead by raids on the neighbouring French villages. When the poor wretches died he would not allow them Christian burial nor even allow the bells of the churches in the city to be rung to summon the devout to Mass; to him these chimes were "the devil's musical instru-

* Morgan: "History of Algiers."

ment." The cost of feeding and paying his crew he transferred entirely to the French exchequer. Occasionally he sent out a squadron to annoy the King of Spain, according to the terms of his commission. Otherwise he remained at Toulon "lazily engaged in emptying the coffers of the French King."

At length the French could stand the strain no longer; the stay was costing too much. But the going was by no means inexpensive, for Barbarossa collected a large sum for himself and the wages of his men up to their reentry into the Bosphorus, as well as procuring the freedom of four hundred Mohammedan galley slaves, before quitting Toulon for home.

This was his last voyage. He spent his few remaining years in building a magnificent mosque as well as a stately sepulchre for himself, which he required in July of 1546.

A great many legends sprang up about him after his death, amongst them that "his corpse was found four or five times out of the ground lying by the said sepulchre after he had been there inhumed: nor could they possibly make him lie quiet in his grave, till a Greek wizard counselled them to bury a black dog together with the body which done he lay still and gave them no further trouble." For many years after his death no Turkish ship left the Golden Horn without a prayer and a salute to the tomb of the greatest of Turkish seamen and the mightiest of Mediterranean pirates. He survived in Islam as the hero of a living epic.

CHAPTER III

THE SUCCESSORS OF BARBAROSSA

THE immediate successors of the mighty brothers were their lieutenants, picked by them and trained in their school. None of these followers equalled their masters, none of them possessed Kheyr-ed-din's imagination or his capacity for widespread administration; but as a group they were equally daring, more ferocious and inflicted even greater harm on European commerce.

The first of these was Dragut, who was born in Anatolia in Asia Minor, opposite to the island of Rhodes. He was one of the few leaders in the Turkish navy to be born a Mohammedan. His parents were peasants but "this obscure and toilsome Life ill agreeing with young Dragut's sprightly and aspiring Genius, he run away to sea at the age of twelve, enlisted aboard a Turkish warship and soon won for himself the reputation of being a good Pilot and a most excellent Gunner." Before long he became the owner of a galliot, in which he cruised the waters of the Levant with great success.

It was not long before the news of his exploits reached the ears of Kheyr-ed-din who, quick to appreciate talent, invited Dragut to Algiers, gave him the command of twelve galleys and sent him off to seek his own and the Beglerbeg's fortunes. Thereafter he "passed not one summer without ravaging the coasts of Naples and Sicily nor durst any Christian vessels attempt to pass between Spain and Italy for if they offered it he infallibly snapped them up and when he missed his prey at sea he made himself amends by making descents along the coasts plundering villages and towns and driving away multitudes of inhabitants into captivity." *

At length his successes had grown so intolerable to Charles

* Morgan.

V that in 1540 the Emperor sent out a special order to Doria, then engaged in the general pirate hunt as described above, to "hunt him out and endeavour by all possible means to purge the seas of so insufferable a nuisance." The admiral passed on the order to his favourite nephew, Giannettino Doria, who set out in pursuit of Dragut, and surprised him ashore on the island of Corsica while he and his crew were employed in haggling over the division of some plunder.

For once the pirate was caught napping and after a fierce but hopelessly one-sided fight was compelled to surrender. Young Doria made his uncle a present of the captive, and Dragut spent the next four years chained to the oars of his own galley.

He obtained his release during the period of the French alliance, while his master was drifting at anchor in the Bay of Toulon. Jean de la Valette, who afterwards became Grand Master of the Knights of Malta, was on a visit to Andrea Doria and noticed the famous corsair amongst the galley slaves. La Valette himself had once pulled a captive's oar in one of Barbarossa's ships and knew by sight this most distinguished of Barbarossa's lieutenants. He could appreciate the degradation of the other's position through experience; moreover he was a kindly and courteous man, a chevalier of the old school.

"Signior Dragut," he greeted the captive, "Usanza de guerra — it's the custom of war." "Y mutanza de fortuna," replied the corsair chief, "the luck's changed."

The Christian undertook to act as mediary between Doria and Kheyr-ed-din, and in the end Dragut was ransomed for three thousand crowns, a bargain which the whole of Christendom as well as the Spanish admiral lived to regret. These bargains were not uncommon, even in the worst fury against the Barbary excesses. In part they were due to greed, since a rich man with friends was more profitable alive than dead, in part to the fear of reprisals by the other side. Even in the next century, when the corsairs were by no interpretation anything but outlaws, and the nations of the West were trying to forge an effective organisation for their suppression, policy required a recognition of the system of ransom.

Dragut's return to command coincided with Kheyr-ed-din's retirement to Constantinople. He was put in charge of all Barbarossa's ships in the Western Mediterranean and soon earned for himself, in the words of an admiring Turkish historian, the title of "the drawn sword of Islam." There seemed to be nothing that his reckless daring would not venture. He seized a Maltese galley in which he found seventy thousand ducats intended for the repair of the fortification of Tripoli which then belonged to "the Religion"—very few of the corsairs ever cared to attack openly the gallant company of St. John. When he decided that Algiers was no longer convenient as a base, and was looking round for another more suitable, he pounced on the island of Jerba, off the coast of Tunis and opposite the island of Malta, which for two hundred years had been the property of the Doria family. The admiral was naturally annoyed but the island remained in Dragut's hands and was fortified into one of the most inaccessible lairs to which ever pirate repaired. In addition he captured in one raid Susa, Sfax and Monastir, which Doria had retaken for Spain only the previous summer, and finally retook, by a Ulyssean ruse, the Tunisian seaport of Mahdiya, or Africa, as it was always called by Christian writers in the Middle Ages.

Again the harassed Emperor was roused to action; to have the Moors once more entrenched on the coast of Tunis after all the trouble and expense he had been put to in recovering and strengthening it was more than Spanish pride could bear. An expedition was sent to Mahdiya in June 1550, once more under the command of old Admiral Doria. It arrived while Dragut was on his summer cruise in the Gulf of Genoa, Doria's home waters, and his nephew, Hisar Reis, was in command of the city. Hisar withstood a long siege while waiting for Dragut to return with help, but a vigorous assault by the Spaniards on September 8th swept the defenders out of the town.

Dragut received warning before his return and fled to Jerba. Not expecting to be disturbed he had drawn up his galleys on the shores of the inland lake of the island in order to careen their hulls, when Doria's squadron suddenly appeared at the mouth of the lake's narrow inlet and effectively bottled the corsair in.

Doria at once sent messengers to Madrid and other capitals to announce his triumph, then settled down to wait at the mouth of the trap till the fox came out. He waited a long time, but no sign of the animal was seen. Ultimately Doria ventured up the narrow channel until he reached the lake, when he discovered that the fox had vanished.

The explanation of the disappearance was simple. Dragut had collected two thousand peasants from the island and put them to work with his own crew and slaves to cut a canal across to the other side of the island, through which the ships could be dragged to the sea. While Doria kept his look out Dragut resumed his interrupted cruise, in the course of which he intercepted a galley from Genoa which was on its way with reinforcements for the Spanish admiral at Jerba.

Dragut lived fifteen years longer, fifteen years which began and ended with two furious efforts by the great Sultan of Constantinople to clear out of the Mediterranean, out of existence even, his ancient and unforgiving enemies, the Knights of St. John of Malta. In both of these expeditions Dragut, delighted to pay off a long score, took a leading part; both were failures, and in the second he perished.

The aristocratic brotherhood of the Knights Hospitallers of St. John of Jerusalem was founded at the time of the First Crusade. It made its headquarters in the Holy City, where its members tended the sick with devotion and fought the infidel with valour until their expulsion by Saladin in 1291.

After wandering about for many years in search of a new domicile they joined forces with a notorious Genoese pirate, Vignolo di Vignoli, and with him conquered the island of Rhodes. Here they constructed a series of massive fortifications wherein they might be safe from any conceivable attack. This was the beginning of the second epoch in their varied and gallant history.

From Rhodes they combined with advantage the two professions of trade and piracy. Their island lay in the fairway of all ships plying with merchandise between Alexandria and

Constantinople and other principal ports of the Eastern Mediterranean. The carrying of slaves was their principal business, but they did not neglect the opportunities offered by the passage of Turkish and Venetian vessels in front of their eyes. At one time or another every Christian nation was either complaining of their depredations or imploring their protection.

The Turks made several attempts to oust them, but were again and again repulsed until in 1522 Suleyman the Magnificent invested the island so thoroughly that after a siege of six months the starving and battered survivors were forced to make an honourable submission. Turned out of Rhodes they resumed their wanderings, flitting from place to place for eight years, while the Grand Porte enjoyed an undisputed hegemony in the eastern half of the Mediterranean and the brothers Barbarossa were threatening to acquire a similar one in the western half.

Their next resting place was Malta, which Charles V ceded them in 1530 together with the neighbouring town of Tripoli. The Emperor was not actuated primarily either by generosity or Christian compassion on the homeless. Malta and Tripoli were of no great value in themselves but of high strategic importance for guarding the surrounding seas from the Turks and the corsairs. His Catholic Majesty reckoned accurately that the Knights, having lost all their property, would be glad to earn a living as an auxiliary of the Spanish high-seas police.

They took their new duties seriously. Once more they built fortifications on a scale never before attempted, and galleys which were the terror of every Moslem vessel, whether legal or illegal, afloat. Their success became proverbial; the strongest and largest of Turkish warships had little chance against an equal number of Maltese galleys, and if the Knights had possessed a sufficient number of ships it is probable that the Turks would have been swept off the Mediterranean. Their fleet numbered only seven large galleys, six of them painted bright red, the flagship of the commander a sombre black. They were of exceptional size, rowed by Mohammedan slaves, and heavily armed. So for many years the Knights of

St. John lived by plundering the enemies of the Faith, and led lives devoted to chastity, piety and charity.

The first of the two Moslem attempts to take Malta was abortive. The fleet, led by Sinan with Dragut second in command, drew up under the walls of the citadel, when the Jew, after reconnoitring the defences and exchanging a few shots, declared the place impregnable and turned south for Tripoli. This secondary stronghold of the Knights was held by only four hundred men, of whom Sinan with his six thousand Turks made short work. He then sailed away, having inflicted more damage on his co-religionists than on his enemy.

The culminating effort of the Mohammedans was made in 1565. The Sultan despatched a huge fleet of a hundred and eighty-five vessels, of which more than one hundred were galleys royal, carrying over thirty thousand fighting men, under the command of Piali Pasha, a Croat — another of the long list of converts from Cross to Crescent. He was joined before Malta by Dragut with a squadron of Algerian war galleys.

The expedition, like the Armada of 1588, was a long while preparing, and the Knights had sufficient warning to enable them to send urgent calls for help to Europe. The Order was fortunate in having for its Grand Master in its greatest hour of peril a man of outstanding wisdom and bravery, the seventy-year-old Jean de la Valette, who had spent almost his whole life in the Brotherhood and had been one of the defenders of Rhodes forty-three years before. He was the most experienced pirate-fighter alive; he had spent a year chained to an oar in one of Barbarossa's galleys; he knew every leading corsair by sight and most of them by name. It was he who had interceded with Doria over twenty years before for the ransom of that same Dragut who now was preparing to disembark his terrible Berbers in the exultant belief that the last chapter of the Crusades was now to be written in the blood of the Crusaders' heirs.

It was one of the great sieges of history. For six months the Turks mined, blew breaches in the walls, and poured in a horde of Believers who were not afraid to die. For six months the defenders, vastly outnumbered, exploded counter-mines, made furious sorties, were driven back, fought with desperate bravery each time the enemy penetrated their defences. The result appeared to depend entirely on the arrival of the Spaniards; the long summer dragged on and still the Spaniards delayed, as they always delayed until they had succeeded in losing half a world. The result seemed so inevitable — the Knights could hold out no longer — and the promised help did not come.

They never came until it was all over, yet it was they who saved Malta. For on a certain day, when the wounded and starving remnant of the Knights were almost at the end of their tether, the Turks heard that the relief from Spain was on the way, broke into panic in the midst of an attack, ran to their ships and scurried away. The great siege was at an end and the Knights of Malta had become immortal. To this day the memory of the Grand Master still lives in the name of the island capital he so nobly defended: Valetta.

Of the thousands who were killed during the siege, almost the last to die was Dragut, who with his Algerians fought on while the main body of the Turks were fleeing in terror — from nothing worse than bad news.

As Dragut represented with distinction the Barbary corsairs in the most magnificent siege of the sixteenth century, so his successor was privileged to represent the same troublesome race six years later in the greatest naval battle of the century, one of the great naval battles of the world, one of the supremely decisive battles of history.

During those six years, although Turkish prestige had suffered at Malta, the Ottoman navy was still formidable and while it held the seas any effort to break up the Algerian organisation could hope for no more than a partial success. In the interval between Malta and Lepanto Uluj Ali, known in Christendom as Ochiali, roamed the ocean with much the same abandon as his predecessors. Ochiali's original intention was to enter the Catholic priesthood, but his studies were interrupted by a pirate raid on his home at Castelli in Calabria and he was carried off to slavery. The profession of Mohammedanism, a striking personality and an aptitude for the sea soon translated him from the rowing bench to the quarter deck, where his proficiency shortly gained him the command of his own ship. For many years he served under Dragut, who had great confidence in him. He was present at the siege of Malta and his services on that inauspicious occasion brought him to the attention of the Sultan of Turkey, who appointed him Beglerbeg of Algiers in succession to Hassan, son of Kheyr-ed-din. Hassan, a competent administrator, had interrupted the maritime tradition of the Algerian pashas and preferred in more characteristic Moslem fashion to keep away from the sea. Ochiali, in the earlier manner of the Barbarossas, went to sea and stayed there as long as the weather permitted; almost his first act after his appointment was the recapture of Tunis (all but the Goletta) for Selim II, who had in 1566 succeeded his father Suleyman the Magnificent.

One day in the July of 1570 he nearly wiped out the stain of the Malta fiasco. While sailing near the coast of Sicily he suddenly happened on four of the Knights' great galleys. Delighted at the encounter Ochiali gave the order to attack. After a fierce battle three of the galleys were captured, including the flagship, which Saint-Clément, the commander of the Knights, ordered to be abandoned, while he escaped with his treasure on shore at Montichiaro. Sixty Knights and serving brothers of the Order were killed or made prisoner.

The pride of the Knights was deeply humiliated. When Saint-Clément returned to Malta he was in danger of being lynched by the mob and was only saved by the intervention of the Grand Master. He was then tried before the secular court, condemned to death, strangled in his cell, and his body placed in a sack and thrown into the sea. Failure, and worse, cowardice were never overlooked or forgiven by "the Religion."

Ochiali's next objective was Cyprus. This island belonged to Venice and the principal activity of its inhabitants was piracy, a practice to which Ochiali entertained strong objection. Cyprus served as the headquarters of the Christian corsairs who preyed on the Syrian coast. In addition its site made it an invaluable base for naval warfare in the Eastern Mediterranean, as well as a convenient depôt for troops and stores. After a siege lasting forty-eight days Nicosia, the capital, fell on September 9th, and Ochiali hurried on to Crete, ravaging every island town and village as he swept on towards the Adriatic.

The following August the conquest of Cyprus was completed and at the end of September the corsair, having joined with the main Turkish fleet under Ali Pasha, Piali's successor, lay at anchor in the Gulf of Corinth, as yet unaware that within a fortnight he would be engaged in the last great struggle of Islam's ocean story.

The capture of Cyprus affected the imagination of Christendom as almost no other aggression of the corsairs had ever done. Venice had not always been on the best of terms with her fellow Christians, but now they responded with rare unanimity to her lamentations and rallied round to teach the Turk such a lesson as he would never forget. The Pope, Pius V, assumed the spiritual leadership of the cause and summoned all Christians to join him in support of the one Italian state above all others that had for centuries irritated the Holy See. The knight errantry of Europe rushed to Italy; even from England, whose Queen this same Pope had excommunicated the previous year, came that doughty Protestant seaman Sir Richard Grenville. Official support was less enthusiastic. Only Spain supplied a large fleet, under the command of Giovanni Andrea Doria, nephew of the dead admiral. The supreme command of all the forces engaged was given to Don John of Austria, the twenty-four-year-old son of Charles V by the beautiful Barbara Bloomberg, most romantic of all the knights errant of the sixteenth century. Amongst the humbler members of his command was Miguel de Cervantes, who was soon to laugh knight errantry out of the world.

The avenging fleet mustered two hundred and six galleys and forty-eight thousand men. Even this powerful force, however, proceeded in its hunt with the utmost caution, dreading lest Ochiali should evade them and scourge the Italian coasts in their rear while they were looking for the main Turkish fleet under Ali Pasha.

On receipt of intelligence that the Christian fleet was at last at sea the Turkish admirals withdrew their squadrons further up the Gulf and anchored in the Strait of Lepanto. Though greater in number than the allies' fleet the Turks were handicapped by their archaic ordnance. Their soldiers still largely used the bow and arrow which the Christians had discarded in favour of the more modern firearm, and their artillery was of an obsolete type.

Early in the morning of October 7th the two fleets came face to face. The first sight of the enemy was called down by the look out on the maintop of Don John's galley; a sail was reported on the horizon, then more and more until the whole skyline was blotted out. The Christian General quickly ran up a white flag, the signal for battle. The slaves were served with meat and wine, a certain indication of hard work ahead. The various principal officers of the allied fleets suggested a council of war, but Don John declined their advice with the reply that "the time for councils is past. Do not trouble yourselves about aught but fighting." He had himself rowed from galley to galley and as he came under the stern of each he held aloft a crucifix and called out encouragement to the men, who responded with cheers. On return to the deck of his own ship he unfurled the Blessed Standard with the figure of the Saviour and falling on his knees commended his cause to God.

It was nearly midday and a dead calm prevailed as the two fleets drew together. There was no attempt at manœuvring and no possibility of it: both fleets were flanked by the shore. Head on they hurled themselves at one another with a shouting and a roar of cannon such as had never been heard before. Ship rammed ship, splintering their oars like match sticks.

The Turks fought like men possessed, boarding again and again with scimitar and sword, only to be mowed down by the deadly hail of musket fire, but in the end the superior weapons of the West told. Towards evening the Turkish resistance weakened, and the discipline of the allied troops converted the defeat into a rout.

By nightfall of that October day the Ottoman maritime empire had been crushed, never to be revived. For centuries the African corsairs continued to harass and plunder Christians in the Mediterranean, but only as outlawed gangs, never again as auxiliaries of a first-rate sea power.

OCHIALI, who escaped from the battle, taking with him the standard of "the Religion" which he had captured from the Maltese flagship and which was hung in Santa Sophia, survived until 1580. He brought to an end the race of pirate kings. There were mighty corsairs after him — not until the nineteenth century was the breed extinguished in Algeria, and their number in the seventeenth was probably even greater than in the sixteenth — but they held no authority apart from what they could win by their individual capacity.

The first of the great independent chieftains was Murad, who learnt his craft under both Kheyr-ed-din and Ochiali. Like so many of his kind he had been born a Christian (of Albanian parents), was captured as a child and carried off to captivity. His owner, Kara Ali, an Algerian corsair, was delighted with his twelve-year-old prisoner and appointed himself the boy's stepfather. Finding him "to be of a daring sprightly genius, he took great delight in him and soon gave him command of a galliot," since he "never failed showing indisputable tokens and superior capacity far exceeding his years." *

The youth was present at the siege of Malta in 1565, but after that disaster became weary of the discipline and monotony of service in the Ottoman navy, gave the fleet the slip and "went on the account" in his master's ship. His seamanship had not yet advanced as far as he thought, for he ran his vessel on the rocks and lost it, but he saved his crew, galley slaves and arms and got them safely ashore on a small island off the Tuscan coast. There the castaways remained until they were rescued by some passing Algerian ships.

Murad was brought back to Algiers to confront an extremely angry Kara Ali who, as a sign of his displeasure, took away

* Morgan.

his ward's slaves and cast him off. Murad, "stung to the quick and having still a violent itch for the cruising trade," managed to get hold of a small galley rowed by fifteen oars and disappeared towards the coast of Spain. Seven days later he was back again, bringing in tow three Spanish brigantines and a hundred and forty Christians. "This lucky hit . . . got him abundance of reputation and so far reconciled him to his patron that he soon gave him another galliot." Murad was off again immediately to try his luck on his new ship, but, somewhat chastened, put himself under the supervision of the older and officially recognised corsair Ochiali. This expedition ended with the capture of three Maltese galleys off the coast of Sicily.

By January 1578 Murad had acquired a squadron of several galliots of his own and was operating as a fully qualified captain or reis. Nothing much of note happened in that year save that he let the Duke of Tierra Nuova, retiring Viceroy of Sicily, slip through his fingers, but in 1580 he carried out an exploit which made his name as famous as that of Francis Drake, who was just returning from his buccaneering tour of the world.

Leaving Algiers in April 1580 with only two galliots, Murad was cruising quietly off the coast of Tuscany when he suddenly spied over a rocky promontory the tall masts of two galleys at anchor. They were the property of His Holiness Pope Gregory XIII, and one of them was the *Capitania* or Papal flagship.

"Murad's mouth watered at the sight" but even his courage stopped short at attacking two well armed vessels with a pair of rowing boats. Just then, while he was wondering what to do, by great good luck along came two other Algerian galliots similar to his own; that is, propelled by oars but with auxiliary sail, and the nimblewitted corsair at once conceived a way of using them. The Papal galleys would be suspicious of four intruders but not of two, for which they would be far more than a match. Murad took the newcomers in tow, ordered them to lower their masts and proceeded to row towards the unsuspecting galleys.

The scheme worked. The Papal crews failed to observe the galliots in tow until all four of the enemy had come round the promontory and were on top of them. The senior officers were on shore, and a panic swept the crews of the large galleys as the turbaned heads showed up over the side. After a short sharp fight both galleys were prizes.

It was a lucky haul for Murad, the galleys being full of treasure as well as of Christians. Chained to the oars were a hundred Turkish and Moorish slaves, and a number of Christian criminals serving their sentences, "many of whom," records the Protestant Morgan with relish, "were priests, monks and friars, there put not for their goodness." There followed much chaining and unchaining. The Mohammedan galley slaves were liberated and their places taken by the late crew of the galleys diluted with the literally unfrocked priests, monks and friars, who merely changed their gaolers without changing the gaol.

Murad's continued success aroused a natural jealousy amongst his rivals. The Admiral of Algiers himself, Arnaut Memi, went off with fourteen galleys to show that the business was not difficult for a competent man to master. Arnaut remained out for two months, and after a thorough scouring of the Mediterranean came back to his station with one blind Christian, captured on the island of Tursia, to show for his summer's work.

The competition proved unfortunate for the competitors. The new Governor-Pasha, recently sent out from Constantinople and entitled by his office to a tenth share of all the plunder brought in by the corsairs, shortly became disgusted with the diminishing return from these ventures. A tenth of one slave, and he blind, would not have enriched the Pasha very much. Sending for all the corsair chiefs to attend him he told them flatly "that they were all a crew of idle dronish poltroons, and that not one of them, Murad Reis alone excepted, was worth hanging." He ended with the announcement "that he himself would show them how to go a-cruising."

And he did. For purposes of instruction he ordered the

masters of twenty-two galliots and galleys to join his own vessels and led the way to Sardinia.

The first lesson was not convincing. The Pasha hid his corsairs on the little island of San Pietro and waited to surprise the town of Iglesia. Unluckily he was discovered, the alarm given and the beach where he proposed to make his landing instantly so crowded with armed and determined Sardinians that the Pasha thought best to postpone his demonstration to another time and place.

He next moved north to Oristano and landed fifteen hundred "fusiliers," who marched to a town forty miles inland under the guidance of a Sardinian galley slave, who was securely fastened to four stout sailors. There they attacked and departed with seven hundred of the inhabitants, whom they carried off to the island of Mal de Vientre (Belly Ache Island). Here the pirates hung out a flag of truce and invited the Sardinians to come and buy their townsfolk back. The invitation was accepted, a delegation arrived and the negotiations were opened. After a long haggle the corsair had descended to thirty thousand ducats and brought the islanders up to twenty-five thousand, but there they stuck. The Moor lost his temper, the Sardinians broke up the conference and the Pasha, "in a fury because he could not prevail with those islanders to come to his demands," departed to sell his prisoners for what they would fetch in the open market.

Continuing north he made a further raid or two, but then learning that Andrea Doria was on his trail with seventeen galleys, decided that the neighbourhood of Corsica and Sardinia was getting too hot for him and turned off in the direction of Spain. On the way he just missed capturing with his staff and his flagship the Viceroy of Sicily, successor to the Duke who had evaded Murad, which caused the Pasha, less controlled in his feelings than the pirate, to "bite his nails and tear his beard for disappointment."

His first landing, a surprise affair not far from Barcelona, netted him fifty Spanish prisoners but so aroused the countryside that he decided once more to look for his luck elsewhere.

This time he chose a spot near Alicante, whence a little while previously some Moriscos had written him to offer substantial payment if he would come and carry them away. Arrived offshore at night the Pasha sent a boat ashore to warn the Moriscos that help was at hand and to be ready to leave. Shortly thereafter a strong force of soldiers rowed ashore and brought back over two thousand men, women and children with most of their possessions. These were quickly got on board and the fleet sailed away without the loss of a single soldier or passenger.

The galleys were now fully loaded with prisoners, passengers and plunder, and the Pasha turned his face for home, only pausing to pick up a corn ship from Ragusa which blew across his path. Three months after leaving Algiers he was back with a fortune in plunder and slaves. Scarcely had he landed when he called a meeting of the professional corsairs and demanded the answer to the question: Who was the best corsair, he or they ?

Meantime Murad Reis, indifferent alike to competitors and Pashas, went his own way. Three years after his superior's return from a cruise which would, after all, have been no more than a weekend excursion for the great Reis, he carried out the most spectacular enterprise of his whole career and did what no Algerian had ever dared to do before. This was to sail through the Straits of Gibraltar and carry out a plundering expedition in the Atlantic. Hitherto the boldest of pirates had preferred to sail in sight of land except for the rare necessary crossings of the Mediterranean.

Murad left Algiers in 1585 with three of his fighting galliots. Calling at Sallee, a thriving nest of pirates in Morocco which was to become as important in a few years as Bougie or Algiers, he was reinforced by several small brigantines. The united squadron then passed Gibraltar and set out across the seven hundred miles of ocean which lay between them and the Canaries, a track as unknown to the Mohammedans as it had been to Western Europe two hundred years before. Murad had picked up a captive who professed to know the course and appointed him pilot, but when, after many days' hard rowing with only occasional assistance from the sails (the mystery of tacking they had not yet explored) they came in sight of some islands, the pilot failed to recognise his goal and confessed to Murad "that he feared they had missed their voyage and were shot far ahead of the Canaries." To this Murad replied, "Though I was never there, I aver what you say to be morally impossible. Therefore keep on your course." *

He was right and the pilot wrong — shortly afterwards they came in sight of the island of Lanzarote, basking peacefully in the hot summer sun.

Immediately on sighting land the pirates took in their sails and lowered their masts so as to be invisible to the islanders. As soon as it grew dark they were again under way. Rowing swiftly and silently to shore they landed two hundred and fifty fusiliers near the principal town. The surprise was complete. The inhabitants had no time to defend themselves, the place was sacked and three hundred captives carried off. The governor himself, a Spanish nobleman, escaped, but his mother, wife and daughter were dragged off to the ship.

By daylight Murad was anchored a little way off shore, and hung out a flag of truce as an invitation to those on shore to come and ransom their friends and relatives. The governor came first, was heavily mulcted and carried back his family. The other well-to-do folk followed so that "none but the unfortunate and destitute remained in their state of wretchedness."

Murad started back without waste of time, but came very near never reaching home. News of his exploit had preceded him, and Don Martin Padilla, whom the winds were to treat so scurvily a dozen years later when Philip II sent him to take revenge on England for the doings of Essex and Raleigh in the Azores, had been despatched to intercept him in the Straits of Gibraltar.

Murad was warned in time to avoid running into Padilla, but not in time to pass the Straits before the Spaniard had taken up his station. To fight through was impossible; the Spaniard had eighteen galleys of the line. Murad stole into an obscure

* Morgan.

port on the Moroccan coast and hid himself for a month, at the end of which he took advantage of a tempestuous night to pilot his minute squadron through the blockaders into the haven of his native waters.

Murad's next exploit took place four years later. This time he was out on a cruise by himself with only one galley — a significant contrast to the days of Barbarossa and Dragut. After picking up a prize or two off Corsica he sailed towards Malta where he met with a French ship, "those fast friends of the Turk," whose amiable master gave him intelligence of a Maltese royal galley, *La Serena,* which was on her way to Tripoli.

Murad promptly took up his station at an island which he believed the Maltese would necessarily pass. His subordinates told him he was wasting their time, but Murad, like most men of his age a firm believer in the black art, consulted his "fortune book" ("an illusion" says Hædo, the learned Spanish chronicler, "truly diabolical" *) and in it learned that the fates had declared he should wait a little longer. Sure enough, early the next morning the great galley appeared, sailing across their line of vision with a Turkish prize in tow. The "fortune book" had been proved right, but the size of the galley put the amiability of the Frenchman somewhat in doubt.

The odds seemed one-sided — a small galliot against a towering galley of the first class — so Murad decided that his crew required moral encouragement. Calling them round him he made them a speech, ending with the inspiring peroration, "Dread not death, since you left your homes in search of wealth and renown and to render service to our beautiful Prophet Mahomet." Occasionally it is just possible to detect a resemblance between the Barbary corsairs and the Knights of the Religion.

The speech had a great success, and the crew cheered it loudly. But by this time the Maltese was well on his way and the slaves were whipped into hot pursuit. The Knights were the last to fly from an enemy, but the commander of the *Serena* could not believe that one solitary galley constituted the whole of the pursuit. Before accepting the action he ordered the look-out to report how many others he could see

* Hædo, "Topographia e Historia General de Argel," 1612.

following behind. On being assured that this was the only one he at once gave orders to put about and capture the insolent corsair. It was afterwards learned that the Knights had agreed, after observing that the galliot was indeed alone, that "this can certainly be nobody but that devil Murad Reis."

Luck this time was again on the side of the foolhardy. At the very first discharge of the corsair's gun, that inefficient weapon scattered its shot so thoroughly that nearly every one of the Christian artillerymen was killed or wounded at his post. This startling exhibition of gunnery decided the contest then and there; disabled at the start the Christians were compelled to give in at the end of half an hour's fighting.

Murad, not unjustifiably pleased with himself, turned back for Algiers, his prisoners sadly rowing his prize home for him. As they were coasting along off the African shore they rounded a point and suddenly came across a Majorcan pirate "which lay plying there upon much the same business as they themselves followed." This form of cut-throat competition on their own doorstep was too serious to be overlooked. Murad snapped up the Majorcan and gave its crew employment by filling up forty-five vacancies on the benches of the Maltese galley. Two days later he entered the port of Algiers with his two prizes, "their colours dragging as is usual in such cases, and with repeated volleys of great and small guns." The whole town turned out to greet its most distinguished son, and the Pasha not only sent him an escort of janissaries but paid him the high compliment of sending his own horse to carry him to his palace.

Murad finished up his career as Admiral of Algiers, an office he received in 1595. He left most of his official work to be done by a deputy and was invariably out "on the account" early in the season. He disappears from the chronicle, wounded in five places by "the Religion's" bullets. It is known that he got back to Algiers after this last encounter with his great foe, but whether he died of his wounds or retired to a fat old age history does not record.

CHAPTER IV

THE SEVENTEENTH CENTURY

BY THE end of the century the evolution in the business organisation of the corsairs was complete. Beginning in the days of the first Barbarossa the Beglerbegs sent out from Constantinople to govern Northern Africa had appointed as governors of Algiers, the principal corsair centre, not Turks or Moors for the most part, but European renegades who had worked their way up through skill and daring to the first rank of the country's leading profession. Some of these converts even rose to the post of Beglerbeg itself. Kheyr-ed-din, the son of a Greek, was followed by a Sardinian, who was succeeded by a Corsican. Ochiali was a Calabrian, his successor, Ramadan, a Sardinian; after him came in order a Venetian, a Hungarian and an Albanian. By 1588 the thirty-five galliots of Algiers were commanded by eleven Turks and twenty-four renegades representing nearly every Christian nation of the Mediterranean littoral and even beyond. Some of these foreigners had been captured as children and subjected to forcible conversion, but others voluntarily submitted to circumcision and took Mohammedan names for the sake of the wealth and adventure promised by the command of a Barbary ship. In 1586 it was reported by Master John Tipton, first English consul at Algiers, that the treasurer to the Pasha was an English eunuch and renegade, son to Francis Rowlie, merchant of Bristol, who went by the name of Hassan Agha. Of the renegades who rose to be high officials nearly all acquired a certain reputation for efficient and even humane administration.

But after Lepanto the character of the administration changed, as it inevitably does when a widespread and decentralizing power offers corrupt servants the opportunity of speedy enrichment away from the eye of the home government. The Pashas sent from Constantinople began to sell the governorship to rich Turks, nearly all of them incompetent and most of them rascals, whose sole ambition was to recompense themselves for the purchase price and put away as much money as possible before their tenure of office ended. During this era the more enterprising renegades were more or less independent of the central authority save for the ten per cent which constituted the Governor's chief source of revenue. These reis or "generals of the galleys" were then free to operate pretty much as they pleased. The days of pure piracy were coming back, and it was now to flourish as it never had before.

In 1606 came a change that revolutionised the art as well as the business of piracy. In that year Simon de Danser instructed the Algerians how to build "round ships," — square-rigged sailing vessels of the type used in the Atlantic — and how to navigate them. It was a transition fully as significant as the change from sail to steam; perhaps even greater, for the sailing vessel could go nearly everywhere the steamship could, and of course range far beyond the remotest possibilities of the oared galley. From that moment not only the coasts but the whole basin of the Mediterranean, winter as well as summer, rough weather as well as smooth, became accessible to the corsairs, and even the long water routes along which travelled the great Spanish treasure flotas were infested with them. The experienced robbers of the North Sea and the Channel, English, Dutch and French, only too often found the golden goose plucked before they could lay their hands on it. Naturally they resented this and trouble followed, for to be deprived of one's loot before one had captured it was as annoying as having it stolen afterwards.

The corsairs' benefactor, Simon de Danser* (sometimes called the elder to distinguish him from his son who followed in his profession), began as an ordinary seaman from Dordrecht. He rose to be commander of a ship and became a privateer in the service of the States General during the rebellion

* For much new material about Danser the author is indebted to Mr. L. C. Vrijman of the Hague.

against Spain. After an unsuccessful Mediterranean cruise he put into Marseilles to refit and victual but found the temptations of that lively port too much for him. Having spent all his money he was forced to sell his ship and spent the proceeds of that as well. Thus deprived of a command he collected a few of the riffraff of the port, stole a small boat and went off "on the account" as an out-and-out pirate. Soon he captured a large vessel, into which he transferred his crew, was joined by a number of English and Moorish seamen and before many months found himself in command of a small fleet, whose largest vessel carried nearly three hundred men and sixty guns. He had now become a power at sea and presently effected a combination with a rival, an English pirate called Warde, which considerably increased his strength.

It was not until 1606, however, that he established himself in Algiers, where he was already famous and assured of a warm welcome. It was then that he taught his hosts the art of modern ship construction, and in return was provided by them with the base and market his activities required. His colleague Warde performed the same service for and received the same reward at Tunis.

For three years the Dutchman cruised the Mediterranean making rich hauls and laying by a large fortune. He built himself a palace in Algiers and hobnobbed with pashas and beys. Then the news reached him that a Spanish and an English fleet were both in the Mediterranean with orders to take him dead or alive. He had also heard unpleasant stories of the uncertainty of life amongst rich foreigners in Algiers. His conscience began to trouble him — he had never forsworn his Christianity like others of his kind — so he decided to retire.

But the problem of respectability offered certain difficulties. It would be hard enough to get out of Algiers with his money; it would be even harder to find a place where he would be welcome, since there was a price on his head in every country that appealed to him as a future home. The second problem was solved first. After some negotiation he succeeded in buying a pardon from King Henry IV of France and prepared to exchange the profits of Algiers for the delights of Paris. The

French ruler had another consideration in mind when closing the deal which he kept to himself for the time being.

The escape from Algiers was contrived with ingenuity instead of cash. Four pirate ships entered the harbour with a choice cargo which they offered for sale. Danser bought almost the whole of it and went on board to pay over the purchase price. As usual the oars of these ships were manned by Christian slaves. While most of the Mohammedan crew were on shore a pre-arranged quarrel broke out between these slaves and the few Moors left on board, who were quickly overpowered and killed, with the exception of some of the officers who were kept as hostages in case things turned out badly. Danser, now master of the four ships, sailed away and in due course arrived safely at his old haunt, Marseilles.

There, despite the Royal pardon, he met with so very hostile a reception that "when crossing the street he was accompanied by part of his bravos, who carried loaded pistols in their hands and formed his bodyguard." Many of the merchants of the city had suffered severe losses at the hands of the Dutchman and in order to get out of Marseilles he had to pay them in full. He then proceeded to Paris in obedience to a royal order. From the capital he wrote in December of 1609 to Zeeland to say that he was in receipt of his pardon from the King of France, and consequently no longer outlawed, adding the apparently irrelevant news "that the Queen of France had been delivered of a young daughter." This infant, christened Henrietta Maria, was in course of time to become the consort of King Charles I of England.

The King of France now divulged the employment he had in mind for his new subject. The French had quarrelled with their former allies, and a fleet was being fitted out to attack the Goletta at Tunis; Henry IV remembered an old maxim about setting a thief to catch a thief and appointed the retired corsair to a place in the expedition. The enterprise was completely successful, the bey's ships were burnt and four hundred and fifty-five guns and booty to the value of four hundred thousand crowns carried back to France.

But seven years later the corsairs were to have their revenge on the apostate. The story is told in full by the author and traveller William Lithgow who was an eye witness of the attack on the Goletta: "When I had stayed here for some five weeks it was my good luck that there arrived here on February 16th, 1616 a Dutch ship the *Meermin* of Amsterdam coming from Tetuan and bound for Venice. On board this ship came a certain captain of the name of Danser, who had been formerly a pirate of renown and a famous commander of the sea, and a very old enemy of the Moors. He was sent as an ambassador by the King of France to take over twenty two French ships that had been captured which were to be restored. This was a stratagem of the Pasha to attract Danser to that town, though the latter had already retired from service and was married at Marseilles. He comes into port, accompanied by two French monsieurs, who go on shore to compliment the Pasha. They meet with a friendly reception and the day after, the Pasha with twelve of his followers goes on board to return the visit. Danser considered it to be a great honour that the Pasha had come in person to visit him; consequently he regaled him with all due honours, with soundings of trumpets and roaring of cannon, and nobody so friendly as the hypocrite Pasha and the gratified Danser, who had taken over the ships, as they had been delivered to him that selfsame morning, fully equipped and wanting nothing. Having drunk more than their fill of wine, the Pasha invited Danser to visit him next morning at the fort to which the unhappy Danser agreed. At the appointed time he came on shore with twelve monsieurs and approaching the castle was met by two Turks. The company passed over the drawbridge, but when entering the gate, the doors were shut as soon as he had entered and his retinue had to stay outside.

Danser was conducted before the Pasha and was charged with having taken many ships, much booty and excessive riches from the Moors and having murdered them without shewing the least mercy. He was beheaded at once and his body thrown into a moat. Having done this every gun was fired, in order to sink Danser's ship but by cutting the cables she managed to escape though with much difficulty.

As to the monsieurs who were on shore they were sent courteously and in safety to their ships, the freed barks, with which they made sail for Marseilles." *

All Europe and Holland in particular was yet to make valuable contributions to the Barbary personnel, but none of them was or ever would be so useful as the seaman from Dordrecht who showed Islam how to build and sail ships as well as Christians did.

The corsairs were quick to learn the lesson Danser had taught them. They went farther and farther afield in their new sailing vessels, finding that these gave them not only a greater cruising range but freed them from the need of carrying provisions for a hundred or two hundred galley slaves. Increasingly the Atlantic commerce became their mark; this had now grown to be of outstanding importance and the coastal raids on Spain less feasible after the expulsion of the last of the Moors from Andalusia in 1610. With no possibility of help from shore the coast raid became risky in proportion as the high seas attack grew more profitable.

It was not long before the terror which had hitherto been felt by the Mediterranean states communicated itself to the northern kingdoms as well. In 1616 Sir Francis Cottington, English ambassador to Spain, wrote to James I's favourite, the Duke of Buckingham, "The strength and boldness of the Barbary pirates is now grown to that height both in the ocean and the Mediterranean seas as I have never known anything to have wrought a greater sadness and distraction in this Court than the daily advice thereof. Their whole fleet consists of forty sail of tall ships of between two and four hundred tons a piece; their admiral (flagship) of five hundred. They are divided into two squadrons, the one of eighteen sail remaining before Malaga in sight of the city, the other about the Cape of S. Maria which is between Lisbon and Seville. That squadron within the straits entered the road of Mostil a town of Malaga, where with their ordnance they beat down the port of the castle, and had doubtless taken the town but that from Granada there came soldiers to succour it; yet they took there divers

* From William Lithgow's "Rare Adventure and Painfull Peregrination," 1632.

ships, and among them three or four of the west part of England. Two big English ships they drove ashore, not past four leagues from Malaga; and after they got on shore also, and burnt them, and to this day they remain before Malaga intercepting all ships that pass that way, and also prohibiting all trade into these parts of Spain."

Between the years 1569 and 1616 the corsair fleet, numbering in all only a hundred vessels, had captured four hundred and sixty-six British ships, whose crews were sold into slavery. The English consuls at Algiers were continually writing home to ask for the alleviation of the lot of English captives and to urge on their government that strong measures be taken to curb the growing insolence of the Algerians. In 1631 the consul wrote direct to the King to say that if ransoms were not speedily sent there would soon be a thousand English slaves in Algiers; in their last cruise alone the corsairs had returned with forty-nine British sail. His letter ended with the warning: "They say that unless you send speedily they will go to England and fetch men out of their beds as they commonly used to in Spain."

The threat was by no means idle. Before long as many as thirty corsair ships were ravaging the Atlantic coasts from their newest base at Sallee in Morocco — one of them was actually captured in the River Thames. In the West of England the populace became so nervous that the Lizard light was extinguished because "it will conduct pirates." The Channel was no longer safe for any merchant ship sailing without convoy; in 1625 the Mayor of Plymouth reported that during that one year the Barbary pirates had captured a thousand seamen of the West Country.

The longest voyage these rovers ever made was to Iceland. The leader of this expedition was, like Danser, a Dutchman, but unlike Danser "took the Turban." His name was Jan Jansz, known to the Moors as Murad Reis, but to prevent confusion with the earlier Murad, the disciple of Barbarossa and Ochiali, his European name will be used hereafter.*

Jan Jansz began his career, as did most of the Dutch seafaring men who ultimately turned pirates, as a privateer of the States

* For the history of Jansz I am indebted to Mr. L. C. Vrijman.

against the Spaniards during the War of Liberation. But this quasi-lawful type of warfare yielded more glory than profit, and Jans presently trespassed on his commission and found his way to the Barbary coast. There he waged war on the ships of all Christian nations alike, those of Holland not excepted, save that when he attacked a Spaniard he flew the standard of the Prince of Orange as a tribute of sentiment to his origin. When occupied against any other nation's shipping he flew the red half-moon of the Turks.

At first he sailed as mate to a famous corsair called Suleiman Reis, of Algiers, but after his chief's death in 1619 settled at Sallee. The port ("its name stunk in all Christendom") was extremely well situated for the new form of piracy, being on the coast of the Atlantic, only fifty miles from Gibraltar, where the corsairs could lie in ambush for everything that passed through the Straits and dash out quickly to meet the East India and Guinea traders. The Sallee fleet was not large, about eighteen all told, and the individual vessels were small, since a bar in the harbour prevented ships of deep draught entering unless they were first unloaded.

The port was nominally subject to the Emperor of Morocco, but shortly after Jansz's arrival the Sallentines declared themselves independent and established what was in effect a pirate republic, governed by fourteen of themselves, with a President who was also the Admiral. The Dutchman was the first to be elected, and to show his adopted countrymen how thoroughly he had become one of themselves he married a Moorish woman, though he had left a wife and family at Haarlem.

Business prospered under Jansz's efficient administration and he was soon compelled to find an assistant, a post for which he selected a fellow countryman, Mathys van Bostel Oosterlinck. The Vice-Admiral celebrated his appointment by following his superior's example, turning Mohammedan and marrying a Spanish girl of fourteen, although he had a wife and small daughter in Amsterdam.

Jansz, what with prizes taken at sea and his perquisites as Admiral, which included all dues for anchorage, pilotage and other harbour revenues, as well as brokerage on stolen goods, soon became an enormously rich man. Nevertheless he occasionally found the routine of business irksome, the pirate in him asserted itself and he went off on a cruise. During one of these, in November 1622, when he was trying his luck in the English Channel, he ran out of provisions and was forced to put in at the port of Veere in Holland to replenish his stock. It seemed a risky undertaking, but the Admiral of Sallee was a subject of the Emperor of Morocco, who had lately made a treaty with the States of Holland; hence Jan could legally claim the privileges of the port, though the welcome he received was a cold one.

The first visitor to come on board was the Dutch Mrs. Jansz, accompanied by all the little Janszes. "His wife and all his children," a contemporary writer records, "came on board to bid him leave the ship; the parents of the crew did the same but they could not succeed in bringing them to do this as they (the Dutch renegade crew) were too much bitten of the Spaniards and too much hankering after booty." Not only did his crew remain, but it was swelled by recruits, despite a stern order by the magistrates that no one was to take service on the vessel. But times were hard in Holland as a result of nearly half a century of war with Spain; the youth of Veere were more tempted by the opportunity of collecting an easy livelihood while getting in a blow at their old enemy than afraid of magisterial displeasure. Jan left Veere with a great many more hands on board than when he entered it.

A few years later, in mid winter, Jansz called at Holland again, this time having barely escaped disaster. Off the coast he had met a big ship flying Dutch colours. Jan, momentarily forgetful of treaties, was "at once enamoured of the fine ship and tried to take her" — it was quite probable that after he had succeeded, the lawyers would again enable him to claim the advantage of the treaty. But the affair turned out quite differently: as he came alongside the vessel the Dutch flag was hauled down, the standard of Spain run up in its place and in a moment Spanish troops were swarming on to his deck. The pirates, outclassed, just managed to escape after a bitter fight, many of the crew being killed and wounded. They were glad to get safe into the harbour of Amsterdam.

Jan applied to the authorities for assistance for his sick and wounded but was flatly refused. The unfortunate corsair had meant to violate the treaty, had failed and been punished, and was now receiving further punishment by having its benefits denied him just as if he had succeeded. He was not even granted permission to bury his dead, so the corpses had to be pushed beneath the ice as the only means of disposing of them.

After several comparatively bad years in the Straits of Gibraltar Jan decided to try his luck where no pirate, Barbary or other, had ever before ventured. In 1627 he engaged as pilot a Danish slave who claimed to have been to Iceland, and instructed him to lead the way to that remote island. Jansz's three ships contained, besides Moors, three English renegades.

The voyage was a daring feat of navigation for the time but the results were not commensurate with the risk. They plundered Reykjavik, the capital, but only obtained some salted fish and a few hides. To make up for their disappointment they caught and brought back four hundred — some say eight — Icelanders: men, women and children.

On his return Jan took up his quarters in Algiers, but not long afterwards was captured on one of his voyages by the Knights of Malta.*

Good Father Dan, who tells the story, also remarks that he was passing Jan's house after the news of his capture had reached Algiers and saw more than a hundred women going in a body to commiserate with the Moorish Mrs. Jansz on her husband's misfortune. How Jan contrived to obtain his freedom is unknown, but in 1640 he was once again free and once more in the service of the Emperor of Morocco.

On December 30th of that year a Dutch ship entered Sallee, where Jansz was Governor of the Castle. The ship brought a new Dutch consul who had with him, as a pleasant little surprise for the pirate, his daughter Lysbeth, now grown into an attractive young woman.

* Père Dan, "Histoire de Barbarie et de ses Corsaires."

The meeting moved all beholders. Jansz "was seated in great pomp on a carpet, with silk cushions, the servants all round him." When father and daughter met, "both began to cry, and after having discoursed for some time he took his leave in the manner of royalty." Lysbeth atferwards went to stay with her father until the following August in his castle at Maladia, some miles inland, "but the general opinion on board was that she had already had her fill of that people and that country." In any event she returned to Holland and we hear no more of her. Presumably she married a worthy Dutchman who had nothing to do with the sea or Morocco.

How Jansz died no one knows. The only hint we have, an ominous one, is contained in the biography of him by the Schoolmaster of Oostzaan, whose concluding sentence is "His end was very bad."

The business of piracy grew so vast in the seventeenth century that it is scarcely any longer possible to pick out isolated picturesque figures. The principal highways of the oceans were as dangerous, apart from the ordinary risks of travel by sea in that time, as the remoter roads of Calabria and Albania before the Great War. Commerce was crippled, famine in cities was not infrequent, families were torn apart and either permanently separated or impoverished by ransoms exacted to preserve the abducted member or members from the horrors of slavery. And at bottom the evil depended for its continuous existence on the villainous state of Christian European politics. The Turks were no longer strong enough to protect their brethren of the Barbary coast. Had all, or even three or four, of the wronged powers agreed to combine their forces, they could at any time have wiped out the North African pirates. But it was exactly this combination which was impossible. If France was at war with Spain she found the Moors useful allies. Policy led the Dutch in the early seventeenth century to adopt a similar course because it suited them to see the pirates preying upon the enemies of Holland's growing trade. At one time or another the Swedes and the English did the same thing. The result was that instead of exterminating the outlaw the civilised states of the West kept paying him tribute not to molest their vessels, a bargain he kept only in so far as it suited him. He was as immune from revenge for broken faith as for acts of barbarity.

Occasionally some nation, driven frantic by a series of piratical aggressions, would make an attempt to retaliate, but these lone expeditions, often ill-prepared, and with half-hearted official backing, did little good. England, France, Spain, Holland or Sweden would send out a fleet which would sail into the harbours of Algiers, Tripoli, Bougie or Tunis and fire off some guns. The commander would then be received by the Pasha or Bey, who would graciously accept a handsome gift and sign a fresh treaty promising never again to molest that particular nation's ships nor hold one of its subjects in captivity. But the moment its fleet had sailed away the pirates would be at it again. In 1620 Sir Robert Mansell was sent from England to extort such a promise and succeeded; before he was back in England forty English ships had been swept from the trade routes into the Algerian harbours.

Cromwell was the first English ruler who declined to compromise with the Barbary corsairs. In 1655 he sent a squadron under Blake with instructions to hunt out and exterminate them, and gave the great seaman a sufficient force for the purpose. Blake sailed boldly into Tunis harbour under the very guns of the port, burnt every ship there anchored, then sailed on to Algiers, whence he brought away all the English, Scotch, Irish and Channel Island slaves imprisoned there. The grim Protector and his heroic admiral had shown Europe what a strong ruler and an able sailor could do to the pests. The victory resounded throughout Christendom and was officially celebrated in a broadsheet:

The barbarous pirates upon Tunis strand
Felt the effects of his avenging hand.

During the next twenty years various punitive expeditions were sent out, none of which achieved anything until Sir Edward Spragg, following Blake's example, burnt the Algerian fleet in the harbour of Bougie in 1671, with the result that the populace rose, murdered the Aga and carried his head to the

English as a sign that they wanted peace. The good effects of this energetic action lasted for five years; it then became necessary to send Sir John Narbrough to bring the Algerians once more to their senses. Instead, however, of bombarding the place Narbrough followed the more usual practice and meekly paid sixty thousand pieces of eight to liberate a number of English captives. He was sent out again in 1677, this time to punish the Tripolitan pirates who had been growing more insolent during the repression of their brothers farther up the coast. After a great deal of parleying with the Dey, Narbrough saw that nothing was to be gained and roused himself to more active measures. At midnight he sent into the harbour twelve boats fitted with "fireworks," under the command of his senior lieutenant, Cloudesley Shovell (afterwards the famous Admiral Sir Cloudesley Shovell). Within an hour all the enemy ships were on fire "to the great astonishment of the Turks." Somehow or other a certain amount of loot was gathered by the way, for on the following day the admiral was able to distribute one thousand nine hundred and fifty-six pieces of eight as prize money to his gallant officers and men.

Until final retribution overtook the corsairs nearly a century and a half later, probably more serious damage was done to them by prospective captives than by invading squadrons. One such encounter is graphically described in a broadsheet of 1681 entitled "A Faithful Account of the Late Bloody Engagement fought between Captain Booth of the *Adventure* and Hadje Ali, captain of the *Two Lions and Crown* of Algiers on September 17th 1681, off Cape Trafalgar."

The Algerian ship was armed with more than forty great guns, and several smaller. She carried three hundred and twenty-seven Turkish and Moorish soldiers, and her crew consisted of eighty-eight Christian slaves. Her commander, Hadje Ali, was a Danish renegade, born at Copenhagen.

It was at dawn, when the *Adventure* was in chase of a small French vessel, that the big pirate ship was first seen, towing an English prize. The Moors in her quickly got on board their own ship and abandoned the prize. Captain Booth took her over, found two English slaves concealed in her, and ordered them to follow him with the vessel while he gave chase to the Algerian.

By one o'clock in the afternoon the two ships were alongside and a furious battle began which raged until nine o'clock, by which time both ships were so disabled in their masts and rigging that both lay off and did what they could to repair and refit. Shortly afterwards they again began to fight and continued to do so all through the night until nine o'clock the next morning, when an accident took place which seemed at first to have sealed the fate of the English ship. To quote Captain Booth's own account of this:

> About nine in the morning, having taken a man from each gun below where they could best spare them, to man those guns on our quarter deck, one of the King's cripples, being quartered there to carry powder from that place, having three cartridges and powder in his hand, went into the round house to secure himself from the shot, we not knowing what had become of the man, till a great shot from the enemy came into the roundhouse and shot the three cartridges of powder which he had by him, which took fire and blew him out of the round house upon our quarter deck and with him all our grenades which were about seven or eight that were left, which granadoes did kill and wound every man that was by me, I escaped very narrowly among the rest, being hurt in the neck by one of the granado shells.

By the greatest good fortune the moment afterwards the Algerian's mainmast went by the board and the pirates at once called for quarter.

Both ships had received heavy casualties. On the pirate they found Hadje Ali wounded, as well as five of his officers. Four of these were renegades from Holland and Hamburg, the fifth being a nephew of the Governor of Algiers. They also found on board an old Turk, Abram Reis, a former admiral of Algiers "who came that voyage for his pleasure." A Christian slave out of the pirate ship told Captain Booth that had it not been for the fierce old pleasure-seeking Abram Reis, the pirates would have yielded much earlier, but "he encouraged the Turks, telling them of his former success he hath had against the Christians, naming his fighting with Dutchmen of War and another time his fighting Sir Richard Beach in the *Hampshire* with several other good actions."

The changing politics and the growing commerce of France under Louis XIV brought that country finally into line with the corsairs' other European enemies, and from then on the French, like the English, several times undertook to punish the Moors, but with no notable success until the nineteenth century.

One of their expeditions, in 1683, is typical both of the method and the brutality of these conflicts. The Marquis Duquesne, commanding the French squadron, fired six thousand shells into Algiers, killing eight thousand persons and destroying many buildings. The populace rose in revolt, assassinated the Dey and elected in his stead the captain of the galleys, Hadji Hasan, nicknamed Mezzomorto (the half-dead) from his deathlike appearance. The new Dey sent a message to the Admiral threatening that if he did not at once stop the bombardment he would blow every Frenchman in Algiers from the cannon's mouth. The threat was not idle: the bombardment continued and the Dey selected his first victim, Jean Le Vacher, Vicar Apostolic. This noble old man, who had given thirty-six years to the service of the unhappy Christian prisoners, was now dragged down to the mole, tied to the mouth of a gun and shot in the direction of the French fleet. The French did not call off their enterprise until the middle of August when, their ammunition being exhausted, they left Algiers. In the meantime twenty other Frenchmen, including the Consul, had followed the venerable priest.

Five years afterwards the French again bombarded the city when forty-eight more Frenchmen were blown from the pirates' guns. There is to be seen in the Musée de la Marine at Paris, an old gun captured at Algiers, called "la Consulaire" from which the French Consul was blown.

So it went on for more than a century, these independent marauders of the coast waylaying commerce, capturing enormous quantities of money and of slaves, suffering punishment, striking back, making alliances, breaking them, and in general exacting toll, whether by aggression or agreement, from every

THE ALGERINES FIRING OFF THE FRENCH CONSUL FROM A MORTAR AT THE FRENCH FLEET

trading nation of the Western world. A small but illuminating incident is preserved which exposes their curious relationship with the rest of Europe. In the year 1780 the Dey of Algiers bought ten cannon from the Swedish government, at a fixed price. These had already been tested by the makers but the pirates, not content, must make a private test of their own. After filling the first gun half full of powder, they applied a match and the gun exploded, killing two of the Algerians outright and wounding many others. Although the accident could only be ascribed to the carelessness of the pirates, the Swedish consul had to pay heavy damages. The Dey demanded five hundred livres for the broken nose of one of the corsairs alone, and the whole affair cost the Swedish government about seven thousand livres.* This reads exactly like the routine business squabbles of two equal states until one remembers that it is a transaction between a Christian government and a nest of outlaws.

At last a power arose, young and not European, which dared to refuse the tribute demanded by the Barbary corsairs. At the very beginning of their existence the United States had been compelled to fall into line and between 1785 and 1799 had to pay the Dey of Algiers an enormous annual tribute in money to obtain nominal exemption for their ships. In 1798 Mr. Eaton, the American consul at Tunis, having been sent to Algiers in charge of four vessels as tribute from the United States, wrote home to his government, "Can any man believe that this elevated brute (the Dey) has seven kings of Europe, two republics and a continent tributary to him when his whole naval force is not equal to two line of battle ships?" Yet the very next year the tribute amounted to fifty thousand dollars, twenty-eight guns, ten thousand cannon balls, beside quantities of powder, cordage and jewels.

Finally public opinion in the United States was aroused to such a pitch that Congress ordered a fleet to be built at once to deal with the corsairs. The threat of strong measures had its effect on the Dey of Algiers: he agreed not to molest American shipping further if the President would send him a present

* "Sjörovarna på Medelhavet och Levantiska Compagniet," Stockholm, 1921.

of a frigate suitably equipped with powder and arms. On hearing of this the Bey of Tunis hurried to write to the President as well, explaining that unless ten thousand stand of arms and forty cannon were sent without delay "it would be impossible to keep the peace longer." Morocco, not wishing to be left out, then put in her claim to payment, but the Yusuf of Tripoli took the line that he was an aggrieved party and proclaimed war on May 14th 1801 by chopping down the flagstaff of the American consulate.

The young republic took up the challenge, but in her own time. In 1803 Commodore Edward Preble sailed for Gibraltar with the squadron of new warships. Of these the *Philadelphia* with thirty-six guns and the *Vixen* were sent to blockade the port of Tripoli.

On October 31st, while the *Philadelphia* was chasing a ship which was trying to run the blockade and reach Tripoli, she ran aground. No effort of the crew could move her and soon swarms of boats were seen coming out towards the ship. The issue of the ensuing fight was never in doubt. The Americans, though putting up a brave defence, were outnumbered, and after consulting with his officers Captain Bainbridge decided, in order to save the lives of his crew, to haul down his flag. Before doing so he had the magazines drowned by boring holes in the ship's bottom and the pumps choked so that she would become a total loss. Soon the pirates clambered aboard, robbed and stripped the officers, and threw both them and the crew into prison ashore. The unfortunate Bainbridge had the bitter experience a month later of seeing the *Philadelphia* refloated by the pirates and brought into harbour with all her guns salvaged and remounted.

On receipt of the news of this catastrophe Commodore Preble, who was preparing his ships for the next year's campaign, immediately laid plans for the destruction of the captive vessel, and selected for this desperate enterprise a young lieutenant, Stephen Decatur, whom he put in command of a ketch, the *Intrepid*. She carried five officers and seventy men, who were packed like herrings on a platform laid across some water butts without even sufficient room for them to sit up straight.

After a wild voyage in stormy weather the little ship arrived off Tripoli. Decatur decided to launch his attack the same night. On entering the harbour only a few of the crew, disguised as Maltese sailors, were allowed on deck, whence they could see the *Philadelphia* riding at anchor a mile away under the walls of the fort.

Sailing boldly in, the *Intrepid* drew up alongside the larger ship and in answer to a Moorish hail the Sicilian pilot replied in Tripolitan that they had lost their anchor in a gale and would like to run a line to the warship so that they might ride alongside of her during the night. Completely deceived, the pirates helped to make the ketch fast—at that moment a cry of "Americanos! Americanos!" rang out and the battle began with the sharp order to "Board!" from the American commander. The Yankee sailors at once clambered over the side and so sudden was the onset that in ten minutes the *Philadelphia* was recaptured with scarcely a casualty on the American side. Everything from now onwards went according to prearranged plan and fires were lighted in several parts of the ship. Once she was well alight, Decatur gave the order to get back on board the ketch and man the sweeps and pull for dear life. And not a moment too soon, for almost every gun in the fort was firing at them.

This scene has been described by one of the officers present, Charles Morriss, who wrote:

Up to this time the ships and batteries of the enemy had remained silent but they were now prepared to act and when the crew of the ketch gave three cheers in exultation of their success they received the return of a general discharge from the enemy. The confusion of the moment probably prevented much care in their direction, and though under fire for half an hour the only shot which struck the ketch was one through the topgallant sail. We were in greater danger from the *Philadelphia* whose broadsides commanded the passage by which we were retreating and whose guns were loaded, and discharged as they became heated. We escaped these also and while urging the ketch onwards with sweeps the crew were commenting upon the beauty of the spray thrown up by the shot between us and the brilliant light of the ship, rather than calculating any danger that might be apprehended from the contact. The appearance of the ship was indeed magnificent. The flames in the interior illuminated her ports and ascending her rigging and masts formed columns of fire which meeting the tops were reflected into beautiful capitals, whilst the occasional discharge of her guns gave an idea of some directing spirit within her. The walls of the city and its batteries and the masts and rigging of cruisers at anchor, brilliantly illuminated and animated by the discharge of artillery, formed worthy adjuncts and an appropriate background of the picture. Fanned by a light breeze our exertions soon carried us beyond the range of their shot.

It was not until the following July that Commodore Preble was prepared to attack Tripoli. Altogether five assaults were made before the pirates' stronghold was compelled to surrender and submit to the American terms. But a strict blockade of the coast was kept up for the two following years. In June 1805 a treaty was finally signed which provided that no further tribute should be paid and that American ships should be free to sail where they would, unmolested by the pirates.

But the sharp lesson America had taught the corsairs was, as usual, soon forgotten. Europe was still willing to argue, threaten and — pay up. But at last the behaviour of the pirates became so outrageous that England decided to deal with them in a thorough way. In 1816 Lord Exmouth was given *carte blanche* to do as he pleased, and duly arrived off Algiers with a powerful fleet, reinforced by a squadron of Dutch warships under the command of Vice-Admiral Baron van Capellan.

The match that lighted the actual conflagration was an order by the Dey of Algiers to arrest all the Italians under British protection at Bona and Oran. These orders resulted in the massacre at Bona of a hundred unarmed Italians who were attending Mass. A hundred more were wounded, and eight hundred robbed and thrown into prison.

The combined fleets of the allies arrived at Algiers on August 27th. In the meantime the *Prometheus* had been sent on ahead to Algiers to rescue the English consul and his family, who were in grave danger of their lives.

The consul's wife and daughters, disguised as midshipmen,

got safely aboard the *Prometheus,* but some other ruse had to be devised to get the baby on board. With this end in view the naval surgeon doped the child with an opiate. Hidden in a basket of fruit and vegetables it was being carried through the gate of the docks when unluckily it cried. Immediately the baby, the surgeon, three midshipmen and the boat's crew were arrested and dragged off before the Dey. Three days later the baby was returned to its mother, "a solitary example" wrote Lord Exmouth in his despatch "of his humanity."

The moment the Fleet arrived at Algiers the Admiral demanded the instant release of the prisoners. No answer was vouchsafed. Without more ado he opened hostilities.

"Then commenced a fire," wrote the Admiral, "as animated and well supported as I believe was ever witnessed from a quarter before three till nine, without intermission and which did not cease altogether till half past eleven. The ships immediately following me were admirably and coolly taking up their stations with a precision even beyond my most sanguine hope and never did British flag receive on any occasion more zealous and honourable support."

The battle raged furiously, even the women, who in those days sailed on board ships of war, serving at the guns with their husbands. By ten at night the main pirate batteries were silenced, and all the ships in the port were in flames, which quickly spread to the Arsenal, storehouses and gunboats, "exhibiting a spectacle of awful grandeur and interest no pen can describe."

Next day a treaty was concluded by which one thousand six hundred and forty-two slaves were set at liberty, and the Dey was forced to make a public apology to Mr. McDonell, the British Consul, who had been imprisoned half naked and in chains in a cell for condemned murderers.*

This lesson might have had and was expected to have a lasting effect for good, yet scarcely was the fleet out of sight of the Mediterranean than the pirates were at their old ways again.

The populace, deciding that their Dey was unlucky, strangled him, and another, Ali Khoja, was put in his place. But this

* Playfair.

rascal, "who greatly affected literature," proved to be a worse blackguard than his predecessor. According to Mr. Shaler, the American Consul, when he and the other foreign Consuls made their first official visit to the new Dey they were made to pass a score of corpses before reaching his presence, where they found him magnificently dressed with a book in his hand as if their entrance disturbed him in his studies."

Owing to the recent action by Lord Exmouth the supply of European women had failed so that the Dey, who seems to have been as fond of the fair sex as he was of literature, was driven to other means than sea piracy to procure additions to his harem. One case of his villainy in particular made a great sensation in Europe and was warmly taken up by Sir Sidney Smith, the President of the Anti-Piratic Association for the Redemption of Slaves in Barbary.

About it Sir Lambert Playfair writes: "A Sardinian girl, named Rosa Ponsombio, who was engaged to be married, was induced on some pretext to go with her mother one evening to the French consulate; on her return she was waylaid by emissaries of the Dey, who throwing a cloth over her head carried her off to his seraglio. The poor girl was forced to change her religion and her dress; but one day she found means of throwing a paper over the wall, addressed to the British Consul, informing him of her sad condition and warning him, as well as the Spanish and Dutch Consuls, to look well after their own daughters, as a similar fate was reserved for them. Indeed, after the Dey's death a book of memoranda was found amongst his effects containing this entry: "Mr. McDonell's daughter, pretty and young, for my harem; the Spanish consul's daughter who is ugly, to serve the favourite; I shall have the English consul's head cut off and that of the Spanish consul also and all the consuls shall be killed if they dare to complain."

Sir Sidney Smith tried in vain to rescue the girl but his efforts, even combined with those of M. de Richelieu, the French Minister, failed to bring about her release and she remained a prisoner in the Dey's seraglio until he died of plague in 1818. The epidemic of this disease had raged for some time in Algiers and was spread all over Europe by the Algerian ships.

By this time the slave trade was in full swing again in spite of all treaties and bombardments, and at the Congress of Aix-la-Chapelle it was decided to take measures against the Barbary pirates. In September 1819 a combined English and French fleet arrived in the Bay of Algiers, full of dire threats which all came to nothing, for in the end they sailed away leaving the Pasha to laugh and go on as he had done before.

And so matters continued, slavery was reestablished, and the rulers of the Barbary states became more and more truculent, insulting and finally beheading consuls, firing on flags of truce and generally behaving like barbarians.

But the day of reckoning was at last drawing near. Driven to desperation, the French, on May 26th 1820, sent a large fleet from Toulon, under the command of Admiral Duperré, with an army of thirty-seven thousand soldiers as well as cavalry and artillery. On June 13th the army was landed and threw up entrenchments. The French then began a slow but steady advance on Algiers, defeating the Moors in every action fought. On July 4th the bombardment of the city began, the principal fort fell and the powder magazine blew up. The next day the French occupied Algiers and the Dey and his family were sent to Naples in a French frigate. Gradually the surrounding tribes, beginning with Tunis, were subjugated by France and after so many hundreds of years the Scourge of Christendom was virtually brought to an end.

There were sporadic outbursts of piracy at intervals during the nineteenth century but in nearly all cases the offenders were caught and punished. With the gradual occupation of the Barbary coast by the various Southern European powers even these occasional recrudescences became less and less serious, and ultimately the last remnants of corsair activity were extinguished at the beginning of the present century.

CHAPTER V

SLAVERY AND REDEMPTION

THE trade in slaves was the reason, the support, the reward, of the Mediterranean pirate, both classical and Barbary, for upward of twenty centuries. The business grew to staggering proportions. Companies were formed in Algiers, Tunis and Tripoli for the sole purpose of financing vessels which were sent to sea with the single object of bringing back living merchandise. There is no record of numbers, but there was scarcely a year in which thousands of Europeans did not disappear into the maw of this traffic. Father Dan, who worked for years amongst them, states that in Algiers alone there were twenty-five thousand Christian slaves in 1634, besides eight thousand Christians who had turned Mohammedan.

When the captives were brought back to port they were first marched off to the bagnios, a strong underground prison. They were then examined by interpreters, who found out each prisoner's name, country of origin and trade or profession; if he had rich connections the amount of his ransom was determined upon and he was put aside until that matter could be adjusted. The other wretches were hurried into the Besistan or great slave market, where they were put up for auction like cattle. Usually they were bought by a dealer who had no direct use for them himself, but hired them out individually or collectively to someone who had — a clerk to a merchant who needed a bookkeeper, a group of labourers to a building contractor.

Some of the slaves were treated with the most devilish cruelty, but, apart from the galleys and public works, this was the exception rather than the rule. The private Turkish or Moorish slave-owner looked upon his Christian captive not as a criminal (even though he considered him an infidel and called him a dog) but as an animal like a horse, who would work best if well fed and looked after. In this the Mohammedans differed rather from the Christians, to whom a Moslem captive was a heretic and subject to be treated as such. There is an account of a Spanish priest who protested at an act of wanton cruelty by the Turks, who answered sharply with a reminder of the Holy Inquisition and its auto-da-fé, which effectively silenced the priest.

The fate of the unransomed prisoners varied enormously. Some of them, if they were skilled craftsmen or professional men, were in great demand by the Moors, especially physicians, who were treated with respect, though because of their value their owners were most reluctant to consider their release. Others accepted conversion and so escaped technical captivity, but were for ever after cast out from the society of their fellow Christians. These renegades enjoyed a certain amount of freedom and would sometimes attain important posts under the Turkish government; others, the offscourings of the European ports, took the turban simply as a means of turning pirate.

The great majority of captives were destined to a short lifetime of intense physical labour. The Moors were indefatigable builders, and at any Barbary port might be seen chained gangs of Christian slaves cutting stone, digging excavations, building houses, forts and harbours.

The fate of women captives is easily guessed. The great majority simply disappeared into the harems if they were young or into domestic labour if old. A typical story of a woman captive will be found in Appendix II.

But by far the worst employment to which a slave was liable was the galley. A man normally unaccustomed to physical labour would be chained to an oar alongside four or five or six other slaves. For food he would be given a few biscuits with an occasional mouthful of gruel, and for drink vinegar and water with a few drops of oil on the surface—all this to sustain a labour in any circumstances beyond normal endurance. Between the two lines of rowers ran a bridge along which walked two *Comiti* or boatswains carrying long whips which they brought down on the bare back of the laggard and the weary.

Two accounts exist from men who had actual experience of the rowing bench, one as slave, the other as witness. The first is by Jean Marteille de Bergerac, who left the following description of experiences in 1707.*

Think of six men chained to a bench, naked as when they were born, one foot on the stretcher, the other on the bench in front, holding an immensely heavy oar (fifteen feet long) bending forwards to the stern with arms at full reach to clear the backs of the rowers in front who bend likewise; and then having got forward shoving up the oar's end to let the blade catch the water, then throwing their bodies back on to the groaning bench. A galley-oar sometimes pulls thus for ten, or even twenty hours, without a moment's rest. The boatswain or other sailor, in such a stress, puts a piece of bread steeped in wine in the wretched rower's mouth to stop fainting and then the captain shouts the order to redouble the lash. If a slave falls exhausted upon his oar (which often chances) he is flogged till he is taken for dead, and then pitched unceremoniously into the sea.

The second is from an anonymous eye-witness:

Those who have not seen a galley at sea, especially in chasing or being chased, cannot well conceive the shock such a spectacle must give to a heart capable of the least tincture of commiseration. To behold the ranks and files of half-naked, half-starved, half-tanned meagre wretches, chained to a plank, from whence they remove not for months together (commonly half a year) urged on, even beyond human strength with cruel and repeated blows on their bare flesh, to an incessant continuation of the most violent of all exercises and this for whole days and nights successively, which often happens in a furious chase when one party, like vultures, is hurried on almost as eagerly after their prey, as is the weaker party hurried away in hopes of preserving life and liberty.

Naturally the stories we have of cruelty are for the most part told with an anti-Mohammedan bias, but there are indications that the other side were no more addicted to humanity in the galleys than their enemies. There is a story of a Moor who

* Whall: "Romance of Navigation."

was chained to a Spanish oar, but finding himself unequal to the work, at last in desperation chopped off his own left hand above the wrist in the hope that some other work would be found for him. But instead, before his wound was half healed he was again chained to the oar with a device attached to his stump, and now received special attention from the men with the lash. Eventually his case came to the ears of the Dey of Algiers, who informed the Spanish Father of the Redemption that he would exchange no more prisoners unless the one-handed rower was first surrendered.

No descriptions of captivities can equal the firsthand accounts contained in letters smuggled home or diaries later published by escaped or ransomed slaves. The following, written by one of these, Thomas Sweet, a "better sort of person," is so typical and so touching that it will bear reproduction in full:

Dear Friends,

It is now about six years since I was most unfortunately taken by a Turks man of war on the coasts of Barbary, captive into Argiere, since which time I have written oft to London to Master Southwood of the upper ground, to Richard Barnard of Duke's Place, Richard Coote of the Bankside, to Master Linger, a haberdasher in Crooked Lane, and in that to Master Southwood I sent an inclosed to my father, if living, and other letters to my brothers and friends if not dead. I could never hear whether any of you were alive or dead, which makes me think the letters are either miscarried, or all of you deceased, or gone to other places, or else I know you are too much Christians and friends that you could have looked upon me in such a condition. O! my friends, once more I tell you I am a miserable captive in Argiere, taken by a Flemish vessel two years after I left the wars in Gilderland. My Patroone is one Baron, a French renegade, that lives in the country, but hires me and another Protestant captive (one Master Robinson, a Norfolk man) out in Argiere, for this time and if we go up to the country, you may never hear of us again. Our misery is that the price of our redemption will be no less than £250, because we are thought to have good friends in England, and we must both go off together. Master Robinson hath written to his friends, and we have deeply bound ourselves to each other, that we will engage our friends to us both equally. Ah! father, brother, friends and acquaintance, use some speedy means for our redemption. Many hundred slaves have been redeemed from their misery since we came hither, which makes us hope still we may be the next and then the next, but still our hopes are deceived. We do pray you, therefore, for the Lord Christ's sake that redeemed you, that you would use all possible means for our redemption. There is now a party in England renowned over the Christian world for their piety this way. Oh make your address to those noble worthies in the name of Christ for whose sake we suffer. We did never so well understand the meaning of that Psalm, penned by those captive Jews, held in Babilonish captivity, as now: "By the waters of Babylon we sat down and wept when we remembered thee Oh Sion," when we remembered thee Oh England. Oh good friends, we hope these our sighs will come to your ears, and move pity and compassion.

We are told there is a merchant in London, one Mr. Stanner of St. Mary Axe, that hath a factor in Legorn, and one Mr. Hodges and Mr. Mico, Londoners, that are dealers there who are able to direct you in the readiest way for our redemption. Deny us not your prayers if you can do nothing else. It will be some comfort to hear from friends. There is a post in London that conveys letters into all parts, and if you have an opportunity of letting us hear from you, if you please, within a month or six weeks. The Lord direct your thoughts with ways of love and strengthen us with faith and patience.

Your sorrowful friend and brother in Christ,

Thomas Sweet

From Barbary: September 29, 1646.

No list of redeemed slaves includes the name of either Thomas Sweet or Richard Robinson, so that it is most likely that they were, as they feared, sent into the interior of the country, whence no slave ever returned.

In spite of the strict guard kept over the slaves there were occasional escapes and the accounts of these adventures are perhaps amongst the most thrilling in all the literature of piracy.

One of these is in the author's possession, a small and very rare volume published in 1675 under the title of "Ebenezer or a small monument of Great Mercy," which was written "By me, William Okeley." The author prefaces his story with a long allegorical poem of which the first two lines are:

This Author never was in print before,
And (let this please or not) will never more.

Despite this disclaimer Mr. Okeley then sets down his narrative in a thoroughly professional manner.

It was in June 1638, he writes, that the "*Mary* of London" set sail from Gravesend for the Island of New Providence in the West Indies. She was armed with six guns and carried a cargo of linen and woollen cloth and some sixty souls made up of crew and passengers. The voyage started unpropitiously. After being weatherbound for five weeks in the Downs, the *Mary* reached the Isle of Wight "but by this time all our beer in the ship stunk, and we were forced to throw it overboard, and to take in vinegar to mix with our water for our voyage." Their next misfortune was to run on to a sand bank, but with much toil they floated the ship off at high water. "These circumstances," observes the author, "seem very inconsiderable to those who were not concerned in the Products of them, but God has given us the advantage and leisure to see what *great things* were in the Womb of *those little things.*"

Our voyagers, who now sailed with two other ships for their mutual protection, met, six days afterwards, three Algerian warships, which attacked them and after a short fight, in which six of the *Mary's* crew were killed, captured all the three English vessels. For several weeks the captives were kept prisoners on board, while the pirates cruised in search of prey, during which time Okeley learnt to speak a little Arabic on the chance that it might be of use to him later on.

Arrived at Algiers the new captives were driven to the slave market. The men fetched various prices, the highest being paid for the young ones with sound teeth and strong limbs. Their hands were particularly examined; those with hard calloused palms being known to be used to hard work, but those with well kept soft hands would often fetch high prices as likely to be merchants or gentlemen and so good for a profitable ransom.

Okeley was bought by a Moorish shipowner, who employed him to do blacksmith's work, but soon afterwards he was ordered to go for a cruise in one of his pirate vessels, against which the Englishman strongly protested, but all in vain. After an unsuccessful cruise Okeley's patron turned his slave out telling him to find some trade or other, out of which he was to keep himself and pay his owner two dollars a month.

Okeley opened a small shop, where he sold tobacco and wine, and as business began to increase he took into partnership another captive, John Randal, a glover by trade. This man, whose wife and child had been captured with him, began to make canvas clothes to sell to the seamen amongst the slaves.

After four years or more Okeley observed that he and other slaves had become "so habituated to bondage that we almost forgot Liberty, and grew stupid and senseless of our slavery; like *Issacher, we crouched down between our burdens, we bowed our shoulders to bear, and became servants of tribute.* I. Chron. iv, 23."

The principal need Okeley felt was for religious comfort and this was soon to be provided in the person of the good Mr. Devereux Spratt, a fellow captive and Anglican priest. "Thrice a week this Godly, peaceful servant of Jesus Christ prayed with us, and preached to us the Word of God; our meeting place was a cellar which I had hired. To our meetings resorted many, sometimes three- or fourscore, and though we were next the street, yet we never had the least disturbance from the Turks or Moors."

After a while Okeley's master, having made several unsuccessful cruises, was forced to sell everything to pay his debts, and his slaves changed hands. Okeley was bought by a "grave old gentleman" who not only treated his English slave with pity and kindness, but as a son, and indeed was so gentle and good natured that for the first time since his captivity at Algiers Okeley felt happy. But in spite of his kind patron, he still yearned for freedom and set about making plans for his escape, but not without great searching of conscience, for the honest slave was worried whether "it was not down-right theft to withdraw myself from his service, who had bought me, paid for me and possessed me as his own proper goods, and now

I was not my own, had no right to myself." At last his conscience, to his great relief, decided that his "Patron's title was rotten at the foundation; Man is too noble a creature to be made subject to a deed of bargain and sale and my consent was never asked to all their bargains." Much relieved in mind, William Okeley then began to make serious plans for an escape. After confiding in Mr. Spratt and getting his consent and blessing, the conspirators, for several were in the plot, began to make a canvas boat, the pieces of which when completed were to be carried down to the sea and there joined together, when it was hoped it would "by the superintendency of Divine Providence, prove an Ark, to deliver us out of the hands of our enemies."

The cellar where the church services were held was chosen as being the safest place in which to make the boat, and in due time a frame was constructed which could be taken to pieces; a canvas cover was also made, well smeared with pitch, which could be stretched over the frame. The parts of the boat were carried down to the seashore by one of the slaves, who was a washerman and each day used to carry some pieces of the boat under the clothes he took to wash, and hide them under a hedge. By the same method the bulky tarred canvas was got out of the city and hidden with the framework.

At last one dark night the seven Englishmen met at the appointed place and hour, quickly put the boat together and launched her, to find to their great relief and joy that she floated. Then, stripping themselves naked, they waded out with the boat and began to get aboard, only to discover to their dismay that when all seven were in she began to sink. Experience showed that five was all the boat would float with, so two had to be left on the beach while the rest ventured out to sea. The voyage began with four men pulling for dear life while the fifth kept on baling without a moment's rest. When daylight came they saw to their horror that they were still in sight of the ships lying in the harbour, but luckily they were unobserved. They rowed for three days until all their bread was exhausted and almost all their drinking water. By the fourth day — it was in July and the heat excessive — the refugees were almost at their last gasp when they managed to catch a tortoise floating asleep on the sea. They drank its blood and ate its flesh and were so revived that they again took up the oars and pulled towards, as they hoped, Majorca and freedom.

At last on the sixth day land was sighted, which encouraged the tired rowers to pull harder, but it was not until the following day that the almost dying runaways arrived safely at Majorca, where they were treated with great kindness, fed, clothed and then sent to Cadiz in one of the King of Spain's galleys. At Cadiz they found an English vessel in which they sailed home, reaching the Downs in September 1644.*

Mr. Okeley's conscience proved a difficulty to him, though fortunately not an insuperable one. There is one story, however, which involves the conscience of an entire ship's crew, all God-fearing Quakers who were compelled by their creed to contrive their escape in a most unorthodox manner. The account is contained in a pamphlet by one of the sailors, Thomas Lurting, and is appropriately entitled "The Fighting Sailor Turned Peaceable Christian."

It was in August 1663 that Lurting sailed as first mate in an English ketch bound from Venice for England. The captain, mate and crew were all Quakers, and in accordance with their creed, carried no arms on board. Just at this time the Barbary pirates were unusually active, but the captain, refusing to listen to the crews' suggestion of waiting for a convoy, insisted on continuing his voyage alone. When off the coast of "May-York," which was the seventeenth century sailors' pronunciation of the name of the island of Majorca or Mallorca, an Algerian vessel chased and took the English ship. Eight Turks were ordered to board the ketch to carry her and the English prisoners to Algiers.

"All this while," says Lurting, "I was under a great exercise of spirit — and going to the side to see the Turks come in, the word of the Lord ran through me thus: 'Be not afraid for all this, thou shalt not go to Algiers.' " After this Lurting lost all

* For an exciting escape of galley slaves from a Turkish warship see Appendix III.

his fear and "received them (the Turks) as a man might his friends and they were as civil to us." Thus the pirates got their first surprise.

The obliging Lurting next showed his visitors over the vessel, explaining all about her cargo. He also found an opportunity to warn his shipmates to be very polite to the Turks and be willing to do all that was told them, as he was certain that he would find means for their escape. The Turks, delighted to find such an unusually docile crew, retired to the great cabin to rest and sleep while the infidels sailed the ship.

Lurting then explained to the still somewhat mystified crew his plan, which was to lash up all the Turks in the cabin and run off with the vessel. The sailors readily agreed to this scheme; indeed one simple Quaker, forgetting for the moment his religious scruples, declared, "I will kill one or two," while another offered to "cut as many of their throats as you will have me." This so shocked the good Lurting that he declared if he heard another word about killing or throat-cutting he would inform the Turks.

In the end, after much discussion, the Turks were all duly lashed up, and the Englishmen were once again masters of their ship. This would be thought to end the story, but no. Lurting was convinced that it behoved good Christians and good Quakers to liberate the Turks. The crew were for taking them to Majorca near by, but this Lurting refused to hear of, for their late captors, now their prisoners, would be seized by the Spaniards and sold for slaves. What he proposed was to put the Turks ashore in their own country.

This, which sounds at first a simple matter, was far from being so in actuality. The ketch was steered close off the Algerian coast and then rose the question: how were the Turks to be put ashore without the Quakers themselves being recaptured? Much argument amongst the crew and much communing with the Lord went on as to how ten Turks were to be safely put on shore in a boat rowed by three sailors. It was a difficult problem to arrange; it was like one of those puzzles in which, whatever is done, at some moment or other there are more blacks than whites in the boat. At last it was decided to carry all the Turks in one trip, and to do this the ingenious Lurting (who refused the obviously simple suggestion of binding the Turks because he said "to bind them would but exasperate them") arranged the Turks as follows:

He first placed the captain of the Turks in the boat's stern with a fellow pirate on either side. On the laps of these he made the next three sit and when all were thus seated, two sailors each took an oar, another sat in the bows armed with a carpenter's axe (for show only), while Lurting steered, the tiller in one hand and a boathook in the other. Under his legs were piled all the Turks' weapons. At last, after committing themselves to the Lord, the crew pushed off.

It was a long pull to the shore and all the longer because the nervous sailors would continue to look over their shoulders and say they saw turbaned heads bobbing up behind the rocks on the shore. At length, after much discussion and panic, the boat was backed into the shore, the captives were landed and thrown their arms and half a hundredweight of bread. The Turks, overwhelmed by this kindness or possibly with sinister intentions, warmly invited the sailors to go with them to the neighbouring town where there was wine to be had and other good things. The cautious Lurting refused, but "we parted in great love, and stayed until they got up the hill, and they shook their caps at us and we at them."

The boat then rowed back to the ship "and as soon as we came on board we had a fair wind, which we had not had all the while the Turks were on board, nor many days before." This reward for good deeds continued until they cast anchor in the Thames. Quickly the news spread and all and sundry came off to hear first hand the story of the Quakers who had "been taken by the Turks and had redeemed themselves and had never a gun." Even the King, Charles II, and his brother, the Duke of York, came from Greenwich, accompanied by many lords, to see so strange a spectacle. The King asked many questions about his men-of-war in the Mediterranean, but Lurting told him bluntly: "We had seen none of them," which must have disconcerted the monarch and his admiral brother.

Occasionally there were desperate mass attempts at escape, but these were rarely successful and were terribly punished in the event of failure. There are various accounts of these concerted dashes for liberty, but they all resemble one another — a well kept conspiracy, the bribing or overpowering of a guard, a ship captured or waiting by pre-arrangement in the harbour, and a race against pursuit into a friendly port. But recorded instances of successful conspiracies of this sort are rare.

The best hope of the captives lay in the possibility of redemption, by friends or the government at home, or else by way of exchange against a similar number of captives in the possession of their own country. The letter of Thomas Sweet is characteristic of the pitiable appeals which were constantly reaching the capitals of Europe.

The two most illustrious prisoners ever to fall into the hands of pirates were both ultimately delivered by this method of ransom. The story of Julius Cæsar has already been told. The other is that of Miguel de Cervantes.

The immortal Spaniard had already served under Don John of Austria at Lepanto, where he lost a hand; two years later he was present at the capture of Tunis, and the following year at that of the Goletta. On September 26th, 1575, while returning from Naples to Spain with his brother Roderigo, the ship was attacked by several corsair galleys under Arnaut Memi, an Albanian renegade, and both of the Cervantes were taken. At Algiers Miguel de Cervantes was sold to an apostate Greek, who on searching his purchase discovered on him a letter of recommendation from Don John of Austria. Don John, then Governor of the Netherlands, and half brother to the King of Spain, was one of the most important men in Europe: the Greek concluded that he had bought a bargain and demanded a heavy ransom. In the meantime the future author of "Don Quixote" was loaded with chains and treated with the utmost harshness.

The restless Cervantes took badly to captivity and was continually planning schemes of escape. Every attempt failed and with each failure the watch over him became stricter. One almost succeeded, when Cervantes hid some fifty fugitives, mostly Spanish gentlemen, in a cave and managed to supply them with food for six months. In the meantime he had arranged with his brother, who had been ransomed after two years by their father, that a ship should be sent to take away the cave-dwellers. The ship arrived and the party was on the point of leaving when an alarm was raised and the attempt frustrated. Cervantes courageously took all the blame on himself and refused to implicate any of his confederates. The Viceroy, Hassan, a monster of cruelty, threatened the Spaniard with every imaginable form of torture to induce him to tell who had helped him with the plot, but not a syllable could the Moor extract. Hassan was so impressed by the prisoner's courage that instead of punishing him he bought him from the Greek for five hundred pounds.

Once again Cervantes all but escaped, and was only betrayed at the last moment by a Dominican monk. At length, after five years, when he was about to be taken to Constantinople, whither Hassan had been recalled, Father Juan Gil arrived with the ransom and he was free. Even old Morgan of Algiers, hater of all papists and Spaniards, owned that Cervantes was "a gallant, enterprising cavalier." If he had been any less, five years in Moorish prisons would have broken his spirit, and the world would have been for ever poorer.

A third famous captive, and the only saint ever to fall into the hands of the Barbary corsairs, was Saint Vincent de Paul, who was captured in 1605 during a voyage from Marseilles to Narbonne. He went through all the excitement of capture at sea and the degradation of public exposure for sale, but subsequently found a kind buyer who was in search of the Philosopher's Stone and implanted in the holy captive a profound interest in alchemy. He was left by will to the old man's nephew and during this second period of captivity was able to enjoy the pleasures of theological disputation with an enlightened schismatic. Finally he escaped. The narrative of this captivity is delightfully told by the saint himself in a letter to a friend, Monsieur de Commet:

The wind would have been sufficiently favourable to bring us to Narbonne, fifty leagues, the same day, if God had not permitted three Turkish sloops coasting the Gulf of Lyons to give chase to us, and make so sharp an attack upon us that two or three of us were killed and the rest all wounded, even myself receiving an arrow wound which has left its reminder for all my life. We were thus constrained to yield to these pickpockets, who were fiercer than tigers, and, as a first expression of their rage, hewed our pilot in a thousand pieces to avenge the loss of one of theirs. After seven or eight days they set sail for Barbary, the robbers' den of the Grand Turk, where, when we had arrived, we were put up for sale with a certificate of our capture on a Spanish vessel, because otherwise we should have been freed by the Consul, who is kept there by the King to safeguard French trading.

We were paraded through the streets of Tunis, where we were brought for sale, and, having gone round the town five or six times with chains on our necks, we were brought back to the ship that we might eat, and so show the merchants that we had received no mortal injury.

I was sold to a fisherman, and by him to an aged alchemist, a man of great gentleness and humility. This last told me he had devoted fifty years to a search for the Philosopher's Stone. My duty was to keep up the heat of ten or twelve furnaces, in which office, thank God, I found more pleasure than pain. My master had great love for me, and liked to discourse of alchemy and still more of his creed, towards which he did his best to draw me, with the promise of wealth and all the secrets of his learning. God maintained my faith in the deliverance which was to be an answer to my continual prayers to Him and the Virgin Mary (to whose intercession I am confident my deliverance is due).

I was with this old man from September, 1605, to the following August, when he was summoned to work for the Sultan — in vain, for he died of regret on the way. He left me to his nephew, who sold me very soon after his uncle's death, on a rumour that M. de Brève, the Kings Ambassador, was coming — armed with powers from the Grand Turk — to emancipate Christian slaves. I was bought by a renegade from Nice in Savoy, and taken by him to his dwelling-place among the mountains in a part of the country that is very hot and arid. One of his three wives, a Greek, who was a Christian, although a schismatic, was highly gifted, and displayed a great liking for me, as eventually, and to a greater degree, did another of them, who was herself Turkish, but who, by the mercy of God, became the instrument for reclaiming her husband from his apostasy, for bringing him back within the pale of the Church, and delivering me from slavery. Her curiosity as to our manner of life brought her daily to the fields where I worked, and in the end she required me to sing the praises of my God. The thought of the "Quomodo cantabimus in terra aliena" of the children of Israel, captive in Babylon, made me, with tears in my eyes, begin the psalm, "Super flumina Babilonis," and afterwards the "Salve Regina" and other things, in which she took so much delight that it was amazing. In the evening she did not fail to say to her husband that he had made a mistake in deserting his religion, which she believed to be a very good one by reason of the account of our God, which I had given her, and the praises of Him which I had sung in her hearing. In hearing these she said she had felt such pure delight that she could not believe that the paradise of her fathers, and that to which she one day aspired, would be so glorious, or afford her anything to equal this sensation. This new representation of Balaam's ass so won over her husband that the following day he said he was only waiting for an opportunity to fly to France, and that in a short time he would go to such lengths as would be to the glory of God. This short time was ten months, during which he offered me only vain hopes but at the end we took flight in a little skiff, and arrived on the 28th of June at Aigues-Mortes, and soon afterwards went to Avignon, where Monseigneur the Vice-Legate gave public readmission to the renegade, with a tear in his eye and a sob in his throat, in the Church of Saint Pierre, to the glory of God, and the edification of all beholders.

Monseigneur kept us both with him till he could take us to Rome, whither he went as soon as the successor to his three-year-old office arrived. He had promised to gain entrance for the penitent into the convent of the "Fate ben fratelli," where he made his vows, and he promised to find a good living for me. His reason for liking and making much of me was chiefly because of certain secrets of alchemy which I had taught him, and for which he had been vainly seeking all his life." *

One hears so much about the terrible effects on a Christian captive of the hardships of slavery that it is pleasant to record a case where a prisoner's physique actually improved during his incarceration amongst the Barbary corsairs.

This exception was "Sir" Jeffery Hudson, a peppery dwarf

* "Vincent de Paul, Priest and Philanthropist, 1576–1660." By E. K. Sanders, London, 1913.

attached to the court of Charles I. In 1630 he was sent to France as escort to a midwife who was to attend the Queen of England in her approaching confinement. The Queen was that same Henrietta Maria, daughter of Henry of Navarre, whose birth had been announced by Simon de Danser in 1609; the child she was expecting was to be King Charles II.

As the dwarf was returning through the Channel with the midwife and the Queen's dancing master, their ship was captured by a Flemish pirate and all were taken to Dunkirk. Besides losing the midwife Hudson lost twenty-five hundred pounds. Ransomed, he contrived in 1658 to be captured again, this time by the Algerians, one of the few cases of the same man suffering two captivities. On his return from the second, again by the method of ransom, he complained to the King that, though he had been only eighteen inches high before his misadventure, the hard labour to which the corsairs had subjected him had increased his height to three feet six inches!

This unique little man had enough adventures in his life to satisfy a giant. Earlier in his career in Paris he had fancied himself insulted by one Crofts. "Strenuous Jeffery," his contemporaries conceded, "though a dwarf was no dastard." He promptly challenged Crofts to a duel. The other, not taking the affair very seriously, arrived at the appointed place armed with no weapon but a water squirt, whereupon the infuriated Jeffery shot him dead. It seems somehow an unfair contest from the point of view of either man: the dwarf's eighteen inches made him a difficult target to hit, but on the other hand he must have found it a serious matter to discharge a lethal weapon nearly as big as himself.

All through the seventeenth century Parliament and the officers of the Crown were being implored in public and private petitions to make some attempt to redeem the wretched captives by ransom, or at least to make some arrangement with their captors to alleviate their lot. It was a frequent sight to behold the approaches of the House of Commons thronged with the wives and daughters of Barbary prisoners, pressing their bereavements on the attention of the members.

The slaves, save the comparative few who had well-to-do

relatives at home, were dependent on the meagre charity of the English government. From time to time the outcry in the country grew so great that the House would raise a special sum, usually by a small extra tax on imported goods, to pay the Turk for the liberation of prisoners. Other means, however, were sometimes employed. In 1624 the House of Lords instructed the Commons to grant letters patent for a collection to be made throughout the whole kingdom for the redemption of English captives. The Lords themselves, to set a good example, made a collection in the Upper House, the barons subscribing twenty shillings and the peers of higher rank forty. The Commons added a resolution that every member who came late to prayers should be fined and the proceeds given to the poor women who attended each day in great numbers at the doors of Parliament.

Unfortunately much of the redemption money was never used for that purpose at all but purloined by the navy. It was admitted in 1651 that out of £69,296 only £11,109 had been used for freeing slaves, the rest having been appropriated by the Royal navy to pay its debts. Sympathy with the captives, however, was not altogether universal, and this may have had something to do with the matter. For a long time England as well as the Continent was filled with broken men returned from Barbary slavery, and a large proportion of them were so unfitted for ordinary employment that a popular impression was created that they were but rogues who "roam up and down Europe as mendicants, in chains and fetters, which they never bore in Africa." It was the usual human reaction to misery too long sustained.

Various ingenious schemes were constantly being drawn up to deal with the question of the captives, and presented to the House of Commons. The anonymous author of one of these, after endeavouring to prove that the Jews of Algiers were the prime cause of all the mischief, since they were the capitalists who financed the pirate ships and principal receivers of slaves, proposed a law to the effect that any loss sustained by Englishmen at the hands of the corsairs should be made good out of the estates of the Jews in England. He held the view, still prevalent in some places, that all the Jews of the world were in league and that to punish English Jews would prove a check on their Barbary co-religionists. Since Jews were not allowed in England until Cromwell's time it is doubtful whether this measure could have been very efficacious.

There were several charities in England for the redemption of slaves, principally founded on legacies. In 1724 a Mr. Thomas Betton left the whole of a large fortune to the Ironmongers' Company, of which he was a member, to be held in trust for charitable purposes, with the direction that half the income should be spent each year for the redemption of British slaves in Turkey or Barbary.

The first organisation in Europe for the redemption of captives was the "Order of the Holy Trinity and Redemption of Slaves," founded at the end of the twelfth century by Jean de Matha. In its first year the founder brought back from Morocco one hundred and eighty-six slaves. Thereafter for centuries the good fathers in their white robes with blue and red crosses on the breast continued fearlessly their dangerous work of bargaining with the pirates. Père Dan, whose history of the corsairs has been quoted several times, was one of its members.

As time went on the Dominicans and Franciscans joined in the work. These priests not only devoted themselves to ransoming prisoners, but did much to alleviate their lot by establishing hospitals for the sick and chapels for the celebration of Mass. As a result the Catholic slaves were in a better position than the Protestants. At times the Protestants were made only too aware of the fact: on one occasion, when the Fathers of the Redemption had arranged to pay three thousand pieces of eight for three French captives, the Dey in a fit of generosity offered to throw in a fourth gratis, but the Fathers refused to take him because he was a Lutheran.

At a later date, however, the Protestant nations founded similar organisations, and the Anti-Piratical Association, of which Sir Sidney Smith was president, carried on its work with notable efficiency until the guns of England, France and America happily dispensed with any further need of it.

BOOK II

THE PIRATES OF THE NORTH

CHAPTER I

THE VIKINGS AND HANSEATICS

THE Norse seamen known as Vikings began to infest the coast of Western Europe during the Middle Ages, reaching the height of their power in about the eleventh century and ultimately carving out for themselves a chain of foreign dominions which extended from the River Tweed to the Straits of Messina. The word Viking in itself signifies a sea rover or pirate, but these Scandinavian freebooters were more than mere banditti, for they were organised and possessed a strictly enforced code of law governing the division of booty and punishment for desertion, treachery or theft. To the well to do young Norseman participation in a Viking cruise was considered as much a part of his education as was the Grand Tour to the English gentleman of the eighteenth century. Though cruel and wild, even for a wild and cruel age, the Norsemen had a strong sense of government and a feeling for colonisation (though not in the sense of a dependency on a homeland), and left their mark ineradicably wherever they settled, especially in Normandy and England.

Their ships, according to modern ideas, were unseaworthy; yet in them the Vikings made voyages of great length, not only into the Mediterranean but even to the coast of America five hundred years before Columbus. These craft were long, narrow and of shallow draught, pointed at both ends, propelled by oars but carrying a mast with a large square sail which was hoisted when wind and weather permitted. The earlier ships did not carry more than ten oars on each side, with a crew of sixty men who took turns at rowing; later, as bigger vessels were built, as many as sixty rowers were employed at a time. Unlike the galleys of the Mediterranean the Viking ships carried only free men, each one a trained warrior. On the sides of the ship were hung the round Viking shields painted with the emblems or crests of their owners. Their arms were spears, javelins, axes, arrows and swords, and their armour consisted of a shirt of mail.

The first appearance of the Vikings in force off the English coast occurred in 789 A.D., when three ships arrived off the Dorset coast and landed a party who killed the port reeve, plundered the neighbourhood and ran away. From then on the raids on England, Scotland and Ireland were annual events and soon the Norsemen had established themselves in islands off the coast, their favourite custom, whence they could dash across to the mainland and take what they wanted, food, women, and even monks. Ultimately they would conquer the adjacent territory, settle, intermarry with the native women, and form independent communities whose chief occupation was further piracy. This is in large measure how the conquest of England was achieved, as will be seen later.

Ireland received her first visit in 795, when the Vikings seized the Island of Lambey in Dublin Bay, and from there made steady inroads into the country. The most formidable of the Viking invaders of Ireland was Turgesius, who gradually extended his conquests until he became ruler of half the island. He then established his wife as high-priestess of Ireland's most famous and learned monastery at Clonmacnoise. Turgesius was killed fighting in 845, but left two colonies at Dublin and Waterford. By this time his pirates had spread to Scotland and wiped out all the communities on its west coast.

The middle of the ninth century saw the Northmen looking for richer plunder than the British Isles could afford. They had ventured up the Scheldt, the Rhine, the Somme and the Seine, and by 912 had conquered the country which has ever since borne the name of Normandy. From there their successors achieved the second conquest of England in 1066.

In the meantime Hamburg had been burnt and fleets of Viking ships had sailed to Spain. Thence they crossed to the opposite African coast, one day to shelter an even more formidable race of corsairs, and gradually spread east to the mouth of the Rhône, and so on along to Italy.

Until they finally settled down to enjoy their widespread conquests they remained the terror of the inhabitants of every seaboard in Christendom, to whose litanies in time was added the fervent prayer: *A furore Normanorum libera nos.*

The Hanseatic League, one of the most celebrated institutions of the Middle Ages, had its origin in the terror which the corsairs of the far north inspired. In 1241 the cities of Lübeck and Hamburg combined to protect their merchant ships from the attacks of the corsairs who lurked at the entrance to the German rivers emptying into the North Sea and the Baltic. Gradually other free cities were enrolled and the power of the League increased rapidly. Its headquarters were finally settled at Wisby in Gothland.

A long history of fighting between the League and the pirates ensued, in which the League gradually gained the upper hand, but since sailors in the Middle Ages were used to playing all sorts of parts at sea and the temptation to deviate from the narrow line of fighting or trading was irresistible, Hanseatic mariners soon learnt by imitation the business they had been hired to suppress, and became as efficient at it as the best. The growing English trade in the second half of the fourteenth century was the particular sufferer, but as the English corsairs had by this time become the worst enemy of German shipping, the complaints were about equal on both sides. From the records of those years it is difficult to see how a North Sea merchant carried on business at all — probably he made up his losses in part by overcharging, partly by a little piracy on the sly, which enabled him to gain on the swings what he lost on the roundabouts.

There were two particularly notorious Hanseatic pirates at large in the North Sea during the second half of the fourteenth century, Godekins and Stertebeker, who generally sailed together and whose names appear in innumerable claims for compensation made by outraged merchants and shipowners. Both of these gentlemen were murderers as well as robbers, but Stertebeker, a ruined nobleman and a drunkard (his name means "a Beaker at a Gulp"), was the worse of the two, though as a pirate he was the superior.

The pair finally turned against their employers and went off on their own. It was what the League might have expected, for the League itself had adopted the dangerous policy of encouraging piracy by making alliances with the pirates in its wars with Denmark, the same shortsighted policy that the European powers were to pursue with the Barbary corsairs.

Godekins and Stertebeker joined with two other outlaws, Moltke and Manteufel (the man-devil), to form a gang calling itself "The Victual Brothers" or, more familiarly, "The Friends of God and the Enemies of the World." This brotherhood recruited its crews from the scum of all the Baltic coast towns and yearly grew more powerful and dangerous. By 1392 it was strong enough to sack and burn Bergen, then the principal city of Norway, take the leading merchants away and hold them to ransom. No ordinary trading vessel in the North Sea or the Baltic could hope to outrun or outfight one of the brotherhood, and after the sack of Bergen even the great herring fisheries had to be abandoned, for no fishing boat dared to go out.

The menace to life as well as to commerce became so serious that several royal expeditions were sent out to end it. The first, equipped by Queen Margaret of Sweden with the help of Richard II of England, failed utterly. A second, despatched in 1394 by the Hansa towns, and consisting of thirty-five warships and three thousand men, had only a meagre success against its own creatures.

The "Victuallers" were finally brought to book in 1402. Under Simon of Utrecht, who flew at his masthead the emblem of the Spotted Cow, to this day the favourite name for a Hamburg ship, the Hamburg fleet met and dispersed the pirates. Stertebeker, its commander, was captured alive, carried to Hamburg and there executed. It was said at the time that the mainmast of his ship was found to be hollow and filled with molten gold, of such fabulous value that when sold it was sufficient not only to pay the whole cost of the war and an indemnity to the merchants for all they had lost, but to make a golden crown for the spire of the sailors' Church of St. Nicholas in Hamburg.

CHAPTER II

THE EARLY ENGLISH PIRATES

WITH some of the best pirate blood in the world in their veins, Norse, Danish, Saxon and Norman, it was not remarkable that the English race grew in time to be the first corsair nation of the earth. But even before the conquest and settlement of the island by the invaders from across the North Sea and the Channel, the Britons had already acquired a more than local reputation for proficiency in the art to which they were to give the most illustrious exponents.

It was the mischievous sea folk of southern England who were directly responsible for Julius Cæsar's invasion of Britain in 55 B.C. The fierce Veneti pirates of Britanny had proved exceedingly troublesome to the conqueror of Gaul, and a large part of their strength was recruited from across the Channel. Cæsar realised that the best way of subduing the Veneti was to put down the Britons first, and the invasion followed. It was a lesson which Philip II of Spain might have used to his great advantage sixteen centuries later if he had invaded England before exhausting himself in the attempt to subdue his rebellious Dutch provinces.

The ships of the Veneti and of the Britons both were of shallow draught, stoutly built of oak fastened with iron, and carrying chained cables instead of rope. Though provided with oars, they depended principally on their sails of tanned hide. Their decks were a foot thick, and altogether these small craft were so well and strongly built that the Romans were unable to sink them by their favourite method of ramming. It was not until he took to cutting the pirates' rigging with sharp hooks attached to poles that Cæsar at last defeated them at sea.

By 43 A.D. the Roman conquest of England was complete and the country became part of the Roman Empire for more than three hundred years. Yet piracy continued to flourish, even under Imperial dominion and in spite of Rome's formidable *Classis Britannica.* Not until the reign of the Emperor Maximian in 286 A.D. were effective measures taken to gain proper control of the Narrow Seas. An expedition was organised and conducted with typical Roman efficiency. The command was given to Marcus Aurelius Carausius, a man familiar from birth with the waters he was to police. From his station at Boulogne Carausius swept north and west across the Channel and soon dispersed Frankish and northern pirates to their respective lairs.

Carausius was a Scotsman or a Belgian — it is not quite certain which. As a young man he had been employed as a pilot and was known as a first class seaman. Later he entered the Roman army, where by extraordinary talent and energy he quickly gained high rank.

But the rewards of professional merit presently began to seem inadequate and Carausius, like so many before and after him, entered into an arrangement with the pirates to give them protection in return for a share in their plunder. The Imperial Government found him out and he was condemned to death, but receiving timely warning escaped across the Channel into Britain. Here he proclaimed himself an independent ruler and was joined by the Roman legion on garrison duty in the island, as well as by large numbers of Frankish pirates. For seven years he maintained himself as a sort of corsair king of Britain, building and equipping a fleet which was strong enough to rout the Roman fleet sent to capture him. He was murdered in 293, after the accepted fashion of the Roman emperors, by the Prefect of his own Guard.

The break-up of the Roman Empire left England quite unprepared and unprotected from invasion by the Picts and Scots from the north and the hordes of Norse pirates who soon began to pour into the country. The latter particularly, for several centuries after the departure of the Romans, used the unfortunate island as a happy hunting ground to raid and plunder and gradually to settle in.

Under King Alfred a temporary halt was put to the depredations of the northern pirates. With a strong administration the country became comparatively settled and strong enough to fight in its own defence. Moreover in 897 Alfred set about the creation of the first English navy. According to the Saxon Chronicle his ships were of a new type, some of them twice as big as any previously known, pulled by sixty and even more oars. He promulgated a law to the effect that henceforth all Norsemen would be treated as pirates, without mercy — there was to be no more paltering or purchase of temporary exemption by payment of tribute money. The efficiency of Alfred's preparations was shown during the reign of his grandson, Athelstan, who led the English fleet against an invading force of Danes who were plundering Sandwich and routed them in the first real sea fight in English history. Nine of the enemy's ships were captured and the rest scattered to the winds.

The lesson was unlearnt. When the Danes came again in 991 they found the King, Ethelred, busily engaged in earning the title which posterity has added to his name. They harassed the coast of Essex, meeting with only the feeblest of opposition, and had to be bought off with ten thousand pounds of silver, raised by a tax called the Danegeld. They were soon back and by 1014 had conquered the whole country and sent the unready Ethelred flying for safety to Normandy. The new rulers brought with them one benefit, a strong fleet, which for a long time procured the country comparative immunity from further pirate raids.

During the later Middle Ages, as England assumed a position of importance amongst the nations and her trade in consequence increased, piracy in adjacent waters, particularly the Channel, again began to flourish. By the reign of Henry III the risks run from Irish, Scotch, Welsh and French outlaws by merchantmen plying between France and England had become so great that ships scarcely dared to leave harbour. The familiar process of declining trade and rising prices set in. An increase in the fleet and a vigorous naval policy under Henry and his successors, Edward I and Edward II, once more put a temporary stop to the worst of the evil. But by the death of Edward II, "the King of the Sea," in 1327, the navy had been allowed to fall into neglect, many of the best ships were sold to private merchants, and the old story began all over again. It finally became necessary for the merchants of the maritime cities to employ their own resources, after the manner of the Hanseatic League, to keep their commerce from being strangled altogether.

This was the origin of the league of the Cinque Ports. The original union, dating back a century or more, comprised at first five towns, Hastings, Romney, Hythe, Dover and Sandwich, to which were later added the two "ancient towns" of Winchelsea and Rye. The duty they undertook was to protect the south-east coast of England from pirates and to police the neighbouring seas. In return for these services they were granted certain privileges by the Crown such as "Soc and Sac," "Tol and Team," "Bloodwit and fledwit" to say nothing of "Pillory and Tumbril," "Infangenthoef and outfangenthoef," "mundbryce" and other mysterious mediæval rights. The highest officer of the federation was the Admiral of the Cinque Ports, who to this day has residence in Dover Castle.

Not the least profitable of these prerogatives was the right to plunder all merchant ships — except English — which passed up and down the Channel. It is not difficult to see where this would lead. The Cinque Port vessels put their own interpretation on their privileges and soon ships of friendly powers, and even English vessels themselves, began to suffer from the protection the league was affording. Conditions in the Channel and even the North Sea very quickly became worse with these authorised pirates about than they had been before. The high officials of the towns themselves became robber chiefs — in 1322 the Mayor of Winchelsea, Robert de Battayle, robbed two Sherborne merchants of their ship and cargo — and the Privy Council was besieged with innumerable such complaints annually. The Crown was before very long disgusted with its own creatures and began to punish individuals with severity. In 1435 William Morfote, member of Parliament for Winchelsea, is found sueing the King's pardon for having broken out of prison at Dover Castle, where he was under arrest for acts of piracy with a ship manned by a hundred of his own constituents.*

The other coast towns of England naturally resented the privileges of the Cinque Ports and the high-handed manner in which they interpreted them. On one occasion this feeling rose so high that a fight broke out between the Yarmouth and Cinque Ports squadrons at Helvoet Sluys while both were engaged against a common enemy, and only ended when twenty-five of the Yarmouth ships had been burnt. For nearly two hundred years outbursts of recriminations followed, and as the result of the introduction of the Channel police the last state of piracy in the Narrow Seas was worse than the first.

By far the most uncompromising of the Cinque Ports' rivals were the towns of Devon and Cornwall. The depredations of the West Country men had been confined at first to neighbouring towns and villages or to ships sailing close to their harbours, but before long they became bolder and sailed further afield in search of victims, often plundering the opposite coast of France. The Bretons were not the kind of folk to sit down quietly under such treatment, and the West country men soon found that they had their hands full protecting themselves and their own homesteads.

The activities of the Breton corsairs are outside the scope of this chapter, but one of them is perhaps the most romantic personality ever to command a pirate vessel and is deserving of a momentary divagation. On August 2nd, 1313 Lord Olivier de Clisson, one of the foremost knights of Nantes, being accused of an intrigue with the English, was carried to Paris and beheaded. His head was taken to Nantes and hung on the walls of the city as a warning in the usual manner.

His widow, Jeanne de Belleville, a lady famous for her beauty throughout the entire kingdom of France, swore to be revenged on her country for the death of her husband. She mortgaged her estates, sold her jewels and the furniture of her châteaux, and with the money so realised bought and equipped three stout ships. At the head of this little squadron la Dame de Clisson, as she is known to the annals of piracy,

* Roberts: "Social History of the Southern Counties of England," 1856.

cruised abroad, devoting particular attention to the coast of France, showing mercy to none that fell into her hands, cutting throats, sinking ships, burning villages. In naval engagements she was always the first to board an enemy, at her side her two young sons, youths as courageous and ferocious as their mother. Her end, unfortunately, is unknown.*

Dartmouth was a particular sufferer from the attacks of the French corsairs. In 1399 John Hawley, the hero of Dartmouth's mediæval maritime history, decided upon an "enterprise against those pestilent rogues," chartered the whole of the shipping then lying in Dartmouth harbour and set sail for the shores of Normandy and Brittany. This private war of merchant captains proved satisfactory to everybody but the French. Hawley captured thirty-four of their ships, with cargoes which included amongst other things one thousand five hundred tuns of wine, with the result that in the ensuing celebration Dartmouth "ran red with the luscious wine of France."†

Hawley was a typical example of the merchant adventurer who combined trade and piracy with gratifying success. He became a very rich man and also distinguished himself in his country's service as Admiral's deputy. Even while holding this office he did not abandon his private concerns and in 1403 went off on a little venture of his own with armed vessels from Dartmouth, Plymouth and Bristol, returning with seven Genoese and Spanish galleys.

More famous even than Hawley was his eminent contemporary, Harry Pay of Poole in Dorset. Pay in many respects anticipated the methods and outlook of Drake nearly two hundred years later. He was the self-appointed scourge of the Spaniards, by whom he was known as "Arripay." At the close of the fourteenth and beginning of the fifteenth century he was an incessant torment to the coast of Castile, but the one act of his which shocked and angered Spain more than any other was his carrying off the Holy Crucifix from the Church of Santa Maria of Finisterre.

* Nicollière-Teijeiro, "La Course et les Corsaires du Port de Nantes."
† Clive Holland, "From the North Foreland to Penzance."

Occasionally, like Drake, Pay got into hot water with his own government but always managed to get out of it again, particularly when they needed the help of his remarkable seamanship. Then he went his own way once more. Thus in 1405 he served in an expedition under Thomas Berkeley, the Lord Admiral; the next year the record states that with fifteen ships he captured a hundred and twenty French merchantmen on his own behalf. He was a hero to Poole as Drake was a hero to Plymouth, and when he returned with his prizes a public holiday was proclaimed. Once when he came back from an expedition to the Breton coast with over a hundred captured vessels (how many of these remarkable totals of the early chronicles included fishing smacks we are not told), the rich and busy town gave itself over to a spree in which "many puncheons of good Porto wine and kegs of brandy were broached . . . so that there was scarcely a sober man in the town, and for days no one thought of business or anything save eating and drinking and merrymaking."

But the pirate was not an unmixed blessing to his native town. Pay's principal victims were not yet the foremost nation of Europe, but they were a proud and virile race none the less. In the very year that he was pursuing French prizes off the Breton coast, 1406, the Spaniards swept down on Poole's landlocked harbour under the terrible Pero Niño and gave it the same thorough treatment that Spain was to mete out intermittently to the Barbary ports in the next century. One Philpot, an eminent citizen of the town, hired a thousand men and sent them to sea in search of revenge. A certain measure of it was obtained by the capture of fifteen Spanish merchantmen with their cargoes, but it was small compensation for the desolation which ended for good Poole's commercial importance.

It is difficult to imagine that the sleepy little town of Fowey ever enjoyed a similar maritime splendour, but in the fourteenth, fifteenth and sixteenth centuries Fowey was as conspicuous as Dartmouth, Poole and Plymouth amongst the seaports of England. John Leland, the antiquarian, describes it at the height of its prosperity as "partly by feats of war and partly by piracy and so waxing rich fell all to merchandise so that the town was haunted with ships of divers nations and its ships went to all nations."

None of the Cornish ports was held in worse repute for its piratical exploits than this small town whose sailors, styling themselves "the Fowey Gallants," burnt and plundered the Normandy coast in the reign of Edward III. During the Hundred Years War the King was glad enough to have their help against the French. In times of peace the Fowey Gallants fought the men of the Cinque Ports, natural enemies of all Devon sailors. Once the Gallants refused to "vaile their bonnets at the summons of those towns" when sailing past Winchelsea and Rye, with the result that the men of the Cinque Ports, mad with rage at this insult, "made out with might and maine against them, howbeit with more hardy onset than happy issue, for the Foymen gave them so rough entertainment as their welcome that they were glad to depart without bidding farewell." *

But every port in the West of England had its chief pirates, who came and went as they liked, always hand in glove with the local magnates and county landowners. Exmouth boasted of Captain William Kyd, a name borne some three hundred years later by perhaps the most celebrated of all pirates, and Portsmouth of Clays Stephen, whose name was feared many leagues beyond the waters of the Isle of Wight. St. Ives had too many of these gentry to catalogue, and their reputation was as great for drinking as for piracy. There were famous bouts at the taverns down by the quay whenever a St. Ives ship returned from the Bristol Channel. For many years after the last St. Ives pirate ended his life on the gallows or by the rum bottle, the girls of the town used to sing to one another this warning of the exciting temptations of the Cornish port:

Shun the bustle of the bay,
Hasten Virgins, come away;
Hasten to the mountain's brow,
Leave, O leave St. Ives below,

* Hals, "History of Cornwall," *circa* 1750.

Haste to breathe a purer air,
Virgins fair and pure as fair;
Fly St. Ives and all her treasures,
Fly her soft voluptuous pleasures;
Fly her sons and all their wiles,
Lushing in their wanton smiles;
Fly the splendid midnight halls;
Fly the revels of her balls;
Fly, O fly the chosen seat,
Where vanity and fashion meet.

Now and then a strong government did what it could to put an end to the national infliction, but as a rule its efforts were obstructed by the local landowners. Practically all the West Country squires living near the coast had a hand in the big enterprises and many of them made the Crown's writ ridiculous because as justices of the peace they served on the commissions instituted to investigate the alleged piracies. It was extremely unlikely that they would assist their profitable employees to the gallows. Moreover, during the almost constant warfare of the fourteenth and fifteenth centuries, the pirates were the best available seamen at England's command.

Henry V made decided progress, using the sensible method of a treaty with France and Spain whereby each country bound itself not to use the services of the corsairs and to stamp them out by joint effort. The treaty provided that no armed ship should be allowed to leave port without a proper licence and the deposit of a heavy surety for the captain's good behaviour. To strengthen the effect of these measures Henry enacted strong regulations for the punishment of robbery at sea and originated the issue of safe-conduct passes to vessels engaged in lawful business. A slight improvement followed, but within twenty years the King's navy had again declined and the merchants were once more compelled to reimburse themselves by force for their losses.

During the reign of Henry VI the evil was worse than ever, English pirates now plundering English ships without shadow of hesitation or scruple. Things became so bad that the sea, the natural and normally cheapest route for the transport of goods, was almost closed, and it became actually cheaper to send goods from London to Venice for instance by the overland route, up the Rhine and across the Alps, than by water. This additional expense was entirely due to the huge cost of defence against the pirates. One Venetian captain who had dared the water way reported on arrival in London that he had shipped a hundred extra hands and twenty-two gunners for fear of attack, a fear which proved justified, since he had only completed his voyage after beating off a Norman pirate.*

In the reign of Henry VII a new method was instituted which it was hoped would check piracy, but it only made matters worse. This was the issue of letters of marque or reprisal, a device to be extensively used for several centuries, which gave the bearer the right to take the law into his own hands. For example, if an English merchant had been robbed by a French pirate of goods valued at five hundred pounds he procured a letter of marque from the government which authorised him to seize goods of a like value from any other French ship. This on the very face of it was looking for trouble. We get a very good instance of what this kind of law led to in the history and activities of Sir Andrew Barton, the Scotch merchant, pirate and hero.

Claiming that his father had been robbed many years before by the Portuguese, Barton was issued a letter of reprisal by James IV of Scotland. Armed with this, Barton sailed with two powerful ships, the *Lion* and the *Jennet Purwyn,* to the coast of Flanders, where he robbed and plundered the ships of all nations that traded with the Flemish ports, particularly English ones. At last there arose such an outcry over this that King Henry VIII sent the two sons of the Earl of Surrey, Edward and Thomas Howard, to bring the villain to account. After a fierce fight off the Goodwin Sands Barton was slain, his Scotch pirates defeated, and their two ships brought in triumph to Blackwell on August 2nd, 1511 to be added to the English Navy, over which King James IV was "wonderfull wrothe."

Several ballads were written to celebrate this great victory

* J. A. Williamson, "Maritime Enterprise."

and one, of eighty-two stanzas, can be read in the publications of the Navy Records Society.*

As time went on and bigger ships were built, the English sailors became more daring and skilful, and we find them venturing on longer and longer voyages. Though it was quite true, as a contemporary writes, that the "pick of all seamen were pirates," yet, bad as all this fighting and plundering was for trade, it unquestionably bred that race of wonderful seamen who, whether pirates or no, shared with the Queen and her poets the glory of Elizabeth's reign.

* "Naval Songs and Ballads," Vol. XXXIII.

CHAPTER III

THE ELIZABETHAN CORSAIRS

THE reign of Queen Elizabeth saw a growth of fierce nationalism which ultimately brought employment to the adventurous sailors of England as members of an unofficial yet recognised and highly capable navy. But in the beginning of her reign all the conditions favourable to piracy prevailed in a high degree. The country was poor, trade was slack, with consequent unemployment amongst seafaring men (Richard Hakluyt, than whom no man was ever better qualified to speak, accounted for the prevalence of piracy amongst the English and French in contrast with Spain and Portugal by the fact that, whereas the two Iberian countries had full employment for their sailors and "bred no pirates . . . we and the French are most infamous for our outrageous, common and daily piracies"), rich merchandise was constantly passing through the Channel, and the English navy had been so allowed to deteriorate both in numbers and quality under Edward VI and Mary that effective policing was out of the question.

The habit of preying on Spanish and Portuguese merchantmen had already become so fixed under Philip and Mary that it naturally did not diminish under a sovereign whose very accession ruptured the Anglo-Spanish tie and whose first important act was to sever the strong bond of religious community by breaking away from the Catholic faith. In the reign of Philip and Mary the Portuguese had been the principal sufferers, but now the English seamen appeared to think that they could molest Spain with equal impunity.

The Portuguese and Spaniards both used Antwerp as their principal port of entry for the distribution of their wares over central and northern Europe, as in fact did the English until the outbreak of trouble with Spain in 1568. There the Spanish traders brought their wines from Spain and Gascony, wheat and salt from the Mediterranean, and all the strange and various products of her Americas; there also the Portuguese conveyed the wines of Madeira, the spices of the Far East, the rare woods from Brazil. And their way inevitably led through the waters whose every tide and current was known to the inhabitants of the Cornish and Devon coasts as a man knows the garden he has laid out himself.

As one reads through the diplomatic correspondence of the early years of Elizabeth's reign one is struck by the fact that protests against acts of piracy make up the largest item of ambassadorial routine. There is voluminous correspondence over Thomas Wyndham, son of a Norfolk man who had served at sea against the French and became a councillor and Vice-Admiral under Henry VIII, "a fierce and masterful man making more enemies than friends among his equals, but always able to command the loyalty of his crew; just the type of character of which the service and personality of King Henry VIII bred such numerous examples and whose traditions were handed on to the golden age of Elizabeth's sea captains." *

Wyndham's particular enterprise was the seizure of sugar ships in the Channel and the transfer of their cargoes into Waterford, where they were sold to London receivers who had agents there and at other Irish ports.

When the Queen had only been on the throne two years the Spanish ambassador was complaining of the seizure, as the climax to a series of outrageous acts, of Spanish gentlemen at sea and their subsequent sale at auction in Dover — the purchasers were paying as much as a hundred pounds for a well-dressed Spaniard who looked as if he might fetch a solid ransom. The particular ire of Bishop de Quadra, who was then representing Philip II at Elizabeth's court, was directed against two men called Poole and Champneys, who had been capturing Spanish vessels homeward bound from the West Indies between the Azores and the Canaries. In 1560 they landed at one of the Canary ports, where they were arrested by the Spaniards and thrown into jail. Here they languished

* J. A. Williamson, "Sir John Hawkins."

until the following Christmas Day, when they seized the opportunity of escape while the whole population of the island was at Mass, slipped on board a vessel lying in the harbour and so got back to England.

The escape maddened the Spaniards even more than the offences for which the men were awaiting trial. All English merchants and ships in the Canaries were at once seized and all kinds of punishment inflicted on innocent people, which nearly precipitated a crisis between the two nations. The affair blew over, however. Elizabeth and Fate were conspiring together to put off the day of conflict for as long as possible. She soothed the wrath of the Spaniards by apologising, and made a really determined effort to put down her irresponsible rovers.

In 1564 she wrote to Sir Peter Carew that "forasmuch as that the coast of Devonshire and Cornwall is by report much haunted with pyrattes and Rovers" he was "to cause one or two apt vessels to be made ready with all speed in some ports thereabout" for their apprehension. With her usual feeling for economy Her Majesty proposed that the crews of the apt vessels should take "their benefit of the spoil or be provided only by us of victuals"; in other words, that they were to look for their pay to what they could get out of the pirates. She ended her letter with the practical suggestion that "ye said rovers might be enticed with hope of our mercy to apprehend some of the rest of their Company which practice we have known do good not long ago in the like."

On the whole the Queen tried sincerely in these early years of her reign to reduce her adventurous subjects to order, but the habit of piracy had grown too strong in the course of centuries to be broken by her limited resources. Moreover it had become a vast and complicated business with vested interests extending from Dorset to Kerry. She did contrive to clear the Channel of the lone corsair who worked independently of the great pirate combines, and who soon felt the weight of the royal hand sufficiently to find it advisable to seek more congenial quarters in the south of Ireland, the islands off the west coast of Scotland (where Bothwell was a few years hence to find refuge) and the Barbary coast, but piracy as a big business defeated her. Its executives were too closely intertwined with the administration of the law of England, too close in blood to the ruling caste, to be rooted out without a campaign that would have amounted to civil war. Occasionally a pirate belonging to one of the combines was caught, but as a rule influence freed him after a short term of punishment served in the Queen's navy.

The props of the whole business were the powerful squires, who acted both as receivers and as administrators of the law in their areas. Local sentiment was with them — the small county gentry were quite content to receive a preposterously high rent for a little cove which ordinarily would not have been worth more than a few shillings a year. The petty officials at the ports had for so long taken their pay to overlook offences of this order that they had begun to think of it as the principal perquisite of their office. The records are full of instances such as that of the Mayor of Southampton who, after a bribe from the rich brokers of the town who traded in stolen property, released several pirates caught redhanded, and of other mayors, lieutenants of ports and deputy searchers of Customs who were almost openly in league with the pirates.

But more important than these were the high officers of the navy, the lord lieutenants and sheriffs of counties, who directed the operations of the business in dignified safety. Time and again an ambassadorial complaint or the self-exculpation of a small official, when sifted to the bottom, disclosed some august servant of the Crown in the background. Historic names are often involved, such as William Hawkins, brother of the famous treasurer of the navy, and Sir Richard Grenville, the immortal hero of the *Revenge,* both of whom were at one time up before the Privy Council on charges of piracy.

By far the greatest of these magnates of piracy were the Killigrews of Cornwall. From this ancient family, which provided many a distinguished minister, diplomat and soldier to the nation, arose a veritable oligarchy of corsair capitalists. The seat of the family was Arwenack in Cornwall and its head in Elizabeth's time was Sir John Killigrew, Vice-Admiral of

Cornwall and hereditary Royal Governor of Pendennis Castle, who acted as a sort of managing director of the family business. He was closely connected by blood with William Cecil, Lord Burleigh, the Queen's principal minister.

Sir John's father had been a pirate and his uncle Peter had sailed the Irish Sea as a rover in his younger days. Even his mother, as will appear presently, was to be tried in a court of law for piracy. One of his relatives, Sir John Wogan, Vice-Admiral of South Wales, looked after the family interests on that coast; he too once stood his trial for piracy. Another relative, John Godolphin, acted as agent in his own district of Cornwall, while the important base at Tralee in Ireland was in charge of an old friend and neighbour of Sir John's, the Vice-President of Munster and member of parliament for Liskard. Various other cousins looked after the branches along the Devon and Dorset coasts. Amongst his associates was the Irish Lord Conchobar O'Driscoll, the famous Sir Finian of the Ships and "the terrible John Piers" who worked in partnership with his remarkable mother, a well-known Cornish witch.

Not only the receiving and distributing, but all the other details of the business save the actual robbery at sea was in the hands of this family: payment of the crews and other expenses, including bribes to officials, the purchase or charter of ships, the provision of supplies and the underwriting of the finances, which were subscribed by the gentry of Dorset, Devon and Cornwall, though occasionally a Somerset gentleman was allowed to take a share. The pirate captain received only one-fifth of the value of any plunder he brought in, the bulk of the profit going to the receivers — the usual division in this sort of transaction, and one that is, it seems, the general practice amongst the bootlegging gangs of America. The actual value of the individual captures was not great, a cargo worth a thousand pounds being unusual. But the regularity with which the prizes were brought in made the business extremely profitable, and laid the foundation of many a great family fortune of later times. It may seem surprising that a Europe so thinly populated as it was in the sixteenth century (England's inhabitants then only numbered about three million) should have possessed so much shipping, but it must be remembered that the evil state of the roads made the sea the easiest and cheapest means of local transport. Unless the pirates overreached themselves by their own greed and stopped traffic by water, it was generally less expensive and more expeditious to send goods from one part of England to another by ship.

Although plunder was often disposed of at the bigger ports, such as Plymouth or Southampton, smaller and more secluded bays were preferred. Lulworth was a favourite and the furthest east; there were also several in Devon and Cornwall, as well as in the south of Ireland, at the disposal of the Killigrew syndicate.

Falmouth was probably as important as any English port for the trading of pirate plunder, for it was the home of the Killigrews. Their great house of Arwenack stood close to the sea in a secluded part of Falmouth Harbour, and had a private and secret way down to the water. Pendennis Castle was the only other building near and although armed with over a hundred cannon it was more a refuge than a menace to visiting pirate ships. At Arwenack Lady Killigrew dispensed hospitality to the more respectable pirates, and the Killigrews' connections did the same at their houses. One notorious pirate chief who worked the Bristol Channel and South Wales made his residence when on shore with the Sergeant of the Admiralty. The syndicate provided rest and comfort for the crews in recognised lodging houses for pirates in the receiving ports.

The extent to which Falmouth offered a haven to the outlaws is illustrated by a characteristic incident. A pirate one day brought his ship into the harbour to find himself suddenly confronted by several royal men of war lying at anchor. The situation was awkward, but it was soon relieved by the tact of Sir John Killigrew. The Vice-Admiral of Cornwall promptly had himself rowed out to the flagship of the squadron and was there closeted for some time with the senior naval officer, Captain Jones. As the result of the conference it was settled that Captain Jones should enjoy a little excursion inland at the expense of the Killigrews. With a hundred pounds in his pocket he departed, and the pirate was free to land his cargo.

It was very rarely indeed that one of Killigrews' employees was ever seriously interfered with. Here and there a guardship was stationed in the Channel, but there is no record of their ever catching one of his men red-handed. On the contrary, at times quite the reverse happened, as when in 1578 some pirates attacked and plundered *The Flying Heart,* the guardship of the Vice-Admiral, off the Welsh coast. During the whole of this period there is no record of a pirate ever being captured in the Bristol Channel, although they swarmed round Lundy Island and committed innumerable robberies.*

Only when really important people suffered did retribution come down heavily, and then from the hands of the central authority in London. Thus in 1573, when the Earl of Worcester was crossing from Dover to Boulogne with a christening present of a golden salver from Queen Elizabeth to the infant daughter of Charles IX, his ship was attacked by pirates, and although the Earl escaped with the salver he was robbed of five hundred pounds, while a dozen of his retainers were killed or wounded. As a result there was a general round up of Channel corsairs; several hundred were captured and arrested but only three were hanged. Probably influence again stepped in.

It was a mistake in the selection of her victim that finally brought old Lady Killigrew to justice. This extraordinary woman had been assistant to her father, Philip Wolverston, a distinguished gentleman pirate of Suffolk, before becoming a valuable helpmate to her husband. But in 1582 she overreached herself. On New Year's Day a Hansa ship of a hundred and forty-four tons burden was driven into Falmouth harbour by a storm. She dropped anchor directly opposite Arwenack — since the house was the residence of the Commissioner of Piracy for Cornwall and since England was at peace with the world, the master might reasonably think that he had nothing to fear. But from her drawing-room window

* David Matthew: "Cornish and Welsh Pirates in the Reign of Queen Elizabeth," "English Historical Review," Vol. XXXIX.

her ladyship noticed the foreign vessel, made enquiries and learnt that there was valuable merchandise on board. In the meantime the owners of the vessel, two Spanish gentlemen, Philip de Orozo and Juan de Charis, had gone to Penryn to stop at the inn until the weather turned favourable.

On the night of January 7th a boat put off from shore filled with armed retainers of Sir John Killigrew and steered by Lady Killigrew herself. On coming alongside, the Cornishmen, headed by her ladyship, scrambled on deck, slaughtered the unsuspecting crew and threw their bodies over the side. Lady Killigrew and two of her servants, Kendal and Hawkins, returned to Arwenack House with several bolts of holland cloth and two barrels of pieces of eight, while the Cornish sailors took the captured ship to Ireland where the rest of the plunder was disposed of. The owners at once laid formal complaint before the Commissioners of Piracy in Cornwall, of which the offender's son was president. After enquiry it was found that there was no evidence to implicate any known persons. The jury returned an open verdict: the ship had certainly been stolen, but by whom they found it impossible to say.

Charis and Arozo were persistent, however. They went up to London and laid their complaint before the highest authorities, with the result that the Earl of Bedford, a member of the Privy Council, instructed Sir Richard Grenville and Mr. Edmund Tremayne to conduct a searching investigation into the affair. At the conclusion of their enquiry Lady Killigrew, Hawkins and Kendal were sent for trial at the assizes at Launceston, where they were duly found guilty and condemned to death. The two men were executed but Lady Killigrew received a reprieve at the last moment.

Gradually, as Elizabeth's reign lengthened and the clouds of war gathered over the country, her government began to override privilege and either suppress the pirates or put them to useful employment in the navy. In 1581 Lulworth was closed to the syndicate by Lord Howard of Bindon, Vice-Admiral of Dorset, who built a castle at East Lulworth and maintained strict guard over the harbour. In 1583 the Privy Council was prompt to provide the people of Weymouth with the means of defence against the threats of a notorious pirate named Thomas Purser, who made a "very insolent and rebellious attempt" on the town, was driven off after capturing a Rochelle ship and retired shouting a promise to return and destroy the town and all the shipping in the harbour. There are frequent entries in the archives of the old seaport town which indicate increased activity in arresting and imprisoning the outlaws. The following, a list of charges paid by the Mayor of Lyme Regis in 1586 for sending ten pirates to Dorchester under arrest, is an example:

Money disbursed about the Pirates as followeth:

		s.	*d.*
First,	paid for the use of eleven horses and eight men to carry the prisoners to Dorchester	28.	2
Item	paid for the prisoners' meat and drink during the time they were here	2.	6
Item	for the watchman to watch the prisoners		12
Item	paid for two mayling cords to bind the prisoners	1.	2
Item	paid to the gaoler of Dorchester for receiving the prisoners (ten in number at 4d. each)	3.	4
Item	paid for Mr. Hardes charges, dinner and supper and for his horse meat for two days and to take the examinations and to make the mittimus	14.	6

Space does not permit a record of the activities of all the independent pirates, and their careers resemble one another so much as to be monotonous. A characteristic one is Captain John Callys, like many of his profession a man of birth and education. Amongst his relatives was the Earl of Pembroke, one of the leading peers of the realm. Callys first sailed as an officer of the royal navy under Sir John Berkeley, but afterwards turned pirate. His base was Glamorgan in Wales, where he was much respected by the local gentry, at whose houses he visited when on shore. Generally he sailed alone, but sometimes joined forces with two foreign corsairs, Count Higgenberte and Symon Ferdinando Portingale, or else with his old friend Captain Robert Hickes of Saltash, who was afterwards hanged.

Callys was captured off the Isle of Wight on May 15th 1577. On his person was found the sum of twenty-two pounds seven shillings which was offered as an incriminating piece of evidence against him at his trial. Though his record was bad he escaped punishment by turning Queen's evidence and supplying information against his receivers. This, together with the bribe of five hundred pounds offered by his friends for his release, got him off.

Possibly alarmed at his narrow escape, Callys disappeared from his former haunts and was not heard of again till 1580, when he barely missed capture at his old trade in the Orkneys, losing his ship and all his belongings. He was then reduced to lower employment, sailing in a humble capacity on a pirate ship, the *Minikin,* belonging to a Mr. Bellingham. There is some doubt as to how Callys met his death. According to Captain John Smith, the founder of Virginia, "this ancient pirate Collis, who most refreshed himself upon the coast of Wales . . . grew famous till Queen Elizabeth of Blessed Memory hanged him at Wapping," but it is more likely that he joined the Barbary corsairs and died fighting in a sea engagement.

Only one other pirate can be mentioned specifically and that not for his dexterity at his trade but his name: Captain Arystotle Tottle. In fact the only other information we have about him is that he once made a hundred pounds on a pirating adventure and the verdict of Mr. Oppenheim, a highly competent judge, that he was "a timid pirate."

If Elizabeth was on the whole severe with pirates operating in home waters, she was more than indulgent with those who ventured further afield. As the national hostility to Spain increased she not only shut her eyes to their aggressions against the Spaniards but even took a financial interest in their ventures. Piracy in wartime had always been more or less sanctioned by the state, but under Elizabeth it was connived at while England was at peace with all the world. As a result of this unofficial encouragement not only was much wealth brought into a poor country but, a matter of far greater importance, a race of tough seamen was evolved which was to save England in her need, bring about the downfall of her principal enemy, and make her the proud mistress of the seas.

It was to the West, to the vast, little known lands of America where the gold came from, that Elizabeth's more adventurous subjects looked with envious eyes. The Pope at Rome might draw lines on the map of the world and decree where Spain should rule supreme and where Portugal, but the heretic swash-bucklers cared very little about that. As pressure was brought to bear on the more aggressive pirates in the home waters they tended to go further and further from England and the law.

Thus some sailed to Barbary, living in one of the Moorish strongholds and turning Turk; while others, who preferred to retain their birthright as Englishmen and Christians, wandered off to the western islands or the Canaries and cruised to and fro in the Atlantic in the hope of catching some galleon lumbering home to Spain with a heavy cargo of gold and precious stones. Great prizes also awaited the boldest of sailors who were willing to go to the West Indies and the Spanish Main. It was this, the most daring and glittering of adventures, that called out the great breed of English corsairs: Hawkins, Drake, Grenville, Frobisher, Cumberland and their kind. It was the French who led the way to the Spanish settlements in that rich preserve, but they were soon followed by the English and the Dutch.

This last was the newest of European sea powers. After the first defeat of William of Orange in the Netherlands, numbers of the Dutch rebels took to the sea as a means of escape from the appalling conditions at home and of harassing the national enemy. They adopted the collective title of "Beggars of the Sea," the comprehensive name of "Beggars" having been fastened on all of Orange's followers by the Cardinal Granvella, Philip II's minister in the Netherlands. Their principal stronghold was Rochelle, where the Huguenot Prince de Condé had gathered corsairs from the several Protestant nations and issued to them letters of marque against all Catholic shipping, whether French or Spanish.

This strange motley of colleagues, Dutch, English and French, roamed the seas together and found ready shelter for some years in the Channel ports. The commander of the "Beggars" was the Count de la Marck, and though for some years his English headquarters was Dover, the other Channel towns as far west as Plymouth knew him and his men well. Recruits came pouring in to him from all the West of England, and soon his fleet, whose original aim had been patriotic and religious, became little better than a pack of wolves who preyed on the ships of all nations indiscriminately. At the end of the first year of their existence the "Beggars" numbered almost a hundred ships and had taken over a hundred prizes.

For three years the strange floating republic flourished under the political sympathy of the English nation and the practical support of the English merchants. But gradually, as trade became almost paralysed in the Channel, as less and less plunder was brought into English harbours, the same merchants began to call upon the government to suppress their late friends and allies. Since the "Beggars" were stirring up unpleasant complications for Elizabeth, she was disposed to comply. She shut Dover to the Dutchmen at the request of the Spanish ambassador and in January of 1573 sent Sir William Holstocke, Controller of the Navy, with two powerful battleships to make war on the "Beggars." Holstocke's big guns were too much for the rovers, and his ruthless methods soon paralysed their larger activities.

Meanwhile more and more Englishmen were sailing in search of loot to America, and one of them even ended such a voyage by circumnavigating the world. The Spanish ambassador strongly protested in person to the Queen and clamoured that El Draque be hanged. But times were changing. Her Majesty's answer was to order her barge and row down the river to knight the "master thief of the known world" on the deck of his *Golden Hind*. And so she put her seal on the school of pirates who were to form so large a part of that navy which in July of 1588 sallied forth to meet the "Invincible Armada" as it came sweeping up the Channel and drove it off the face of the ocean.

CHAPTER IV

THE JACOBEAN PIRATES

THE accession of James I brought a profound change to Great Britain's foreign policy. The long war which Elizabeth had waged with Spain, at first without a declaration of hostilities, later with proper formality, had by the end of the century absorbed the energies of the nation's seafaring folk. Peace brought the familiar difficulties. Ships were taken out of commission, crews disbanded and the country was flooded with unemployed sailors. Legitimate merchant shipping could not use more than a small part of the superfluous seamen and the rest, whose only trade was the sea, turned again to the sea for a means of a living.

The situation was vividly summed up by Captain John Smith, adventurer, coloniser and author, who observed it with keen eyes and reflected upon it with troubled mind: "After the death of our most gracious Queen Elizabeth . . . King James, who from his infancy had reigned in peace with all nations, had no employment for those men of war so that those that were rich rested with what they had; those that were poor and had nothing but from hand to mouth turned pirates; some because they became slighted of those for whom they had got much wealth; some, for that they could not get their due; some, that had lived bravely, would not abase themselves to poverty; some vainly, only to get a name; others for revenge, covetousness or as ill." *

Employment was not hard to get if accepted on the employer's terms; trade unions and benevolent government did not yet exist to regulate the relations between owners and workmen. A speculator would invest in a ship, arm her and call for men to man her on the basis of "No prey, no pay."

* Smith, "Travels and Adventures," 1629.

Before long English trade was crippled as it had been before Elizabeth's accession, while that of Spain was in even a worse state and had indeed practically disappeared from the northern seas. The Barbary corsairs too were becoming bolder at this time, owing largely to Danser and his sailing vessels, and their ships were scouring the North Atlantic and even the English coasts. Simultaneously the fast sailing pirates of Dunkirk were swarming up and down the Channel.

The Government sent out ship after ship to catch the pirates, which they sometimes did, but the captor usually released the culprits after relieving them of their accumulated plunder. Those who were brought to trial did not seem to mind particularly, knowing that they were only liable to "a little lazy imprisonment." * And in spite of increased pressure from London the outlaws still maintained friendly relations along the Devon and Cornish coasts. If authority gained a momentary ascendancy in the English ports, the corsairs could always be sure of a welcome in the south of Ireland, where even Barbary ships could put in for repair or supplies.

The best means of obtaining a comprehensive picture of the state of piracy during the reign is to be had in the recorded careers of a few of the more notorious practitioners such as Sir Henry Mainwaring, Captain John Warde, Sir Francis Verney and one or two others.

The story of Sir Henry Mainwaring is of particular interest. Not only was he a most successful pirate himself — "without equal in England" — but he later accepted the King's Commission to hunt down his old confederates and published a full account of his own past which is one of the principal textbooks of piracy.†

Mainwaring was one of those geniuses who lived at the wrong time. There can be little doubt that had he been born fifty years earlier, his fame would have rivalled that of the great navigators Drake and Raleigh. His particular talents were to

* Oppenheim.

† By some inexplicable oversight no account of Mainwaring occurs in the Dictionary of National Biography and I am largely indebted to Mr. G. E. Manwaring, the editor of the "Life and Works of Sir Henry Mainwaring," (Navy Records Society, Vols. LIV, LVI) for the particulars which follow.

a large extent wasted in the more peaceful and far less adventurous reign of James I.

Born in Shropshire of an old county family, he was educated at Brasenose College, Oxford, where he matriculated at the age of twelve and received the degree of Bachelor of Arts in 1602, at the age of fifteen. After various vicissitudes as lawyer, soldier and sailor, he decided to turn pirate, and bought a small ship of a hundred and sixty tons, the *Resistance,* which although small was a beautifully built craft, fast and handy, well armed and manned by a first class crew. They left England ostensibly to sail to the West Indies, but when near Gibraltar the young captain assembled his crew and announced his intention of fighting any Spanish ship they met.

Since every pirate must have a base from which to work, Mainwaring steered for Marmora on the Barbary coast, a place of very ill repute. From here the new pirates met with the greatest success, taking ship after ship from the Spaniards, and in a short while Mainwaring found himself master of a strong fleet. Although he never spared a Spanish vessel he never molested an English one, and so powerful had he become that he was able to forbid his fellow pirates at Marmora to pillage any ships of his nation.

His fame spread rapidly; he was fêted on the Barbary coast, and in the south of Ireland his wealth and generosity made him an almost legendary hero. The King of Spain at first threatened, then tried with promises of great rewards and a high command in his service to win the corsair over, but he turned a deaf ear to these overtures as he did to those of the Dey of Tunis, who offered to take him into equal partnership if he would abjure Christianity.

In 1614 he sailed for the favourite recruiting ground of pirate crews, the fishing banks of Newfoundland. From the Colonial State Papers, which contain frequent references to his exploits in those waters, we learn that

Captain Mainwaring with divers other captains arrived in Newfoundland on the 4th of June, having eight sail of war-like ships, one whereof they took at the bank, another upon the main of Newfoundland, from all the harbours whereof they commanded carpenters, mariners victuals, munitions and all necessaries from the fishing fleet after this rate—of every six mariners they take one, and the one fifth part of their victuals; from the Portuguese ships they took all their wine and other provisions, save their bread; from a French ship in Harbour Grace they took 10,000 fish; some of the company of many ships did run away unto them. They took a French ship fishing in Carbonear, and so after they had continued three months and a half in the country taking their pleasure of the fishing fleet, the 14th of September 1614, they departed, having with them from the fishing fleet about 400 mariners and fishermen; many volunteers, many compelled.

Having got all he wanted out of the Newfoundland fishing fleets, Mainwaring returned across the Atlantic to his old haunts at Marmora, only to find that the port had been captured by the Spaniards and was firmly in their possession. But there was a new port now open to pirates, Villefranche in Savoy, where Mainwaring took up his quarters and was joined by another aristocratic English pirate, Walsingham.

Prize after prize was captured and five hundred thousand crowns of Spanish money taken in the space of six weeks, until the Spaniards scarcely dared show their noses outside their harbours. The King, driven to desperation, issued licences to all who were willing to go privateering against any English ship, and himself sent out a squadron of five royal ships with orders to destroy the English corsairs and bring back the pirate himself, dead or alive.

Leaving Cadiz, the royal fleet happened to meet Mainwaring with only three ships and a fierce fight ensued, which raged until nightfall, when the Spaniards were glad to escape, battered and broken, to Lisbon.

Finding force of no use, the Spanish king again offered Mainwaring a free pardon and twenty thousand ducats a year if he would take command of a Spanish squadron; but tempting as such an offer must have been to this soldier of fortune he resisted it.

By now the pirates had become so intolerable that both the Spanish and French ambassadors threatened King James that extreme measures would be taken if Mainwaring were not called off.

James, who desired peace above all things, sent an envoy to the Barbary coast with instructions to offer Mainwaring a free pardon if he promised to give up piracy, or to threaten him with a fleet strong enough to defeat and crush him if he refused.

Mainwaring made up his mind at once, accepted the first alternative, and with two ships sailed to Dover. On June 9th, 1616 "Captain Mainwaring, the sea captain, was pardoned under the Great Seal of England," on the curious grounds that "he had committed no great wrong." At the same time a general amnesty was granted to all of his crew, who on returning to England had promised never to go pirating again.

The forgiven and reformed corsair, to show his gratitude and sincere atonement, at once went to sea to search for any pirate he could capture. There was plenty of material, for the Barbary pirates were just then in the Channel, doing much harm to shipping, one of their worst deeds being the capture of the whole of the returning Newfoundland fishing fleet. The boldness of these Turkish pirates was astounding, for Mainwaring reported finding three of their ships lying in the Thames as high up the river as Leigh. These he boarded, releasing a number of Christian captives whom he found on board.

This energetic conduct on the part of Mainwaring so much impressed the King that he appointed him a Gentleman of his Bedchamber. As a result the mariner became for a while a courtier and an intimate of the King, who had a high esteem for his advice in nautical matters and enjoyed his conversation.

Life at Court soon became tedious to the restless sea-rover, and another, more congenial, post was found for him, that of "Lieutenant of Dover Castle and Deputy Warden of the Cinque Ports." Four years later, in 1623, he was elected M.P. for Dover.

The forts of all the Cinque Ports had been allowed to go to ruin, and Dover, the most important of all, was no exception. Mainwaring did all he could to improve the fortifications and have them properly armed. His discovery that, instead of gunpowder some dishonest official had supplied ashes and sand shows to what a state of decay they had sunk.

In the interval of his many duties the new Deputy Warden of the Cinque Ports found time to write a book, the first of several. This particular work was addressed to the King, as a token of gratitude for his pardon. The original manuscript lies in the British Museum and has the following title:

> Of the beginnings, Practices, and Suppression of Pirates
>
> To my most Gracious Sovereign, that represents the King in Heaven, whose mercy is above all his works.

The forty-eight pages of neat handwriting contain the whole history of piracy, especially Barbary piracy, under the Stuarts. The author, to show how it could best be suppressed, explains what caused sailors to turn pirate, and how many honest sailors were driven to that trade by hunger and unemployment.

He has much to say about Ireland which "may be well called the Nursery and Storehouse of Pirates," and so agrees with Sir W. Monson, who a few years afterwards described Broadhaven on the west coast as being the "well-head of all pirates." Ireland was the great clearing house, rendezvous and playground of pirates from Iceland and the Baltic to the Straits of Gibraltar. In those out-of-the-way bays and harbours "a Pirate may trim his ships without affront from the Country . . . as also victual themselves. . ." At this time the Vice-President of Munster, Sir Richard Moryson, reported that at Youghal he found eleven pirate ships with one thousand sailors, and that owing to the remoteness of the place and the wildness of the people he dared do nothing. "In Ireland" Mainwaring adds, "they have all commodities and conveniences that all other places do afford them," also, a matter of some importance, "good store of English, Scottish and Irish wenches, which resort unto them and these are strong attractions to draw the common sort of seaman thither."

There were no secrets of the trade that the reformed pirate did not give away. In one chapter devoted to suggestions for suppressing these gentry, after naming the favourite trade routes where prizes may be looked for and the proper time of year to go after them, he describes how an attack begins: "A little before day they (the pirates) take in all their sails and lie a-hull till they can make what ships are about them." If the enemy approached, the pirates would pretend to escape, clapping on all sail, but at the same time tow over the stern empty hogsheads to slow her down so that she could be easily overtaken, when the unsuspecting pursuer could be the more easily surprised and captured.

Mainwaring describes the various Barbary strongholds; how the inhabitants of Tunis are to be treated, the Dey being "a very just man of his word." At Tituan, on the Morocco coast, "a pirate may water well, having good refreshment and buy store of powder," and he adds the enlightening information that this gunpowder was brought there by English and Flemish merchants.

Newfoundland he considers the best of all places for an honest pirate to refit, but he must be strong enough to deal with any opposition. "On the bank of Newfoundland they easily get bread, wine, cider, and fish enough with all necessaries for shipping," writes this pirate Baedeker.

This portion of Mainwaring's book, devoted to the good and bad points of the innumerable pirate ports in Ireland, North Africa, the Canary Islands, Azores, West Africa and Newfoundland, reminds the modern reader of the Automobile Association's handbook with its recommended hotels and garages; and one almost expects to find some of his more attractive resorts for pirates "starred" to indicate their quality.

As to punishing captured pirates, Mainwaring advised clemency; not from any maudlin ideas of pity but because he thought it would be more profitable to the state to employ the undoubted talents of such skilful seamen rather than hang them out of hand. He recommended using them as galley-slaves to patrol the coast and for any other useful services which might be found.

Mainwaring was deeply concerned about the growth of piracy in his time: "since Your Highness's reign there have been more Pirates by ten to one than were in the whole reign of of the last Queen." This estimate appears rather startling when it is compared with the census of the four hundred pirates known to the authorities in 1563, when Elizabeth's reign still had forty years to run. The great bulk of the increase was due to the turbulent and discontented Irish; as Mainwaring says, "Ireland, which I hold the most material of all, being that this is as the great earth for foxes, which being stopped they are easily hounded to death."

The authorities were only too well aware of the fact, and the King in response to urgent calls for protection from his native Scotland had already tried to do something about it. In 1614 he had collected a fleet and sent it to the Irish Sea to intercept the raiders on the coast between Ireland and Scotland. Mainwaring's estimate of a later date proves that the effort was not notably successful.

Nevertheless it was conducted with energy and efficiency. The commanders were Sir William Monson, an experienced Elizabethan admiral, and Sir Francis Howard. Monson's own account of the voyage is one of the most interesting and valuable of contemporary documents relating to the suppression of piracy.* It will be seen that the mere name of the great Henry Mainwaring procured him ready admission to the principal pirate lair in the whole of the British Isles.

The English ships called first of all at Edinburgh to get particulars. On being informed that there were known to be twenty pirates in the Orkneys, Sir William hurried north to try to catch them, calling on his way at Sinclair Castle, the seat of that firebrand, the Earl of Caithness. Only two pirates were surprised but one was of peculiar interest to the admiral, for he proved to be a certain Mr. Clarke, an old boatswain's mate of his. The mate was the guest of the Earl, whose castle offered hospitality to all rovers and pirates.

Admiral Monson then passed over to the Orkney Islands, where he met with a very civil reception. Here he left Sir

* "Naval Tracts," 1703.

Francis Howard to guard the coast while he himself went on to the Hebrides. His welcome here was a very different one, which caused him to write that "The Brutishness and Uncivility of those People of the Hybrides exceeds the Savages of America; . . . there cannot be greater difference between Day and Night, than betwixt the Conversation of those of Orkney and those of the Hybrides."

The Admiral then decided to sail straight to Broadhaven on the west coast of Ireland, a famous stronghold of freebooters and the like, but his little squadron of four ships met with a terrific storm "fit only for a Poet to describe." One of his vessels foundered, and the other two he did not see again until his return to England. At last he arrived off Broadhaven. None of the crew had ever been there before but luckily it was discovered that their one and only prisoner knew the coast well and he offered to pilot His Majesty's ship into harbour.

Being at last safely arrived at "the well-head of all Pyrates" the Admiral had recourse to strategy. On close enquiries being made quite a number of his crew admitted to having been at some time or other in the pirate trade, so these men were ordered to row ashore and the ringleader was told what tale to spin when he should meet the local chieftain. This was to say that Captain Mainwaring—the famous pirate had not then reformed—was on board with his ship full of "purchase" and that he was as generous as he was reported to be to those who served him willingly.

The story of how the English admiral hoodwinked the Irish is so diverting and human a story that, although of some length, it would be a pity to condense it:

The gentleman of that place (Mr. Cormat or McCormac) like a wily fox, absented himself, and left his wife and hackney daughters to entertain the new welcome guests, till he beheld the coast clear; and when he saw his time he returned, and to make his credit and reputation seem the greater with Captain Mainwaring, expressed the favours he had done to sundry pyrates, tho' it was to his eminent peril, which he did not esteem, if he might do Capt. Mainwaring any service; so much he was devoted to his person, when he heard the report of his wealth; and to endear him the more, he promised to send two gentlemen of trust the next morning on board him, to give him the better assurance of his fidelity; and in the meantime because he should not be unfurnished of victuals, he directed him to send his men ashore armed and in a warlike manner, that it might appear their cattle were taken by violence, which he would appoint in a place with their ears slit, to be distinguished from other beasts.

The messenger being fully satisfied, and having executed his stratagem, returned aboard that night. At the dawning of the day the play began, for that was the hour appointed for the wolf to seek his prey; and Capt. Chester with 50 armed men in a disorderly manner like pyrates, went on shore, and acted so much as was agreed on; and the cattle being killed he was, in a secret manner, invited to the house of the gentleman, but as his intreaty was to make it appear publickly that he came not by invitation, but of his own accord. Here he was welcomed and friendly entertained by the daughters, whose desire was to hear of their sweet-hearts, and to receive their tokens; but all in general coveted to see Capt. Mainwaring, also they confidently believed would enrich them all. The gentleman, Mr. Cormat by name, was punctual in all his undertaking, and the two ambassadors he promised came aboard, and delivered a friendly message of their love and assurance of their service to Capt. Mainwaring. The message ended, Sir William wished them to observe and consider, whether they thought that ship and company to be pyrates, for they could well judge of pyrates, because of their familiarity and acquaintance with them.

It was a folly to dissemble any longer; for tho' they would yet they could not betray Sir William's design, and therefore in as rough and rude a manner as they delivered their message, he told them how they had transgressed, and the next thing they were to expect was Death, and commanded them to be put in irons, in dark and several places, being careful to permit neither boat nor man to go ashore until his own landing.

The time approached that Sir William promised to visit them; and for his greater honour they had drawn down four or 500 people to attend on the shore side, which he perceiving and seeming to be jealous of their number, pretended to be shy of going ashore for fear of treachery; but if oaths, vows, or any kind of protestations would serve him, he had them, and when they saw him thus convinced of their sincerity, and that he put himself upon them, three of their principal men ran up to the armpits in water, striving who should have the credit to carry him ashore. One of these three was an Englishman, a late tradesman of London, and attended the arrival of pyrates. The second had been a schoolmaster and a man attended like another Apollo amongst those rude people. The third, a merchant of Gallaway, but his chiefest trade was to buy and sell with pyrates.

These three gallants, like gentlemen-ushers, conducted Sir William to Mr. Cormat's house; and the meaner sort followed with acclamations of joy. At his landing happy was he to whom he would lend his ear; falling into discourse, one told him that they knew his friends, and though his name had not discovered it yet his face did shew him to be a Mainwaring. In short, they made him believe he might command them and their country, and that no man was ever so welcome as Capt. Mainwaring.

Entering into the house of Mr. Cormat, his three hackney daughters rose to entertain him and conducted him to the hall newly strewed with rushes, as the richest decking their abilities or the meanness of the place could afford. In the corner was a harper, who played merrily to make his welcome the greater.

After some discourse, and several questions, asked by the three daughters concerning their acquaintance and friends, but above all, being desirous to handle the tokens promised, and laughing and jeering at their two messengers aboard, who they did not suspect were detained prisoners, but drinking and frolicking in the ship, as the use was upon the arrival of pyrates; after these passages the women offered to dance; one chose Sir William which he excused, but gave free liberty for the rest of his company. The Englishman was so pleased and merry that he seemed to have new life infused into him; he told Sir William, the Heavens did foresee he was born to serve him, and to relieve him; he shewed him a pass procured upon false pretences from the Sheriff of that country, authorising him to travel from place to place to make inquisition of his goods, which he falsely pretended he was robbed of at sea; he laughed at his pass, and urged the advantage that might be made of it, in sending to and fro in the country without suspicion.

He proffered Sir William the service of ten mariners of his acquaintance, that lay lurking there-abouts, expecting the coming in of men-of-war, which seafaring men he had power to command.

His antic behaviour was enough to put the melancholiest man in good humour; sometimes he played them part of a commanding sheriff; then he acted his own, with many witty passages how he deceived the sheriff. Sir William embraced his offer of ten mariners, with a promise of reward, and caused him to write effectually for them, as may appear by this that follows:

"Honest Brother Dick, and the rest, we are all made men; for Valient Capt. Mainwaring and all his gallant crew are arrived in this place. Make haste, for he flourisheth in wealth, and is most kind to all men. Farewell and once again make haste."

This letter being writ, and the pass enclosed in it, Sir William took it into his own hand, offering to hire a messenger to carry it; but night drawing on, which required his return on board, and having drawn from the Company all the secret he desired, he caused the harp to cease playing, and commanded silence, because he was to speak.

He told them that hitherto they had played their part, and he had no part in the comedy: but though his was last, and might be termed the epilogue, yet it would prove more tragical than theirs. He put them out of doubt that he was no pyrate, but a scurge of such; and was sent by His Majesty to discover, suppress and punish them, and their abettors, whom His Majesty did not think worthy the name of subjects: he told them that he had received sufficient information of the protection given to pyrates in that harbour, and by Cormat; and that he could find no better expedient to confirm what had been told him, than by taking upon him the habit of a pyrate, and one of their associates; and that they had made themselves in the law, without further accusation: and now there remained nothing but to proceed to their execution, by virtue of his commission; and to that purpose he had brought a gallows ready framed, which he caused to be set up, meaning to begin the mournful dance with the two men they thought had been merry dancing aboard the ship.

He told the Englishman he should be the next, because his offence did surpass the rest, being an Englishman, who should be a pattern of good life to those people we have fought to reduce to civility since we first possessed that country; and seeing man naturally is rather apt to follow evil example than good, he should be hanged for example.

He told the schoolmaster he was a fit tutor for the children of the devil, and that he had apt scholars to follow his damnable instructions; and, that as the members are governed by the head, the way to make his members sound was to shorten him by the head; and therefore willed him to admonish his scholars from the top of the gallows, which should be a pulpit prepared for him. He asked the merchant, whether he imagined there could be thieves if there were no receivers? And as the contriver and plotter of evil is worse than he that executes it, so is the abettor and a receiver to be condemned before the thief. He told him that pyrates could no more live by their occupation, were it not for buyers, than a poor labourer work without wages; that the offence in a merchant was more heinous than in another man, because his trade must be maintained and unheld by peace; his time he told him was not long, and wished him to make his account with God, that he might be found a good merchant and factor to him, though he had been a malefactor to the law.

At this point Sir William brought his speech to a close, possibly from want of breath, for there can be no doubt that he, if not his hearers, most thoroughly enjoyed it.

Meanwhile, as night was drawing on, the English admiral retired on board his ship, leaving his carpenter to erect and prepare the gallows for the executions. Early next morning the culprits were marshalled, in irons, at the foot of the scaffold, when Sir William arrived, and to the surprise and joy of all declared that if they gave their solemn promise never again to have any dealings of any kind with pirates, he would pardon them. The prisoners, having spent the night in chains and lamentations, were only too ready to give their solemn promise to amend their wicked ways and were freed.

"The Englishman," Sir William continues, "was banished, not only from that coast, but from the seaside throughout Ireland, and a copy of his pass sent to the Sheriff, with advice to be more cautious for the future in granting his safe conduct."

Before leaving Broadhaven, the wily Admiral by means of another cunning stratagem captured a whole ship full of pirates, whose captain, already twice pardoned, he hanged as an example to the rest and, one may be forgiven for believing, to test the gallows he had brought with him from England.

"This severe justice gave a terror to the people of that country," concluded Monson, so that "the pyrates ever after became strangers to that harbour of Broadhaven, and in a little time wholly abandoned Ireland, which was attributed to the execution of that man; for before that time, they were in those parts rather connived at than punished." But Mainwaring's statement indicates that Monson rather overestimated the results of his own vigour and cunning.

Another pirate of this time, whose early career resembled that of Mainwaring, was Captain Peter Easton or Eaton, alias Cason, nicknamed by the fishermen of Newfoundland the Arch-Pyrate.

The first time we meet with his name is in 1610, when he had already achieved the distinction of being described as a "notorious pirate." At this time his fleet of forty ships was holding up all the traffic of the Bristol Channel at the mouth of the Avon, and his incessant plundering had driven the Bristol merchants to seek the aid of the Lord Admiral, the Earl of Nottingham.

A year later Easton turned up on the Newfoundland coast in command of ten ships of war, on the same errand as Mainwaring had been, to replenish his crews and ships. We get particulars of his doings there from Sir Richard Whitbourne in his "Discourse and Discovery of Newfoundland." At this time there was no force, civil or military, to keep order amongst the large unruly population which numbered in the summertime from fifteen to twenty thousand fishermen.

In 1612 Easton arrived at Harbour Grace and stole five ships, one hundred pieces of ordnance, and various goods to the value of ten thousand four hundred pounds. Also he took, or induced, five hundred English fishermen to join him in piracy. He robbed French ships of goods, mostly fish, valued at six hundred pounds, a great Flemish ship of a thousand pounds, and twelve Portuguese of three thousand pounds.

On shore also the pirates did great harm; robbing the settlers of their goods, burning down the forests, and committing murders and theft. The English "erring captains," as Whitbourne euphemistically calls them, were by far the worst rogues of all, and he adds that the "Portugals, French and all the other nations frequenting that trade are more conformable to good order than the English."

Whitbourne, who spent a large part of his life in Newfoundland and lost a fortune in attempting to colonize the island with Welshmen, was made prisoner by Easton, who kept him "eleven weeks under his command." This captive proved quite unlike any other the "arch-pyrate" had ever met with, for he so earnestly and severely admonished Easton on the wickedness of his life that the pirate ended by imploring Whitbourne to return to England "to some friends of his and solicit them to become humble petitioners to the King for his pardon." Whitbourne agreed to do this but refused an offer of "much wealth" for his services. It was arranged that the penitent pirate should follow by easy stages, so as to give time for the pardon to be granted before he arrived back in England.

While waiting Easton decided to have one more fling before becoming an honest seaman, and sailed to the Azores to intercept one of the Spanish Plate fleet. Then with his fourteen ships heavily laden with plunder, he hung about the coast of Barbary for the hoped-for pardon, until despairing of it, he went to Villefranche, the favourite pirate haunt. Here he purchased a palace, stored his booty, which was said to be worth two millions of gold, and lived in luxury for the rest of his days, the first of many wealthy magnates to retire to the Riviera.

During the Elizabethan and early Stuart periods men of the highest station in life took to piracy either from necessity or for love of adventure. One such, Sir Francis Verney, had the additional incentive of escape from henpecking.

Married as a boy by a scheming mother-in-law to her determined daughter, he was sent to Trinity College, Oxford, where he matriculated in 1600. He was famous for his good looks, his great personal courage and magnificent dress. Directly he came of age he appealed to Parliament to revoke certain orders which his mother-in-law had got legalized to deprive him of his fortune. He lost his case, quarrelled with his nagging wife, sold his estates and disappeared from England.

For the next few years he wandered about Europe, fought several duels, and squandered his fortune. When his money was gone, he joined a relation, Captain Philip Gifford, who commanded a company of two hundred English adventurers in the service of Muley Sidan, Pretender to the throne of Morocco.

After the crushing defeat of Sidan, Philip Gifford became a pirate, commanding a ship, the *Fortune*. Sir Francis Verney joined him in this enterprise, "making havoc of his own countrymen and carrying into Algiers prizes belonging to the merchants of Poole and Plymouth." Verney did nothing by halves; when at Algiers he "turned Turk and wore the Turban and the habit of the Moors."

At last he was defeated in a fight with some Sicilians, taken prisoner, and for two years pulled at the oar of a galley as a slave. His life ended in tragedy, for according to William Lithgow, the traveller, he "found the sometime great English gallant, Sir Francis Verney, in the extreemest calamity and sickness in the hospital of St. Mary of Pity at Messina in 1615, where he died on September 6th." An English merchant John Watchin, sent back to Claydon, his home in Buckinghamshire, his belongings which, with his portrait, are still preserved there.

Some years later another pirate rose to cause endless trouble to the English authorities. This was Captain John Nutt of Lympston in Devon, about whom there is much to be learned in John Forster's "Life of Sir John Eliot."

In 1623 King James needed sailors for his navy and Sir John Eliot, as Vice-Admiral of Devon, was ordered to press seamen for the service. Somehow Nutt got to hear of these orders before they were issued and gave warning to the West Country. By the time the hated press gangs got to work hundreds of sailors had escaped to Newfoundland in the fishing fleet or gone into hiding inland.

This pirate Nutt commanded several ships which scoured the Channel and the coast of Ireland. Originally he had gone to sea as a gunner on a Dartmouth ship bound for Newfoundland, but arriving there he joined up with several other refugees from the press gang, seized a French vessel and went "on the account." Fortune soon smiled on the newly fledged pirates, for they captured a big Plymouth ship, as well as a

Fleming of two hundred tons. With this little squadron Nutt and his crews plundered the fishing fleets and then returned to English waters. His fame and reputation for good luck drew to his service crowds of discontented or starving seamen. His robberies and plunderings in the Channel and North Sea soon brought a shower of complaints, but Nutt, from his safe retreat in Torbay, simply laughed at the threats of the authorities in London.

Sir John soon saw that as long as Nutt was at large there would be no peace at sea, nor sailors to be got for the royal navy. One sound reason for this was that Nutt paid his men good wages and paid them regularly, while the common seamen whose privilege or misfortune it was to serve their King were half-starved, and lucky if they drew any pay at all.

The Vice-Admiral tried in every way to catch Nutt and set ambushes to seize him when he came on shore to see his wife and children. But the pirate never landed unless escorted by a strong bodyguard of armed pirates who would have been daunted by nothing less than a regiment of soldiers.

Urgent orders came from the King that Nutt was to be arrested forthwith, but they merely increased the Vice-Admiral's difficulties. With one hand the King issued warrants for the pirate's arrest, while with the other, through the influence of certain high persons at court in Nutt's pay, he promised one free pardon after another to the pirate if he would deliver himself up by certain dates.

In May, with a view to escaping arrest and receiving one of the pardons he knew had been issued, Nutt wrote a letter to the Vice-Admiral from aboard his "man-of-war" in Torbay offering the sum of £300 for his pardon. Eliot at once rode over to Torbay, but the pirate's heart failed him at the last moment, for he sent a messenger to say "that he would willingly have come ashore, but his company would not suffer him, and therefore he desired to be excused." The one chance left of persuading the pirate to come on shore seemed to be for Eliot to visit him on board his ship. This was naturally a very risky proceeding, for it put the Vice-Admiral at the mercy of the toughest gang of cut-throats then afloat.

The two met and Eliot at once discovered that Nutt while negotiating for his pardon had stolen a Colchester ship with a cargo of sugar. Eliot's enemies later accused him of dismissing with contempt the owner's plea for restitution, but the Admiral's answer was that he had insisted on the restoration of the prize as a preliminary to further negotiations with the pirate, who, however, burst out into such abuse that Eliot realised the impossibility of pressing the matter at the moment.

After much haggling and many recourses to the flask of wine which stood on the table between them, it was agreed that Nutt should come ashore, surrender himself, and receive a pardon on payment of five hundred pounds. On the day appointed his ship arrived at the entrance of Dartmouth harbour, when Nutt seems to have become suspicious of a trap, which indeed had been laid for him, and he sent word to Eliot that he would not land until the Vice-Admiral came aboard his ship. But the wily Sir John, who knew quite well that the date on the pardon he had in his pocket was by now expired, refused "knowing the danger of the first adventure he had made going aboard in Torbay with the pardon out of date and not willing to trust himself again with people of that condition."

At last the pirate landed and was put under formal arrest until orders should come from London regarding his fate and that of his crew. While waiting, the pirates swaggered about the quay at Dartmouth, dressed up in fine clothes "boasting," wrote the Mayor of the town to the Council, "and not ashamed to wear the clothes of those poor men in their sight, from whom they took them few days since; a part so audacious and barbarous as was never heard or seen in our nation."

At last, after endless orders and counter-orders instructions came down from London that Nutt was to be sent a prisoner to the capital, while his crew were to be locked up in the town jail. Sir John also seized the pirate's plunder and made a minute inventory of it, including this tantalizing item: "One chest I yesterday recovered, wherein it was supposed treasure lay; but I find it so unfit to mention in this place as I dare not speak what it does contain."

In the meantime a friend of Nutt's, Sir George Calvert, afterwards Lord Baltimore, the King's principal secretary, was busy in London plotting his release. Calvert, the proprietor of a "plantation" in Newfoundland, had received certain favours from the pirate captain while in that country and was now repaying them. On a trumped-up charge Sir John Eliot was arrested and clapped into the Marshalsea prison to await his trial. While the Admiral was confined in prison, awaiting the return from Spain of his patron, the all-powerful royal favourite, the Duke of Buckingham, the pirate was pardoned, released and presented with a hundred pounds by way of recompense.

Scarcely was Nutt free than he was again causing trouble. Again royal orders were issued for his apprehension, and a Captain Plumleigh was sent to the Irish coast, with one royal ship and two "whelps" to catch the pirate. Plumleigh found him in command of twenty-seven Barbary vessels as well as his own ship, with the result that the pursuer himself was attacked and only just managed to escape. As Nutt's historian remarks: "With great propriety had the successful Villain repaid during three years, by a series of such humiliations as this, the royal favour and state protection which alas saved him from the gallows Eliot had built for him." He had become "incomparably the greatest nuisance in His Majesty's dominions. Nothing on the seas was safe from him, and he struck at the highest quarry."

Shortly after his brush with Plumleigh Nutt captured a ship which was carrying the luggage, furniture, wardrobe and plate of Lord Wentworth, the new Deputy-Governor of Ireland, to Dublin. This was his way of showing his gratitude to his benefactor Calvert, of whom Wentworth was the intimate friend.

From the point of view of literary fame few pirates of the early seventeenth century excel the famous Captain John Warde, but he was also the hero of several popular ballads, and there are two rare pamphlets about his piratical adventures in the British Museum.

He is first heard of as a drunken ragged fellow who haunted the taverns of Plymouth, where he was regarded as a sullen, foul-mouthed ruffian, seldom sober and given to speaking "doggedly, complaining of his own crosses and cursing other men's luck." * His career at sea had begun as a fisherman, and he had served during the end of Elizabeth's reign as a privateer. When King James came to the throne with his new fangled ideas of peace with the Spaniards, Warde was one amongst hundreds of his kind to be thrown out of employ.

His situation at last became so desperate that Warde was forced to take service in the royal navy, the last resource of the starving mariner, and shipped aboard His Majesty's pinnace *Lion's Whelp.*

He was not a model sailor. Discipline sat uneasily on him, the pay was insufficient to support him in the state to which he aspired, and he bred discontent amongst his mates by lamenting the good old days under Elizabeth "when we might sing, swear, drub and kill men as freely as your cakemakers do flies; when the whole sea was our Empire where we robbed at will, and the world was our garden where we walked for sport." With this kind of talk he worked on some of his shipmates until they too were ready for any roguery.

An opportunity soon came. Lying alongside their ship in Portsmouth harbour was a small bark which, Warde discovered, had been bought by a Catholic recusant who had sold his lands at Petersfield and was shipping all his worldly possessions in her to France. It was arranged by Warde and his friends that one night they would go aboard the boat and steal the treasure.

Getting leave to go ashore for a merrymaking the thirty rascals met at an alehouse where they elected Warde their captain, kneeling round him with their tankards in their hands. That night they stole a boat and rowed out to the bark, which they seized, and went off to sea in her.

They were hugely disappointed next morning, when ransacking their prize, to find nothing of value in her save provisions for the intended voyage. It appears that a friend of the owner,

* J. S. Corbett, "England in the Mediterranean," 1904.

becoming suspicious, had warned him to be on his guard, and the valuables had been taken for safe keeping to the *Golden Lion,* a man-of-war then lying in Portsmouth harbour. The mutineers, knowing it was now out of the question to return, consoled themselves with the excellent victuals on board and sailed down Channel.

Off the Scilly Isles they met a tall French ship of eighty tons and five guns which by a clever trick they managed to seize. Naming her *Little John* after Robin Hood's lieutenant, they put back into Plymouth Sound and there had no difficulty in completing their numbers with the sort of seamen they wanted. The new pirates then set sail for the Mediterranean, taking a couple of prizes on the way.

Arrived at Algiers Warde proposed to the Dey that he should be allowed to take service under him, but to this the Dey would not consent. Going on to Tunis Warde met with a warm reception from the Bey, who allowed him to use his port in return for half of all the plunder Warde and his men should bring in. In the meantime Simon Danser, the Dutch renegade, had settled at Algiers, and the English corsair made the alliance with him previously described. With two such past-masters of the trade the Barbary corsairs soon learnt to build and navigate sailing ships in place of their small rowing galleys.

Warde, fighting beneath the colours of Tunis, made no bones about attacking Christian ships and was so successful that when he had been there but one year the King of France found it necessary to send a special mission to Tunis to protest against the English pirate's outrages on his ships and sailors. The protest seems to have been effective, for after this Warde left the French alone and turned his undoubted talents to capturing and pillaging Venetian ships and those flying the flag of the Knights of St. John of Malta.

It was in the hulls of the Venetian vessels that Warde found most of the great fortune which enabled him to build a palace at Tunis only second in grandeur to that of the Bey himself—a noble edifice "beautiful with rich marble and alabaster . . . more fit for a prince than a pirate," according to one who had seen it.

In 1611 William Lithgow, the traveller, happening to be in Tunis, dined and supped with Warde on several occasions and speaks of him as having "turned Turk" on account of being banished from England.

ELIOT's detention was an all too typical example of what a conscientious official had to contend with. On his release and return to his office in Devon he again attempted a vigorous enforcement of the law, but the inertia and dishonesty of Whitehall again frustrated his zeal. Each year of James's reign more and more money was raised by special taxes to supply ships and build forts, and each year the bulk of it was frittered away or misappropriated. The Barbary pirates began to infest the Channel as never before, and even made light of attacking coast villages by daylight and carrying off the whole population. Fishermen dared not go to sea, trade dwindled, prices mounted. How much the feebleness of the Government in dealing with piracy had to do with Stuart unpopularity would be an interesting subject for a historical study.

Indignant attacks were made in Parliament against the Duke of Buckingham as Lord High Admiral by Sir Robert Mansell, the Admiral who had commanded the unsuccessful expedition a few years previously against Algiers. In one speech he said "the Turks were still roving in the West, the Dunkerks in the East, the cries came out of all parts. Their losses great, their dangers more, their fears exceeding all. No merchant doth venture on the seas, hardly they thought themselves secure enough on land. It was alleged by some, that as the king's ships were stopped from going to relieve them when it was ordered by the council, so they were then. Though ready on the coasts, or in the harbours near them, where these rogues were most infectious, nothing might be done. Nay in some cases it was proved that the merchants had been taken even in the sight of the king's ships, and that the captain being importuned to relieve them, refused their protection or assistance, and said they were denied it by the instructions which they had."

These accusations were backed up by petitions which came

before Parliament on August 11th, 1625 from the Devon Grand Jury, and from the Mayor of Plymouth, as well as from several leading merchants in the West, in which complaints were made that the Admiral of their station, Sir Francis Stewart, had allowed pirates to capture English ships before his very eyes, and done nothing to stop them. The member for Hull, Mr. Lister, also told of the wrongs done to shipping by the Dunkirk pirates and said that trade on the East coast was almost at a standstill. But Parliament was adjourned — as so often was the case during the Stuart period — without coming to any definite conclusion on a matter of such grave importance to the country.

The renewal of war against Spain under Charles I showed how James had allowed the great navy of Elizabeth to degenerate in barely a score of years. When the futile attack on Cadiz in 1625 broke down, investigations showed that the ships and their rigging were falling to pieces. Officers were ignorant of navigation and incapable of keeping discipline amongst their crews, who consisted of the scourings of the ports, half starved, half naked and riddled by disease. Levet recounts in his "Relation of the Cadiz Voyage," in the Cope MSS, how the confusion in the English fleet on the way to Spain was so great that the ships kept colliding with one another. Occasionally one would chase another in the belief that it was an enemy, despite the quite different construction of the Spanish and English vessels, which would have been easily recognisable by any trained sailor. Most extraordinary of all, during the voyage out, two ships of the fleet, thinking — and with good reason as matters turned out — that they could do better for themselves elsewhere, deserted and turned pirate. It was a sorry contrast with the expedition of 1597, when the English squadron under Howard and Essex had sailed into Cadiz harbour and in a day and a night destroyed every ship and captured the citadel itself.

During the new reign the crop of petitions seeking help against pirates, Turkish and Dunkirk alike, and pathetic appeals from English slaves in the Barbary ports continued to pour in. Yet very little could be done. To execute prisoners was dangerous since there were too many English captives in Barbary and reprisals could be inflicted at the rate of ten for one. A half hearted overture was made towards the exchange of prisoners, some of them being ransomed for guns which were certain later to be turned against the English. "It was a poor way," as Mr. Oppenheim remarks, "but since the cruisers could not clear the Channel it was the only way open."

If the south-west coast suffered from the Barbary pirates, the east coast was no way better off, for the Dunkirk privateers were practically blockading the whole coast from Northumberland to Suffolk. Newcastle cried out that its coal trade was being destroyed, and at Norwich no trade could be carried on at all, fifty-eight ships being laid up there, not daring to go out, for already in that year they had lost shipping worth four thousand pounds. At Lynn things were as bad or worse; one thousand men were unemployed, and the pirates landed when and where they chose, plundering and burning houses.

The pride of the ancient Cinque Ports was now a thing of the past, and they had to petition for help against the "force and fury" of the Dunkerkers by whom they were "miserably oppressed . . . and dare not go about their voyages to Scarborough and Yarmouth, or fish in the North Sea."

It was several years before Charles I and his advisers could be brought to the point of doing anything definite but in 1637 Admiral Rainborow was sent with a punitive force to Sallee, which brought about a sudden if temporary change for the good, and the English coast was at last free from Barbary pirates. This was the solitary occasion during the whole of this reign on which any really comprehensive measures were taken, and soon after Rainborow returned the pirates were back in their old haunts.

With the death of Charles I and the rise of the Commonwealth a rapid change for the better took place in the navy. Immediate improvements were introduced; ships were repaired and made seaworthy; even more important, consideration was shown to the hitherto abused seamen. They now received proper wages and were paid punctually; their food, although poor, was infinitely better in quality and quantity than under the previous government. All this encouraged the right sort of sailor to man the navy ships, as did the award of medals, introduced for the first time by Oliver Cromwell.

The first to notice the difference were the pirates, for in a very short while both the Turks and the Dunkerkers were swept from the Channel. Here and there a few still lurked, in such places as Lundy Island in the Bristol Channel and Jersey in the Channel Islands, from which latter stronghold they were driven by Admiral Blake in 1651.

The first Dutch war found employment for English sailors, and the majority of the English pirates were not slow in coming to their country's aid when there was fighting to be done. It was at the end of this first war, in 1654, that Blake was sent with a strong fleet to deal with the Tunis corsairs.

With the end of the Commonwealth the navy again deteriorated and there followed a corresponding increase of the Channel pirates. After the Restoration Charles II sent Sir Thomas Allen to the Barbary coast; he bombarded Algiers, and in 1671 Sir Edward Spragge did the like to Bougie. Ten years later, owing to the interruption of French trade in the Mediterranean, Admiral Du Quesne took out a fleet and in the port of Scio in the Archipelago destroyed eight corsair galleys, which brought the pirates to terms.

From then on, as has already been related in the chapter on the Barbary Corsairs, the menace of the Moors in the Atlantic rapidly waned and they became a problem largely local to the Mediterranean.

BOOK III

THE PIRATES OF THE WEST

CHAPTER I

THE BUCCANEERS

THAT strange and sinister school of piracy known as "The Brotherhood of the Coast" had its origin in certain definite developments in European politics. Spain had declined from her lofty position in the world; other nations were less and less inclined to respect her claim of monopoly in the West Indies and the Caribbean, and to subscribe even without the excuse of war to the doctrine of "No peace beyond the Line." (The "Line" was Pope Alexander VI's parallel of longitude which granted Spain her monopoly as the result of Columbus's discoveries.)

The Spaniards' use of this monopoly was excessively, though not uniquely, stupid. They, in common with all other countries at the beginning of colonial enterprise, attempted the hopeless task of trying to prevent all intercourse between their colonies and foreigners. Spain was obsessed with the belief that she would gain the greatest profit for herself if her colonies traded only with the mother country, notwithstanding the fact that she had not the means at home to provide her colonists with more than a small part of the goods they required in exchange. Not only was trade prohibited on these grounds, but for reasons of religion as well all heretics were in particular forbidden to intrude in His Catholic Majesty's western domains — very early an edict had gone forth that no "corsarios luteranos" were to land at any Spanish settlement or to sell or buy goods or victuals of any kind whatever.

But the edict was easier to issue than to enforce. The colonists needed the goods that the corsairs had to sell and bought them. This fundamental need explains the success of the Hawkinses and their kind in the second third of the sixteenth century. But in a short time a more serious danger than the rovers appeared — the intruders began to colonise the forbidden territory and attempt the establishment of a permanent trade with their Spanish neighbours. The first colony founded by the French in Florida in 1562 was ruthlessly wiped out. Indeed the Spaniards hesitated at no cruelty to protect their monopoly. In December 1604 the Venetian ambassador in London wrote that "the Spanish in the West Indies captured two English vessels, cut off the hands, feet, noses and ears of the crews and smeared them with honey and tied them to trees to be tortured by flies and other insects." This information from an English source may have been exaggerated or exceptional, but it is not surprising to read that "the barbarity makes people here cry out" and that small attention was paid when "the Spanish here plead that they were pirates, not merchants, and that they did not know of the peace." Yet the colonisation went on. The first permanent English settlement in America was made at Jamestown in Virginia in 1607, and in 1623 the first in the West Indies was established at St. Kitts, although two years later the island was divided between the English and the French.

Whatever the original traders in the Spanish possessions were, whether pirates, privateers or honest merchantmen, they were not buccaneers. A pirate was a criminal who robbed the ships of all nations in any waters, but the original buccaneer preyed only upon Spanish ships and property in America. The buccaneers owed their existence largely to the shortsightedness of the Spaniards, who could not supply their colonists with what they needed, or did so at prohibitive prices fixed by the authorities at Cadiz at a time when foreigners were bringing all kinds of merchandise to the settlements to be sold at reasonable prices.

The first base of these free lance traders from whom arose the fraternity of buccaneers was Hispaniola, now called Haiti

A BUCCANEER OF HISPANIOLA

or San Domingo, the second largest of the West Indian islands. This large and beautiful island had once been inhabited by Indian races whom Spanish cruelty had virtually exterminated. After the conquest of Mexico and Peru most of the Spanish settlers left the islands to seek their fortunes on the mainland, leaving behind large herds of wild cattle and pigs, descended from domestic stock, which wandered at large over the savannahs. Gradually Englishmen and Frenchmen had come to Hispaniola to hunt these wild cattle, dry the meat, and sell it to passing ships.

Clark Russell, in his "Life of William Dampier," graphically describes this primitive settlement, incidentally giving the origin of the term buccaneer:

> In or about the middle of the seventeenth century, the Island of San Domingo, or Hispaniola as it was then called, was haunted and overrun by a singular community of savage, surly, fierce and filthy men. They were chiefly composed of French colonists, whose ranks had from time to time been enlarged by liberal contributions from the slums and allys of more than one European city and town. These people went dressed in shirts and pantaloons of coarse linen cloth, which they steeped in the blood of the animals they slaughtered. They wore round caps, boots of hogskin drawn over their feet, and belts of raw hide, in which they stuck their sabres and knives. They also armed themselves with firelocks, which threw a couple of balls, each weighing two ounces. The places where they dried and salted their meat were called "boucans," and from this term they came to be styled bucaniers or buccaneers, as we spell it. They were hunters by trade, and savages in their habits. They chased and slaughtered horned cattle and trafficked with the flesh, and their favourite food was raw marrow from the bones of the beasts which they shot. They eat and slept on the ground, their table was a stone, their bolster the trunk of a tree, and their roof the hot and sparkling heavens of the Antilles.

The first trespassers on the Spanish monopoly were the French. Although towards the end of the sixteenth century Scaliger, the French chronicler, wrote "Nulli melius piraticum exercent quam Angli," the freebooters across the Channel were by no means fumblers in the art of piracy. Already by the middle of the century the French from Dieppe, Brest and the Basque coast were plundering in the West. Already such names as Jean Terrier, Jacques Sore and François le Clerc, alias "Pie de Palo" or "Wooden Leg," were as detestable to Spanish ears as were to become those of Francis Drake or John Hawkins. These first pirates had, it is true, no very difficult task, for most of the settlements they attacked were poorly defended, possessed few guns and often as not no gunpowder. The French corsairs soon learnt the favourite routes of the returning gold-laden galleons, and were wont to prowl about the Cuban and Yucatan coasts and the Florida straits on the look-out for a rich prize. When at last a fleet of great unwieldy ships appeared the small low close-sailing pirate vessels hung upon its skirts, waiting an opportunity to snap up any which was so unfortunate as to fall behind or get separated from the main fleet, so that it was no wonder they were said to have "become a nightmare of Spanish seamen."

However these were but the precursors of the buccaneers, who did not begin to flourish until the middle of the seventeenth century. Their real beginning dated from their expulsion from Hispaniola by the Spaniards. That jealous race determined to rid itself of these hitherto harmless "boucaniers" but in dislodging them, a feat accomplished without much difficulty, converted butchers of cattle into butchers of men.

Driven out of Hispaniola, the settlers found a safe retreat in a small rocky island called Tortuga, or Turtle Island, which lies a few miles off the north-west coast of Hispaniola. Here they settled, formed a kind of republic, and built themselves a fort. For a year or two all seems to have gone well with the little colony, until one day a Spanish force from San Domingo swooped down and wiped it out. But the Spaniards did not stay long and after their departure the "boucaniers" began to drift back again. It was not until a few years later, in 1640, that the true buccaneer came to stay and flourish there on and off for some eighty years. In that year a Frenchman of St. Kitts, Monsieur Levasseur, a Calvinist, a skilled engineer and a very courageous gentleman, got together a company of fifty other Frenchmen of the same faith, and made a surprise attack on Tortuga.

This was successful and without much trouble the French took possession of the island. The first thing the new governor did was to build a strong fort on a high pinnacle of rock and arm it with cannon. On this stronghold he built himself a house to live in and named it the "Dove-cote." The only way of reaching it was to climb up steps cut in the rock and up iron ladders. Scarcely had it been completed when an unsuspecting Spanish squadron appeared in the little harbour to be met by a withering fire from the "Dove-cote," which sank several of the ships and drove away the rest.

Under the wise governorship of M. Levasseur the little settlement prospered. French and English adventurers of all sorts gathered there, planters, buccaneers and runaway sailors. The buccaneers hunted cattle on the neighbouring island of Hispaniola, the planters grew crops of tobacco and sugar, while many of the former, now become full-blooded pirates, roamed the neighbouring seas in search of Spanish ships to plunder.

Tortuga soon became the mart for the boucan and hides brought from Hispaniola, and for plunder taken from the Spanish, which were bartered for brandy, guns, gunpowder and cloth from the Dutch and French ships which called there.

It was not long before the fame of Tortuga had spread all over the West Indies, to be followed by a rush of adventurers of all kinds, to whom the attraction of cruising after the Spaniards with its opportunities of sudden wealth was irresistible. Such extremes of fortune have always attracted a certain class of dare-devil character and the situation was not unlike that met with during the days of the "forty-niners" in California, or the rush of gold-seekers to the Klondyke in 1897.

A detailed account of the rise of the buccaneers is impossible in a work of so general a scope as this, but their history has been fully and ably set down by their own historian, Alexander Olivier Exquemelin, or Esquemeling, a young Frenchman from Honfleur who arrived in the West Indies in 1658. His book was first published in 1678 at Amsterdam and appears to have met with instantaneous success. Three years later a Spanish edition appeared, printed at Cologne and translated from the original Dutch edition by a Señor de Buena Maison. The first English translation appeared in 1684 and is entitled:

Bucaniers of America: or, a true account of the most remarkable assaults committed of late years upon the coasts of The West-Indies, by the Bucaniers of Jamaica and Tortuga, Both English and French.

This edition was so well received that within three months it was reprinted and with it was published a second volume. The two volumes are today of considerable rarity and when good copies turn up at occasional sales they fetch a hundred pounds or more.

The second volume is entitled:

Bucaniers of America. The second volume. Containing The Dangerous Voyage and Bold Attempts of Captain Bartholomew Sharp, and others; performed upon the Coasts of the South Sea, for the space of two years, etc. From the Original Journal of the said Voyage.

Written By Mr. Basil Ringrose, Gent. who was all along present at these transactions.

The two volumes of this book are the chief source of information about the life of the buccaneers. It might well be described as the Handbook of Buccaneering, and we can imagine that many a Dutch or English boy at the end of the seventeenth century must, after perusing it, have run away to sea to join its heroes. There have been several good reprints of the History during the last few years, in which those who wish may read more fully of the "bold attempts" of the "Brothers of the Coast."

The author of the book tells us that he went out to Tortuga in his youth as an apprentice in the service of the French West India Company.* This for all practical purposes made him

* Mr. Vrijman has recently communicated to me his interesting discovery, from the "Surgeons' Guildbook 1597–1734," in the Municipal Archives at Amsterdam, that Exquemeling of Honfleur passed his State examination for surgeon in 1679, the year

a slave for a certain number of years. After a while the Governor of the island, who used him so cruelly that his health broke down, sold him cheap to a surgeon. This new master proved as kind as the former was cruel, so that gradually young Exquemeling regained his health and strength, and imbibed from his master the mysteries of the barber-surgeon's craft. Eventually, being given his freedom and a few surgical instruments, the newly "qualified" surgeon began to look round to see where he should practise his profession. An opportunity soon came to serve as a barber-surgeon with the buccaneers of Tortuga, and the year 1668 found him enlisting on board a buccaneer ship, where he shaved and bled his shipmates and dressed their wounds, no doubt surreptitiously keeping a journal all the while.

It was in the year 1665 that a daring exploit took place which may be said to have been the beginning of the buccaneering that was in full swing when Exquemeling arrived on the scene. Up to this time the pirates had sailed in small craft pulled by oars with a sail or two to assist on occasion. In these they roamed along the coasts or lurked in creeks ready to surprise small Spanish craft. It was in such a craft that Peter Legrand set out with a crew of twenty-eight men. For many days they searched for a prize in vain and, having consumed all their victuals, they were in danger of starving. Then one evening they beheld a large fleet of Spanish ships sailing majestically along. Following some way behind was the biggest galleon of all, and this vessel Peter resolved to take or die in the attempt. In the tropics darkness falls suddenly and so the little craft was able to come up astern of the towering galleon unobserved.

Before attempting to board her, Legrand ordered the surgeon — for it seems they were provided with this luxury even before the appearance of Exquemeling — to bore holes in the bottom of their boat so that there would be no question or hope of escape if the project failed. Then the men, barefoot and armed

after the publication of his first volume in the Dutch capital. Until this discovery it had always been supposed that he was a Dutchman who for certain reasons preferred to use a name other than his own.

with pistol and sword, climbed stealthily up the sides of the galleon, killed the dozing helmsman and rushed down to the great cabin where they burst in to surprise the Admiral and his officers at a game of cards. Holding a pistol to his breast Legrand ordered the Admiral to surrender his ship. Well might that terrified officer cry out, "Jesus bless us! are these devils, or what are they?"

In the meantime others of the pirates had taken possession of the gunroom where the arms were stored and had killed every Spaniard who opposed them. In but a brief space of time the incredible had happened and the great ship was in the possession of a handful of French ruffians.

Peter Legrand then did a unique thing. Instead of sailing back to Tortuga and squandering his riches as every other buccaneer after him did, he sailed straight home to Dieppe in Normandy, where he retired to live in peace and plenty and never again went to sea.

The ordinary buccaneer, having won a good prize, generally prided himself on squandering it as soon as possible. Some of them would spend as much as two to three thousand pieces of eight in one night at the taverns, gambling-halls or brothels. Exquemeling, in speaking of this, writes:

> My own master would buy, on like occasions, a whole pipe of wine and placing it in the street would force everyone that passed by to drink with him, threatening also to pistol them in case they would not do it. At other times he would do the same with barrels of ale or beer, and, very often, with both hands he would throw these liquors about the streets and wet the clothes of such as walked by without regarding whether he spoiled their apparel or not, were they men or women.

Naturally the news of Legrand's great exploit spread far and wide. After this there was hope for every buccaneer, however small his craft might be, and the Spanish captains of rich home-sailing galleons sailed in constant fear of attack.

To give an idea of how the buccaneers were organised, and what were the rules or laws they observed when on the war path, it will not be out of place to quote from Exquemeling, who gives the following description of the men he served with:

Before the Pirates go out to sea, [he writes] they give notice to everyone who goes upon the voyage of the day on which they ought precisely to embark, intimating also to them their obligation of bringing each man in particular so many pounds of powder and bullets as they think necessary for that expedition. Being all come on board, they join together in council, concerning what place they ought first to go wherein to get provisions — especially of flesh, seeing they scarce eat anything else, and of these the most common sort among them is pork. The next food is tortoises, which they are accustomed to salt a little. Sometimes they resolve to rob such or such hog-yards, wherein the Spaniards often have a thousand heads of swine together. They come to these places in the dark of night and having beset the keeper's lodge they force him to rise, threatening withal to kill him in case he disobeys their command or makes any noise. Yea, these menances are oftentimes put in execution, without giving any quarter to the miserable swine-keepers, or any other person that endeavours to hinder their robberies.

Having got possession of flesh sufficient for their voyage, they return to their ship. Here their allowance, twice a day to everyone, is as much as he can eat, without either weight or measure. Neither does the steward of the vessel give any greater proportion of flesh or anything else to the captain than to the meanest mariner. The ship being well victualled, they call another council, to deliberate towards what place they shall go to seek their desperate fortunes. In this council, likewise, they agree upon certain articles which are put in writing, by way of bond or obligation, which everyone is bound to observe, and all of them, or the chief, set their hands to it. Herein they specify, and set down very distinctly, what sums of money each particular person ought to have for that voyage, the fund of all the payments being the common stock of what is gotten by the whole expedition; for otherwise it is the same law, among these people, as with other Pirates, "No prey, no pay."

In the first place, therefore, they mention how much the captain ought to have for his ship. Next the salary of the carpenter, or shipwright, who careened, mended or rigged the vessel. This commonly amounts to 100 or 150 pieces of eight, being, according to the agreement, more or less. Afterwards for provisions and victualling they draw out of the same common stock about 200 pieces of eight. Also a competent salary for the surgeon and his chest of medicaments which is usually rated at 200 or 250 pieces of eight. Lastly they stipulate in writing what recompense or reward each one ought to have, that is either wounded or maimed in his body, suffering the loss of any limb, by that voyage. Thus they order for the loss of a right arm 600 pieces of eight or six slaves; for the loss of a left arm 500 pieces of eight, or five slaves; for a right leg 500 pieces of eight or five slaves; for the left leg 400 pieces of eight or four slaves; for an eye 100 pieces of eight, or one slave; for a finger of the hand the same reward as for an eye.

All which sums of money as I here said before, are taken out of the capital sum or common stock of what is got by their piracy. For a very exact and equal dividend is made of the remainder among them all. Yet herein they have also regard to qualities and places. Thus the Captain, or chief Commander, is allotted five or six portions to what the ordinary seamen have; the Master's Mate only two; and the other officers proportionate to their employment. After whom they draw equal parts from the highest even to the lowest mariner, the boys not being omitted. For even these draw half a share by reason that, when they happen to take a better vessel than their own, it is the duty of the boys to set fire to the ship or boat wherein they are, and then retire to the prize which they have taken.

They observe among themselves very good order. For in the prizes they take it is severely prohibited to everyone to usurp anything in particular to themselves. Hence all they take is equally divided, according to what has been said before. Yea, they make a common oath to each other not to abscond or conceal the least thing they find amongst the prey. If afterwards anyone is found unfaithful, who has contravened the said oath, immediately he is separated and turned out of the society. Among themselves they are very civil and charitable to each other. Insomuch that if any wants what another has, with great liberality they give it one to another. As soon as these pirates have taken any prize of ship or boat, the first thing they endeavour is to set on shore the prisoners, detaining only some few for their own help and service, to whom also they give their liberty after the space of two or three years. They put in very frequently for refreshment at one island or another; but more especially into those which lie on the southern side of the Isle of Cuba. Here they careen their vessels, and in the meanwhile some of them go to hunt, others to cruise upon the seas in canoes seeking their fortunes. Many times they take the poor fishermen of tortoises, and carrying them to their habitations they make them work so long as the pirates are pleased.

It is interesting to compare the compensation paid by the buccaneers for injuries received in action with the scales of indemnification paid by modern insurance companies to working men for loss of a limb or eye. I am indebted to Mr. T. W. Blackburn for the following schedule, which appeared in "The Insurance Field" of America.

Pirates	*Pieces of Eight*	*Equivalent in dollars*	*Modern Workman, Dollars*
Loss of Right Arm	600	579.00	520
Loss of Left Arm	500	482.50	520
Loss of Right Leg	500	482.50	520
Loss of Left Leg	400	386.00	520
Loss of an Eye	100	96.50	280
Loss of a Finger	100	96.50	126

It will be noted that the buccaneers drew a distinction between the loss of a left arm and the loss of a right, whereas in modern compensation laws no distinction is made. The buccaneers evidently prized the right member higher than the left. In the case of the loss of an eye the buccaneer schedule is lower than the modern, such a loss evidently not being considered much of a handicap, in view of the number of successful and capable one-eyed buccaneers.

It should be borne in mind that the conditions described by Exquemeling represent the early days of buccaneering, what might in fact be called the "Happy Family" era, which was very different from the conditions found later on under such great leaders as Mansfield, Morgan and Grammont.

In these later days, the grand period of buccaneering, the recognised general or admiral would send forth word east, west, north and south that he was going "on the account" and name the place of meeting. Then from every island and bay came rough men, armed with flintlock and short sword, to enlist under a favourite or lucky leader.

If Pierre Legrand had shewn his fellows that even the largest Spanish galleon was not out of their reach, it fell to another far worse rascal to open up a new and even richer mine of wealth. This was another Frenchman, François Lolonois, probably the most cruel and pitiless blackguard who ever cut a Spaniard's throat, and one who boasted that he had never spared a prisoner's life.

Hitherto the buccaneers had confined most of their attention to Spanish ships, making only occasional raids on shore in order to procure food and drink. But Lolonois conceived a new plan. Getting together a strong force of ships and men at Tortuga he sailed for the Gulf of Venezuela. The large and prosperous city of Maracaibo stood by a vast lake which communicates with the Gulf by a narrow channel. This was guarded by a fort which fell to the pirates after three hours of severe fighting. The way being then clear, the fleet sailed through the channel into the lake, and captured the city without resistance from the panic-stricken inhabitants, who had fled and hidden themselves in the neighbouring forest.

Next day Lolonois sent strong parties of armed men to scour the woods. They returned the same night with many prisoners, twenty thousand pieces of eight, and a string of mules laden with household goods and merchandise. Amongst the prisoners were women and children, and many of these were put to the rack to force them to confess where valuables had been hidden.

In the meantime a Spanish officer who had seen active service in Flanders gathered together a force of eight hundred armed men, threw up earthworks at the narrows and mounted guns to prevent the escape of the buccaneers. The buccaneers attacked and after a fight the fortification was taken. The greedy Lolonois, in revenge, decided to try to squeeze a little more out of Maracaibo and ordered the fleet to return there, with the result that several thousand more pieces of eight were added to the plunder.

After spending several weeks at Maracaibo, the buccaneers sailed away in the direction of Hispaniola. They landed on Cow Island and shared out their plunder. When counted up it was found that they had got the enormous total of two hundred and sixty thousand pieces of eight, as well as goods of all sorts, so that when every man had his share, in money, silver and jewels, he was rich.

We need not follow the further career of Lolonois beyond saying that he came to a horrible end at the hands of the Indians of Darien.

We have mentioned Pierre Legrand and the terrible Lolonois as conspicuous members of the first epoch, but there were others of almost equal fame who won renown and riches on the Spanish Main, such men as Bartholomew the Portuguese, Rock Brasiliano, and Montbars the Exterminator. Also there was Lewis Scot, the Englishman, whom some claim to have been the very first buccaneer, even earlier than the bloody Lolonois, to try his fortune on the Main, when he sacked and pillaged the city of Campeche. This unfortunate town was soon to receive another unwelcome visitor, a Dutchman, Captain Mansfield or Mansvelt, a buccaneer who had bigger ideas than the common run of the brotherhood, for he dreamed of founding a pirate settlement or colony on Providence Island off the Mosquito coast, but he met his death before his plan had matured.

There was also Pierre François, who after being at sea in an open boat with twenty-six companions, began to despair of ever meeting with "any prey," so decided upon a highly original exploit. This was to try his luck among the pearl fisheries off Rancherias, which no buccaneer had ever dared to do before. The pearl fishing fleet, which came from Cartagena, consisted of a dozen vessels and when working on the pearl grounds was protected by two Spanish men-of-war. On approaching the fleet, François ordered his men to take the sails down and row so as to be taken for a Spanish craft from Maracaibo.

With incredible boldness the twenty-seven buccaneers rowed up alongside the smaller man-of-war, the *Vice-Admiral,* a ship armed with eight guns and carrying sixty well-armed men, and called on her to surrender. The Spaniards shewed fight, but notwithstanding their superiority in numbers and arms they were defeated by the buccaneers. So far the enterprise had been successful beyond their wildest hopes but Pierre was one of those who did not know when to stop. Instead of sailing away with his new ship, his prisoners and the catch of pearls, valued by the Spaniards at the enormous sum of a hundred thousand pieces of eight, the foolhardy buccaneer attempted to take the other and bigger man-of-war, but in this mad attempt was defeated, lost his catch and was lucky to escape with his life.

Tortuga was too well suited in every way to be the headquarters of the buccaneers for it to be left very long unmolested by the Spaniards. Again and again they attacked it and killed or drove away all the French and English but they always returned. Eventually, however, the harassed buccaneers decided to look for a new and safe retreat where they would not only be free from attack but where they could sell their plunder, get drunk and, when their money was all spent, find another ship to sail in. Such a spot they found in Jamaica, where at the end of a narrow spit of land stood the little town of Port Royal, which exactly met their needs.

Some years previously, in 1655, Jamaica had been captured from the Spaniards by Penn and Venables, and the new colonists found themselves in a somewhat precarious position. But with several hundreds of the finest seamen afloat they felt safer, and soon money and merchandise began to pour into Port Royal, which became one of the richest and probably most vicious spots on the face of the globe.

The most celebrated of all the men of Port Royal, the greatest of all the buccaneers, was Henry Morgan, son of Robert Morgan, a yeoman farmer of Llanrhymny in Glamorganshire. The story prevalent during his lifetime that as a lad he was kidnapped in Bristol and sold as a servant in Barbados was probably untrue. In fact it served as the basis of a libel action which Morgan brought against Exquemeling's English publisher. He won his suit and was awarded two hundred pounds and a public apology. What appears to have annoyed him more than his portrayal as a perfect monster in his treatment of prisoners was a variant of the above story to the effect that he came of very humble stock and had been sold by

SIR HENRY MORGAN

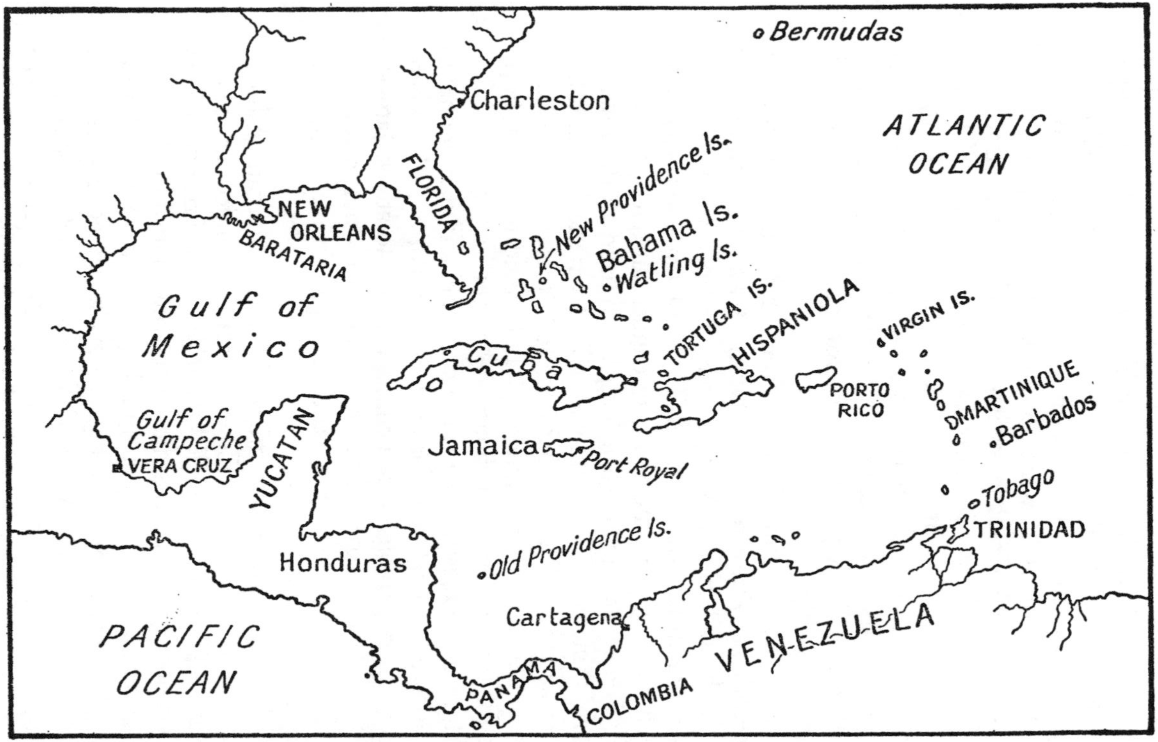

THE DOMAIN OF THE BUCCANEERS

his parents when a boy to serve as a labourer in Barbados.

Morgan seems to have visited Barbados before he turned up in Jamaica, where he at once joined the buccaneers. After taking part in a minor capacity in several expeditions along the coast of Honduras he went up the San Juan river in a fleet of canoes to attack Granada, which was sacked and burnt.

When Sir Thomas Modyford was made governor of Jamaica he proved to be a warm friend to the buccaneers. In 1666 he gave a commission, for what it was worth, to Captain Edward Mansfield, then the leading buccaneer, to capture Curaçao. In this expedition young Henry Morgan had his first command of a ship.

After taking Santa Catalina from the Spaniards the buccaneers met with a reverse. Mansfield was captured and put to death, and Henry Morgan was elected "Admiral" in his place. Getting together a small fleet of ten good ships with five hundred pirates, the new commander sailed to Cuba, where they landed and marched a long way inland to the town of Puerto Principe. This place was so far from the sea that it had never before received a visit from the "Brothers of the Coast." It was soon taken and plundered, and would have been burnt but for the payment of a thousand "beeves."

Morgan's next enterprise was a very bold and daring one: to surprise and attack the fortified city of Porto Bello, where, he had heard, troops were being got ready to attack Jamaica. Porto Bello was expected to prove too hard a nut to crack, so the French buccaneers refused to take part in the scheme and deserted.

Sailing to within a few miles of the city Morgan anchored and at three o'clock the following morning landed his men in canoes. Three forts defended the town. The first two offered only a poor resistance, but the other, commanded by the Spanish governor in person, put up a brave show. Eventually the English made a dozen scaling ladders wide enough for three or four men to mount abreast. With a complete disregard for mercy or pity Morgan compelled a number of priests and nuns to carry these ladders and place them against the walls. Many of these "Religious" were shot down by the Spaniards, who

EXPLOSION ON BOARD A BUCCANEER SHIP

defended themselves bravely but when the governor himself was slain the fortress fell. The town was then entered and sacked, indescribable tortures being practised on the inhabitants to make them reveal where their treasure was hidden.

This is the account given by Exquemeling. If we are to believe Morgan's own official report of the affair, the town and castles were left "in as good a condition as they found them" and the Spanish people were so well treated that "several ladies of great quality and other prisoners who were offered their liberty to go to the President's camp refused, saying they were now prisoners to a person of quality, who was more tender of their honours than they doubted to find in the president's camp, and so voluntarily continued with them till their departure."

On returning to Port Royal Morgan was well received by Governor Modyford, in spite of having far exceeded the conditions laid down in his commission. Probably the huge booty he brought back did much to assuage the anger of the authorities. In any case, the money was soon squandered and Morgan sent forth messages that all who wished to serve under him again should meet him at Cow Island, where he arrived in January 1669 to find a great company of buccaneers waiting for him. Here he gave a banquet to his officers on his great frigate, the *Oxford,* but during the festivities she blew up and only a few escaped, among them being Morgan himself.

But the accident did not cancel the enterprise for which the summons had been sent out, which was another raid on the already sorely tried city of Maracaibo. Morgan forced his way through the narrow entrance of the lake, the place was soon taken and the usual process of torturing the wretched prisoners, with "murders, robberies, rapes and such-like insolences," continued for five weeks.

Once again Morgan returned to Port Royal with vast plunder, and again the Governor reproved him for exceeding his instructions, at the same time handing him a new commission to get together a big fleet and go out and do all the damage possible to Spanish ships, towns, magazines or stores. It was hoped that these strong measures would discourage the increasing attacks by the Spaniards on English shipping along the north coast of Jamaica.

No doubt the commission lent a more respectable appearance to what was actually nothing but a pure piece of piracy, and it is significant that the document concluded with these instructions — "As there is no other pay for the encouragement of the fleet, they shall have all the goods and merchandises that shall be gotten in this expedition, to be divided amongst them according to their rules."

The expedition turned out to be the crowning event of Morgan's career. Sailing to the Isthmus of Darien, a strong party was landed at the mouth of the river Chagres and the castle of San Lorenzo attacked and taken. Morgan left a garrison in the castle to cover his rear, then with one thousand eight hundred men in a fleet of canoes he started with the main body up the river on January 9th, 1671. The march across the Isthmus through the tropical jungle was one of tremendous hardship, the more so since the Spaniards had taken care to remove or destroy all foodstuffs, so that the buccaneers, who had expected to find provisions as they went along, were almost starving when on the sixth day they came across a barn full of maize. On the evening of the ninth day the exhausted men were cheered by the report of a scout that he had seen the steeple of a church in Panama.

Morgan, with that touch of original genius which so often brought him success, attacked the city from an unexpected quarter, with the result that the Spaniards had all their guns in the wrong place and were compelled to do just what Morgan intended they should; namely, come out of their fortifications and fight him in the open.

The enemy began the attack by driving a herd of several hundred bulls before them, intending to rout the buccaneers before they attacked, but this ingenious plan miscarried, for the frightened cattle turned round and stampeded amongst the drawn-up Spanish cavalry, causing the utmost confusion. For two hours the battle raged between the brave Spanish defenders and the equally brave but almost exhausted buccaneers. When at last the Spaniards broke and ran, the buccaneers were too tired to follow up their success and this gave the enemy time to carry away a large quantity of church plate and other valuables from the city in a ship.

As soon as the city was occupied Morgan assembled all his men and strictly forbade them to drink any wine, telling them that he had secret information that all the wine had been poisoned by the Spaniards before they left the city. This was a mere device to prevent the men from getting drunk and leaving themselves at the mercy of the enemy, as had happened so often in previous buccaneer assaults. They now set about plundering the city, which contained many wide streets of fine houses built of cedar. By some means fire broke out and in a little while a large part of the town was burnt to the ground, though whether this was done by the order of Morgan or of the Spanish governor has never been decided. For the next three weeks the buccaneers occupied the city and spent their time making raids into the surrounding country in search of plunder and prisoners, after which they started back across the Isthmus, taking with them a string of two hundred pack mules laden with gold, silver and valuable goods of all sorts, together with a large number of captives.

On reaching Chagres, the plunder was shared out but not without a great deal of quarrelling, for the rank and file declared that they had been cheated of their rightful share. While this wrangling was going on, Morgan slipped away in his ship with the greater part of the plunder, leaving his faithful followers without food or ships and only ten pounds apiece as their share of the spoils.

On reaching home the council of Jamaica passed a vote of thanks to Morgan for his successful expedition, and this in spite of the fact that not many months previously a treaty had been concluded at Madrid between Spain and England for "restraining depredations and establishing peace" in the New World.

On hearing of the destruction of Panama the Spanish government protested strongly to Charles II, with the result that in April 1672 Morgan was brought home, a prisoner in the frigate *Welcome,* to stand his trial for piracy. But no judge or jury dare convict the man who had just become the popular hero of the country. It would have been as impossible as to have convicted Drake after his voyage round the world. The King, with whom he was a favourite, knighted him and sent him back to Jamaica, not as a prisoner but as Deputy Governor of the island.

But the sack of Panama had nevertheless been a serious matter and the government was alarmed that things had been allowed to go too far. Lord Vaughan was sent out as governor of Jamaica with strict injunctions to suppress the buccaneers. His assistant was to be of course the new deputy governor. The decision to make a thief into a constable worked out well, however, and Morgan seems to have undertaken his new duties loyally. He became a man of importance in Jamaica and a very wealthy planter, remaining to his death senior member of the Council and Commander-in-Chief of the island's forces. Unlike most of his kind Sir Henry died in his bed, in 1688, and was buried in the Church of St. Catherine at Port Royal.

The success of the Panama affair had stirred up the imagination of the whole brotherhood and turned their thoughts to the possibilities of wealth in the Pacific Ocean. This inspiration led to the second era, in which the buccaneers reached their greatest height of daring prosperity and power.

Many proclamations had been issued by the home government offering free pardon to the freebooters if they would give up their wicked ways and settle down to lawful pursuits, but threatening with dire punishments those who refused the offer. Some of the rovers gave themselves up, but many, the worst villains, preferred to keep to their old ways. In the meanwhile a revulsion of feeling against the buccaneers was maturing amongst the very merchants and planters of Jamaica who had supported them in the past. Hitherto these had given every encouragement to the pirates, but now they began to see that no regular trade and commerce could flourish as long as the buccaneers plundered in the Caribbean Seas.

The first expedition to the Pacific started from Port Morant in Jamaica in January 1680. The leaders included such famous buccaneers as Bartholomew Sharp and John Coxon. Sailing to Porto Bello they landed some twenty leagues from the town and after an exhausting march, which took the seamen four days, "many of them being weak, being three days without food and their feet cut with rocks for want of shoes," they came in sight of the place.

The surprise was complete and the town was quickly taken and as quickly plundered, for news reached them that strong Spanish reinforcements were coming. Each man in this enterprise got a share of one hundred pieces of eight. Hurrying back to their ships the buccaneers sailed north to Boca del Toro, where they careened and watered. Here they were met by a detachment, headed by Richard Sawkins and Peter Harris, the "brave and stout soldier." In April the force landed on the Isthmus of Darien and began to march towards the Pacific, only stopping on the way to attack and take the little town of Santa Maria.

The weather was hot and the going bad, which probably accounted in great part for the quarrels which took place amongst the leaders. Coxon, who was a hot-tempered man, first quarrelled with the young Sawkins, because he was jealous over his popularity with the men and then started another quarrel with Harris which ended in blows.

Anyhow the squabbles were patched up and the adventurers proceeded down the river in thirty-five canoes, eventually coming out into the Pacific Ocean. As luck would have it they found two small Spanish vessels lying at anchor, which they at once seized and manned. Then with a small flotilla of two small sailing craft and a number of canoes, these fearless explorers steered for Panama. As they approached the city on the "Day of St. George, our Patron of England," the alarm was given and out sailed to oppose them three small Spanish men-of-war. The buccaneers, in no way daunted, pulled towards the enemy ships, clambered up over the sides and, flinging themselves on the surprised Spaniards, after a desperate fight captured the three warships. They then proceeded to attack and capture a great Spanish battleship, *La Santissima-Trinidad* (the *Blessed Trinity*) which they found lying at anchor and into which Captain Sharp transferred his wounded. Thus in a few hours these dare-devil pirates had advanced from canoes to barks, then to small men-of-war, and finally become masters of a great ship-of-war. This was without doubt one of the most remarkable achievements in the history of the buccaneers.

They were now in a position to do almost anything they liked on the unprotected Pacific shore, but the cantankerous Coxon, who had been accused of cowardice at Panama, quarrelled again with his fellows, and with a party of other malcontents set off back across the Isthmus.

Amongst the mutineers were two very interesting men, each of whom wrote and published an account of his adventures. One was the famous buccaneer and naturalist, William Dampier, and the other a surgeon, Lionel Wafer.* Eventually Coxon returned to Jamaica, and although warrants for his arrest had been issued by Lord Carlisle, the Governor, as well as by Morgan, he seems to have so ingratiated himself with the Council that he was sent by them in quest of a notorious French pirate, Jean Hamlin.

For the moment let us follow the fortunes of the rest of the buccaneers who remained behind to partake of those "dangerous and bold attempts performed upon the coasts of the South Sea." The original story, written by Mr. Basil Ringrose, Gent., was published in 1684, but was reprinted not long ago.†

With Coxon gone the crew elected as their leader the popular Captain Sawkins. For many days they cruised in the bay of Panama, robbing ships as they came into port and at night carrying on a clandestine trade with none-too-scrupulous Spanish merchants who came out in boats to sell them food and gunpowder, and buy the valuable spoils taken out of the Spanish ships.

On May 15th they sailed south, anchoring off Puebla Nueva where Sawkins and Sharp landed with a party of sixty armed men and marched to attack the place. But for once the Spaniards were ready with newly made breastworks and trenches.

* "The Isthmus of America," Lionel Wafer, 1699.
† "Broadway Translations." George Routledge & Co.

Sawkins, leading the charge, was shot dead, "the best beloved of all our company."

A new leader had to be elected and the choice fell upon "that sea-artist and valiant commander," Captain Bartholomew Sharp. It was decided to make an attempt on Guayaquil, where they had been told by a prisoner, "we might lay down our silver and lode our vessels with gold."

First of all the *Blessed Trinity* was careened at Gorgona, or Sharp's Island, where they removed all the carved woodwork from her stern and repaired the mast. Mr. Ringrose mentions how they killed a huge snake, eleven feet in length and fourteen inches in circumference, and also how "every day we saw whales and grampuses, who would often come and dive under our ship. We fired at them several times, but our bullets rebounded from their bodies." They found a quantity of the "best provisions" on Gorgona and mealtimes must have been exciting when the diner might find on his plate Indian conies, monkeys, snakes, oysters, conchs, periwinkles "or small turtles, with some other sorts of fish" ! "Here in a like manner we caught a sloth, a beast well deserving that name," but whether this was added to the pot Mr. Ringrose does not record.

They spent so much time here, feasting and shooting at whales, that it was decided to abandon the idea of surprising Guayaquil but to try instead Arica, which was highly recommended by a "certain old man who said that all the silver plate from the mines inland was brought there for shipment to Panama," and that he "doubted not but that we might get there purchase (plunder) at least two thousand pounds every man."

So the long voyage to the Chilean town was begun, with little of interest to beguile the buccaneers' time but the occasional capture of a Spanish ship. Out of each prize they took what spoil they needed, but always put prisoners of any social standing into the *Blessed Trinity*. Some of these prisoners were very chatty and confidential so that the credulous buccaneers gleaned a mass of information, some of it, though not much, reliable.

One of the most garrulous was Captain Peralta, who after his capture at Panama seems to have become quite a favourite on board. As the ship lumbered south the Spaniard acted as a sort of guide to Peru and Chile. Thus, as they passed opposite to a small settlement called Tumbes, Captain Peralta was reminded that this

> was the first place the Spaniards settled in these parts, after Panama. . . That there was a priest went ashore with a cross in his hand while ten thousand Indians stood gazing at him. Being landed on the strand, there came out of the woods two lions and he laid the cross gently on their backs and they instantly fell down and worshipped it — and moreover that two tigers, following them, did the same — whereby these animals gave the Indians to understand the excellency of the Christian religion, which they soon after embraced.

With such pleasant anecdotes Captain Peralta became popular with his pirate shipmates and helped to pass the weary days on the tedious voyage to Arica. At last on October 26th they arrived off the town and the buccaneers left their ship in canoes to land and attack the place, but to their "great sorrow and vexation" found the beach black with armed Spaniards waiting for them.

Disappointed at Arica the buccaneers landed lower down the coast at La Serena, quite a big town which boasted seven churches. But here also the inhabitants had received warning and had time to escape to the hills with their valuables, so the buccaneers had to be content with what little loot they could find and with burning the place down.

It was whilst doing this that they nearly lost their ship, for in the night a Chilean, mounted on an inflated mule skin, swam out to the *Blessed Trinity* and getting under her stern crammed oakum and brimstone between the rudder and the sternpost and set light to it. "Our men both alarmed and amazed with this smoke ran up and down the ship suspecting the prisoners to have fired the vessel, thereby to get their liberty and seek our destruction." However the fire was discovered in time and put out and the buccaneers continued their voyage south.

On Christmas Day they sighted Juan Fernandez, the island

of Robinson Crusoe, and "gave in the morning early three volleys of shot for solemnisation of that great festival." The crew was kept busy hunting goats, which they salted, and filling the water butts. But trouble was brewing, for the men were divided into two factions, those who had saved their share of plunder wanting to round the Horn to get back to the West Indies, while those who had lost all theirs by gambling wished to continue in the Pacific. In the end the latter prevailed and ousted Captain Sharp from his command, put him in irons and elected instead John Watling, a hardened old pirate but "a stout seaman," after whom Christopher Columbus' first landfall in the New World is now named.

One of the reasons given by the crew for displacing Sharp was his ungodliness, and under the new commander all this was checked, for Mr. Ringrose makes the following entry in his journal on Sunday, January 9th: "This day was the first Sunday that ever we kept by command and common consent since the loss and death of our valiant commander, Captain Sawkins. This generous-spirited man threw the dice overboard, finding them in use on the said day." Mr. Ringrose himself seems to have been caught up in this wave of religious fervour, for he slipped away to the island and there with his jack-knife carved a cross and his initials on a tree-trunk. But Captain Watling, in spite of his good intentions, brought no luck to the adventure, for on his advice they returned to Arica where they met with a disastrous repulse. The new commander received a shot in the liver, from which he quickly expired, and many others were killed.

The defeated stragglers, many wounded, managed to get back to the boats and push off just as some Spanish horsemen arrived on the shore. Unfortunately the three surgeons had become so drunk while the fighting had been going on that they were unable to walk to the boats and were taken prisoners.

It was a very disconsolate and humbled crew of buccaneers which now approached Captain Sharp and begged him to re-assume his command. At first he flatly refused to do so, but after much persuasion "our good and old commander consented."

Most of the month of May was taken up with hard work, making alterations in the *Blessed Trinity* for the voyage to the Horn. The top deck was removed, the masts and bowsprit shortened and the rigging and sails mended. The remainder of the Spanish prisoners were given a small boat in which to return home, only some negroes and Indians being kept to work in the ship. From now onwards the journal consists mostly of a daily report of longitude and latitude and the direction and force of the wind, except occasionally when they had the good luck to take a prize.

Thus on July 10th they sighted a sail and immediately gave chase. They overtook her by eight o'clock in the evening, when she proved to be the *San Pedro,* the same ship they had looted a year before. This time they found on board her twenty-one thousand pieces of eight in eight oak chests, and sixteen thousand more in bags, as well as a quantity of silver. A week later they caught a "barco de adviso" or packet boat, in which were three passengers, a friar and two white women. The fate of these Mr. Ringrose fails to mention.

The very next day they met a big Spanish merchantman, which at first they feared was a man-of-war sent after them. The pirates fired a volley of small arms at her and by chance hit and killed the captain, whereupon the crew surrendered. She proved to be the *Holy Rosary* and in her hold was found silver and coined money, as well as six hundred and twenty jars of wine and brandy, the last no doubt very welcome to the English sailors. They also took "the most beautiful woman that I ever saw in all the South Sea" but Mr. Ringrose tells us nothing more of her.

The buccaneers made a most unfortunate blunder over the cargo of the *Holy Rosary.* In the hold they found hundreds of pigs of what they took to be tin and which they threw overboard as not worth keeping. One man kept one, however, which he meant to cast into bullets, and when he eventually got back to England a jeweller found that it was of solid silver. It was calculated that the silver the ignorant buccaneers had thrown overboard must have been worth more than a hundred and fifty thousand pounds.

All the prisoners, including presumably the lovely lady, were put on board the *Holy Rosary,* one of whose masts had been sawn off to make sure she would not get to port soon enough to give the alarm, and they were allowed to go where they would or could.

The buccaneers' next visit was to the Isle of Plata to collect goats but these wily animals had good memories and refused to be caught. In fact it was not a successful or happy visit to the island, apart from the disappointment about the goats. Mr. Ringrose writes, "Here it was that our quartermaster, James Chappel, and myself fought a duel together on shore." Here again the diarist excites our interest and then forgets to mention the outcome of his duel in the excitement that followed, for "in the evening of this day our slaves agreed among themselves and plotted to cut us all to pieces, not giving quarter to any, when we should be buried in sleep." The sleep no doubt was of a heavy sort, for he goes on, "They conceived this night afforded them the fittest opportunity by reason that we were all in drink," presumably due to the brandy taken out of the *Holy Rosary.* Fortunately the godless Captain Sharp was sober and discovered the plot in time. The ringleader he suspected was an Indian named Santiago, whom they had caught at Iqueque, who suddenly jumped overboard and began to swim away but "was shot in the water by our Captain and thus punished for his treason." After this all was settled amicably; "the rest laid the fault on that slave and so it passed, we being not willing to inquire any further into the matter" and no doubt "we" were only too glad to resume "our" slumbers.

The buccaneers now set out in earnest for Cape Horn. On the way to that dangerous passage they almost ran upon some rocks and it was only "the great mercy of God which had always attended us in this voyage" that saved them from perishing. They caught a Fuegan boy who came out to them in a canoe in which was burning a fire; the man and woman with him leaped overboard; "our men in pursuing them inadvisedly shot him dead," but the woman escaped. The boy, who was a lusty youth of about eighteen years of age, was not prepossessing in looks and his eyes squinted; indeed, Mr. Ringrose "was persuaded by his carriage that he was a man eater."

As the *Holy Trinity* approached the Cape the weather became worse, with violent gales and snowstorms, and they were driven far south. We find nothing worthy of note until the date of December 7th, when Mr. Ringrose writes, "This day our worthy Commander, Captain Sharp, had very certain intelligence given him that on Christmas day the company, or at least a great part thereof, had a design to shoot him, he having appointed that day some time since to be merry. Thereupon he made us share the wine amongst us, being persuaded they would scarce attempt any such thing in their sobriety," which all sounds very exciting, but rather difficult to follow. Perhaps Mr. Ringrose made this entry in his diary after drawing his share of wine, which was a generous one of three jars.

After this the days were cloudy with violent squalls. On December 10th "our chief surgeon cut off the foot of a negro boy, which was perished with cold"; next day poor Beafero died, as did another negro.

Christmas Day seems to have gone off peaceably, "This day being Christmas day, for celebration of that great festival we killed yesterday in the evening a sow. This sow we brought from the Gulf of Nicoya, being then a sucking pig of three weeks old, more or less but now weighed about fourscore and ten pounds. With this hog's (*it was a sow before death*) flesh we made our Christmas dinner, being the only flesh we had eaten since we turned away our prizes under the equinoctial."

After terrible hardships the buccaneers rounded Cape Horn and crept up the South Atlantic until at last, on Saturday January 28th, they came in sight of Barbados. This welcome sight was spoiled by the presence of one of his Majesty's frigates, the *Richmond,* and they decided to get away without delay.

In spite of this disappointment Mr. Ringrose exclaims: "Here I cannot easily express the infinite joy we were possessed with this day to see our own countrymen again." Unfortunately his countrymen did not share his emotion.

All disputes and misunderstandings on board the *Blessed Trinity* were now over. They freed a negro shoemaker in return for his professional services to the crew during the voyage. "We gave also to our good Commander, Captain Sharp, a mulatto boy, as a free gift of the whole company, to wait upon him in token of the respect we all were owing to him for the safety of our conduct through so many dangerous adventures." After this there was a general share out of what plunder had not already been distributed, amounting to twenty-four pieces of eight per man.

On January 30th Antigua was at last reached, but even now their trials were not at an end. On sending ashore a canoe to buy tobacco and also to ask permission to come into port, they received a flat refusal from the Governor, although "the gentry of the place and common people were very willing and desirous to receive us."

The only thing left the tired travellers was to go on to Nevis, where they were allowed to land and where the party broke up. Many of the crew had gambled away all their plunder, so it was decided to give the ship to them, while those who had money went off where they would. Mr. Ringrose with thirteen others of the company got passages in the *Lisbon Merchant,* Captain Robert Porteen, and landed safely at Dartmouth on March 26th, 1682. As to the bold and valiant Captain Sharp and his master, John Cox, they also returned to England in order, says Cox in his journal,* "to give the King an account of their Discoverys" but actually to be clapped in prison at the complaint of the Spanish ambassador and tried for piracy, though in the absence of any direct evidence both defendants were acquitted.

When Port Royal ceased to welcome the buccaneers, the adventurers of the islands had to seek other places where they could sell their plunder and refit their vessels. Next to Jamaica no place could have suited them better for this than the Bahamas. This nest of islands of all shapes and sizes lay in an excellent position for pirate enterprises, and incidentally possessed a most obliging Governor in Mr. Robert Clarke, who

* MS journal of Captain Sharp's voyage: in the possession of the author.

resided at New Providence Island. Governor Clarke was always ready to supply commissions — for a consideration — to unemployed pirates. Many a buccaneer who would not, or dared not, give himself up at Jamaica, sailed his ship to New Providence and procured a letter of marque to retaliate for real, or more often, imaginary Spanish wrongs.

According to Dampier * some of the governors, such as that of Petit Guaves in Hispaniola, supplied blank commissions which the pirate captains could themselves fill in as they liked. He also declares that many of these French commissions were only to grant the holder permission to fish, fowl or hunt.

It is on record that one filibuster, who plundered Spanish ships, sacked churches and burnt towns, did so under a commission issued to him by the governor of a Danish island who was himself an ex-pirate. This precious document, adorned with florid scrolls and a big impressive-looking seal, was written in Danish. One day some one with a knowledge of that language, having the opportunity or curiosity to translate it, discovered that it entitled the bearer to do nothing more than hunt for goats and pigs in the Island of Hispaniola.

Other new pirate resorts soon sprang up, especially in the Carolinas and New England, where the pirates were always sure of a warm welcome and a fair price for their plunder. Michel Landresson, alias Breha,† a pirate who for a long while played havoc among the Jamaica sloops, used to resort to Boston to dispose of his booty of gold, silver, jewels and cocoa to the godly New England merchants, who were only too ready to take advantage of so profitable a trade and gladly fitted him out for his next cruise. Breha flourished for several years, until in 1686 he was so unlucky as to fall into the hands of the Spaniards, who hanged him and several of his companions.

All sorts and kinds of odd characters were to be found serving amongst the buccaneers. Physicians, naturalists, criminals, poets and broken men of fortune and title; none came amiss in that strange assembly. Possibly the strangest of all was the future Archbishop of York, Lancelot Blackburne.

* "A New Voyage Round the World," 1697.

† C. H. Haring, p. 251, "Buccaneers in the West Indies."

His enemies, for he had enemies as well as many staunch friends during his long life, declared that in the years 1681 and 1682 the newly ordained graduate of Christ Church, Oxford, was roaming the Spanish main and the West Indies with the buccaneers. Certain it is that he went to the West Indies in 1681 and that after his return to England he was paid the sum of twenty pounds "for Secret Services."

One story which was told of him was that one day a buccaneer turned up in England and enquired what had become of his old chum Blackburne, to be informed that he was now Archbishop of York. Horace Walpole believed, or pretended to believe, that Blackburne had been a buccaneer when he wrote of "The jolly old archbishop of York, who had all the manners of a man of quality, though he had been a buccaneer and was a clergyman, but he retained nothing of his first profession except his seraglio." *

Quite recently Archbishop Blackburne's sword was presented to Christ Church and is now a valued if somewhat suspicious object of interest, for with the sword goes a tradition that calamity will befall anyone who draws the sword from its scabbard, and I understand that no member of that ancient seat of learning has yet taken the risk.

In any case it is, I am informed, most unusual for an Archbishop, or even a Bishop, to own a sword, so that this one at Christ Church may indeed have been wielded by its clerical owner on the Spanish main.

I may perhaps venture to repeat here a story ascribed to the present Archbishop of Canterbury, himself once Archbishop of York. This is that Archbishop Blackburne had as butler the famous highwayman Dick Turpin, and it was not long before people noticed that on every night the Archbishop and his butler left Bishopsthorpe, the North Mail coach was held up and robbed.

To those who have not made a close study of such matters it may appear grotesque to believe that a man who had once been a pirate or a buccaneer could ever reach a high position in a learned profession as did Lancelot Blackburne, but there

* Walpole's "Last Ten Years of George II" (1822), I, 75.

are other better substantiated cases, amongst them that of a highwayman, John Popham, who rose to be Lord Chief Justice of England under James I. This office he held for fifteen years, acquiring a reputation for extreme severity to prisoners, particularly those charged with highway robbery, who had little if any hope of acquittal when tried before Popham.*

A story from the pen of Père Labat, a Jesuit, one of the principal authorities on the daily life of the buccaneers, is interesting for its light on the curious religious streak which often existed in the wildest of these rovers; it is a surprising phenomenon which has already been encountered and will appear in startling form in the account of the eighteenth century pirates. Labat, who flourished at the end of the seventeenth century, was a jovial priest who made friends wherever he went and with all kinds of men. He entertained a strong affection for the buccaneers of the West Indies, though he generally refers to them by the less ambiguous name of pirates.

The story is that Captain Daniel, a pirate, finding himself short of provisions, anchored one night off the "Saintes," small islands lying south of Hispaniola. A party landed and, without opposition, seized the house of the curé. The priest and his household were carried off to Daniel's ship, while a search was made for wine, brandy and chickens. While this was being done it occurred to Captain Daniel that the time would be well spent if Mass were held on his ship for the spiritual benefit of his crew. The poor priest dared not refuse, so the sacred vessels were sent for, and an altar improvised under an awning on the poop. The Mass began with a discharge of artillery, and other salvos were fired at the Sanctus, the Elevation, the Benediction and a last one after the Exaudiat, the service closing with a prayer for the King, followed by a hearty "Vive le Roi" from the throats of the assembled buccaneers.

An unfortunate incident slightly marred this ceremony. One of the buccaneers adopted an indecent attitude during the Elevation, and on being rebuked by the captain, replied with a fearful oath. Quick as a flash Daniel whipped out his pistol and shot him through the head, swearing by God to do the

* "Lives of the Chief Justices of England," John Campbell, 1849.

same to any other who failed in his respect to the Holy Sacrifice.

The shot had been fired close to the priest, who, not unnaturally, was much alarmed, but Captain Daniel, turning to him, said, "Do not be troubled, my father, he is a rascal lacking in his duty and I have punished him to teach him better." "Quite an effective method," remarks Labat, "of preventing his falling into a like mistake." When the Mass was over, the body of the dead man was thrown into the sea, and the priest rewarded for his preaching by several valuable presents, which included a negro slave.

The very last appearance of the buccaneers occurred in 1697. The war between France on one side and Spain and England on the other was still being waged. The Sieur de Pointis, Jean-Bernard Desjeans,* had been sent out by the King of France at the head of a powerful fleet to attack Cartagena in Colombia. M. Ducasse, the Governor of the French port of Hispaniola, and the friend and abettor of the buccaneers, was ordered to call in all the freebooters to fight under the command of de Pointis.

On March 18th the combined royal and buccaneer fleets sailed from Cape Tiburon and on the 13th of the following month dropped anchor two leagues to the east of Cartagena. The buccaneer contingent, six hundred and fifty strong, was commanded by Ducasse, for they refused to serve under the haughty De Pointis, who made no effort to hide his contempt for his swashbuckling allies.

After a bombardment of fourteen days the city fell. The treasure found was enormous: some said it was of the value of twenty millions sterling. Then the trouble began between de Pointis and the buccaneers. The former insisted that the buccaneers should receive only the same small share of prize-money which was granted to the royal troops, while the buccaneers demanded that the whole of the plunder should be divided equally amongst them, as had always been their custom.

After much wrangling, de Pointis consented to allot the

* "De Pointis' Expedition to Cartagena," London 1699.

sum of forty thousand crowns to the buccaneers, who would have broken out into mutiny but for the efforts of Ducasse. This matter settled, the French admiral got his troops on board and hurried off to France, glad to get away from the rowdy mutinous buccaneers and to escape the English fleet which was known to be searching for him in the neighbourhood.

The buccaneers also ostensibly sailed away for Hispaniola, but on the way decided to turn back to Cartagena and reimburse themselves for the scurvy way they had been treated over their share of the plunder.

Ducasse, the only man who had any influence over the rough seamen, was too ill to protest, and his officers were useless. Within a few days the buccaneers reached Cartagena and for four days put the city to the sack, torturing the unhappy citizens to make them give up their last valuables, and plundering the churches and monasteries of several millions more of gold and silver.* With this they sailed off to their old haunt at Cow Island to share out the spoils. But on the way retribution overtook them in the form of an allied English and Spanish fleet. Of the nine buccaneer ships the two which carried most of the booty were captured, two more were driven ashore and the rest only just succeeded in escaping to Hispaniola.

Ducasse sent a mission to the French court to complain of the ill-treatment he and his buccaneers had received at the hands of de Pointis and demanding his own recall. To make the peace the King constituted him a Chevalier of St. Louis and sent one million four hundred thousand francs to be divided amongst the buccaneers. Needless to say the greater part of this sum never reached the buccaneers, for it passed through too many hands on its way.

With the capture of Cartagena in 1697 the history of the buccaneers may be said to have reached its termination. "Their great importance in history," wrote David Hannay,† "lies in the fact that they opened the eyes of the world, and specially of the nations from whom these buccaneers had sprung, to the whole system of Spanish-American government and commerce,

* Haring.
† "Encyclopædia Britannica," 1911.

the former in its rottenness and the latter in its possibilities in other hands. From this then, along with other causes, there arose the West Indian possessions of Holland, England and France."

CHAPTER II

THE PIRATES OF NORTH AMERICA

Two changes at the close of the seventeenth century again altered the character of piracy. The first was the increasing vigilance of state ships in home waters, which gradually compelled the less adventurous sea rovers to turn to more social pursuits, while the irreclaimable corsair was driven to find new fields for the exercise of his talents; it was this vigilance in part, combined with the growing distaste of the colonists for their operations, which sent the buccaneers into unfamiliar waters. The other change lay in the new relationship between Great Britain and her North American colonies.

In 1696 Parliament passed a Navigation Act whose object was the exclusion of all nations save England from trading with English colonies. Spain had already shown the folly of such laws, yet her experience did not prevent the English, French and Dutch from attempting to enforce similar ones. These laws benefited England only, and were naturally hated by the American colonists. For example the Navigation Act prohibited the import of goods from the East to New England or any other of the American plantations save by way of England, thereby adding enormously to their cost. The colonists in consequence took to cheap illegal buying whenever they could, and thus it was that a new school of piracy appeared which for a while prospered exceedingly.

Following close on the Navigation Act came the Peace of Ryswick in 1697 which put an end to most of the privateering in the West Indies, while sixteen years later the Wars of Succession which had dragged on for nearly half a century were brought to a close by the Peace of Utrecht, between England and France.

Thousands of privateersmen were thus thrown out of employment, and there was not nearly enough merchant shipping to give honest work to all the crews. Some men no doubt settled down on shore to one kind of work or another, but hundreds of the roughest sort were still without means of making a living. The consequence was that these formed companies and went to sea as before, but now without a commission. To such desperate men nothing came amiss, and in truth was it said that they had "declared war upon all nations."

By the end of the seventeenth century a regular "pirate round" was in force. A company of seamen would fit out a ship at one of the New England ports, and sail away to the Red Sea, Persian Gulf or Coast of Malabar. The great Mogul Empire of India was then in a state of decadence and anarchy, and had no warships for defence. Yet a considerable native trade went on, carried by coasting vessels manned by "Moors." These fell an easy prey to the well armed and ruthless English and American pirates who lay in wait for them at certain chosen points. Having filled their ships with plunder, costly Eastern silk and embroideries, jewels and gold and silver ornaments, the pirates would return to the ports of the Plantations, where no questions were asked, and ready buyers were to be found.*

In 1698 information, on oath, was given to the Secretary of State to the effect that "Thomas Too, William Maze, John Ireland, Thomas Wake, and others who were all known as pirates and had made several piratical voyages from which they had returned with great wealth" were living in New England and made no secret of it. Nor was there any reason for them to be ashamed, since all pirates agreed with Darby Mullins, one of the crew sent with Captain Kidd to apprehend Too, Maze and Ireland, who in his evidence at the Old Bailey voiced the universal pirate opinion that it was no sin for Christians to rob heathens.

There were always plenty of volunteers at Boston and New York to make up the crews on these ships. In the West Indies there were numerous safe harbours where the voyagers could get provisions and other supplies. Once round the Cape of

* "Sea Trader," David Hannay.

Good Hope the great island of Madagascar gave shelter to every ruffian who wished to go ashore.

Arrived in the Eastern seas their only serious risk was a meeting with Dutch men-of-war. If they happened to be caught by one of the English East India Company's ships and taken to one of the Company's factories, they were practically safe from punishment, since the Company had no rights over any but their own servants and had no Admiralty jurisdiction to try prisoners charged with the crime of piracy. The same thing applied to New England, where there were no Admiralty courts, and the expense, time and trouble of sending prisoners and witnesses home to England meant that practically none of the culprits came to justice.*

Of the many pirates who worked the "pirate round" the two most famous were Avery and Kidd.

Captain John Avery, alias Henry Every, alias Bridgman, was in some ways the most popular of all pirates and like all popular characters was known by a nickname, "Long Ben." Some admirers described this hero as the "flower and pattern of all bold mariners"; others dubbed him the "Arch-pyrat." Many "lives" of Avery were published: Defoe took him for his hero in his "Life, Adventures and Piracies of Captain Singleton," while a popular play written about his life in Madagascar by Charles Johnson and called "The Successful Pyrate" was performed with acclamation at the Theatre Royal in Drury Lane.

Avery was born near Plymouth about the year 1665 and was bred to the sea. After serving on board a merchantman for several voyages, he was appointed first officer on an armed privateer, the *Duke,* commanded by a Captain Gibson. They sailed from Bristol for Cadiz, having been hired by the Spanish Government for service in the West Indies against the French pirates. For many days the *Duke* rode at anchor in Cadiz harbour waiting for orders and the idle sailors had nothing to occupy them. Avery began to talk to the men and, finding many of them willing, plotted a mutiny. The Captain and several of the crew who refused to join were put into a boat and allowed to go ashore, while the *Duke,* loyally

* See Appendix IV.

renamed the *Charles II,* sailed off with Avery in command.

Their first exploit was to visit the Isle of May where they seized the Portuguese Governor as a hostage until provisions had been sent on board. They next sailed towards Guinea, capturing and rifling three English ships on the way. After stealing some gold and negroes on the Guinea coast, they rounded the Cape of Good Hope and reached Madagascar. From there they sailed to the Red Sea to wait for the fleet from Mocha which was soon due to arrive.

At length the expected fleet appeared and Captain Avery, picking out the largest vessel, fought her for two hours, when she struck her colours. She proved to be the *Gunsway,* belonging to the Great Mogul himself, and out of her they took one hundred thousand pieces of eight and a like number of "chequins," as well as several high officials of the Mogul's court who were on a pilgrimage to Mecca. It was popularly believed that the beautiful daughter of the Mogul was captured as well and that Avery took her to Madagascar, where he married her and lived in royal state.

Although the story of the beautiful princess may have been added to please the reader of the numerous little pamphlets and broadsheets which claimed to tell of Avery's exploits, there is no doubt whatever that the pirates did capture plunder of enormous value.

One unlooked for result of this successful scoop was that the Mogul, infuriated at the outrage, threatened to retaliate on the East India Company by laying waste their settlements. The Company's urgent appeal for help to the British Government brought many a pirate to the gallows, but Avery was destined for a less sensational end.

He was next heard of on his arrival at Boston in 1696, where he appears to have bribed the Governor to let him and his crew land unmolested with their spoils. He did not stop long at Boston but sailed to the North of Ireland, where he sold his sloop. The company broke up, every man going off where he would with his share of the spoils. Avery tried to sell some of his diamonds at Dublin, but was unsuccessful. Thinking that England might be a better place for a transaction of this kind he went to Bideford in Devon. Here he lived very quietly under an assumed name, and through a friend communicated with certain merchants at Bristol. These came to see him, accepted his diamonds and a few gold cups, gave him a handful of guineas for his immediate wants and returned to Bristol with the goods, promising to send him the money they realized.

Time dragged on, but neither news nor money came from the Bristol merchants and gradually it began to dawn on Avery that there were pirates on land as well as at sea. His frequent letters to the merchants brought him at the most a few shillings, which were immediately swallowed up in paying for the bare necessities of life. At length, when matters were becoming desperate, Avery was taken ill and died "not being worth as much as would buy him a coffin." Thus ended Avery, the "Grand Pirate," whose name was known all over Europe and America, and who was supposed to be reigning as a king in Madagascar when all the while he was hiding and starving in a cottage at Bideford.

Probably the most famous name in the annals of piracy is that of William Kidd,* yet if Kidd's reputation was in just proportion to his actual deeds, he would have been forgotten as soon as he had been "turned off" at Wapping Old Stairs. His fame in piracy was as undeserved as the glory of Dick Turpin, the reputed king of all "gentlemen of the road," who was in life a mere pickpocket but after death stole the famous ride to York from Nevinson, a genuine and daring highwayman.

It was politics that brought William Kidd both to fame and the gallows. Born at Greenock about the year 1645, the boy received a good education, his father being, it is supposed, a Calvinistic minister of that small but growing seaport town.

For many years Kidd sailed as an honest seaman and eventually commanded an English privateer in American waters. He had a good house in New York, where his wife and children lived, and he must have been well off, as he owned several trading vessels.

In 1695 the Governor of Massachusetts, the Earl of Bello-

* "Trial of Captain Kidd," "Notable British Trials," Hodge, 1930.

mont, received instructions from England to take measures to suppress the pirates who infested the New England coast. The man chosen for this difficult task was Captain Kidd, who received from King William III a commission authorising his "beloved friend William Kidd" to apprehend certain pirates, particularly Thomas Tew or Too of Rhode Island, Thomas Wake and William Maze of New York, John Ireland, as well as "all other Pirates, Freebooters, and Sea Robbers of what Nature soever."

Such an enterprise boded no good from the first, for instead of being paid for their work the Captain and crew were put on the evil "No purchase,* no pay" basis. Nor did the Government fit out the expedition. The ship and all her equipment and stores were paid for by a company, each member of which took a share in the expenses and was to receive a dividend from the plunder when the ship returned. The aristocratic shareholders were Lord Bellomont, Lord Orford, first Lord of the Admiralty; Lord Somers, the Lord Chancellor; Lord Romney, Secretary of State; the Duke of Shrewsbury and others holding important positions of trust. Last but not least, Captain Kidd bought a big share of one fifth of the whole.

Kidd's ship, the *Adventure Galley,* with a crew of a hundred and fifty-five men left New York in September 1696 and nothing more was heard of her for many months. Then some very ugly rumours began to be spread about. News reached England and Massachusetts that Kidd, instead of capturing pirate ships, had himself turned pirate and was doing mischief in the Indian Ocean. Peremptory orders were sent to Bellomont to arrest Kidd if he should return to North America.

One day in July 1699 Kidd arrived back at Boston, was immediately thrown into jail by his fellow company promoter, Bellomont, and in due time sent in chains to England in H.M.S. *Advice* to stand his trial for piracy.

After the *Adventure* left New York, Kidd had sailed direct to Madeira for fruit and wine, then called at the Cape Verde Islands for water. He then rounded the Cape of Good Hope

* Plunder.

and did not reach the Red Sea until a year after leaving America. On September 20th he robbed a Moorish ship of several bales of pepper and coffee and some myrrh. He next sailed along the Carwar coast, but met nothing in the way of a prize and his crew began to get out of hand. One day he had words with William Moore, his chief gunner, whom he called "a lousy dog." "If I am a lousy dog," retorted the gunner, "then you have made me one." Kidd's answer to this was to pick up an ironbound bucket and strike Moore such a savage blow on the head with it that the gunner died the next day, and it was this act, rather than piracy, which eventually brought Kidd to the gallows.

Hitherto Kidd seems to have tried to carry out his orders in a half-hearted way, but after the murder of Moore he took to definite piracy. It was on the 27th of November that they met with the *Maiden,* which he took and plundered. As a pirate Kidd proved himself much more successful than as a pirate-catcher. After taking several small ships, he met the best prize of all. This was the *Quedagh Merchant,* a vessel of some five hundred tons bound from Bengal for Surat, which he captured off the Malabar coast. On board her was found a valuable cargo comprising silks and muslins, sugar, iron, saltpetre and gold.

Finding they had now enough to make each man's fortune, the pirates sailed to the well-known pirate stronghold of Madagascar. All the plunder was taken out of the *Adventure* and her two prizes, and carried on shore where it was shared out. Kidd took forty shares for himself, the rest being divided among the hundred and fifty members of the crew. Here Kidd met a notorious pirate, Culliford, who was "wanted," but instead of arresting him, Kidd and he fraternised and drank each other's health in "Bomboo," a drink made of limes, sugar and water, which leads one to believe that these two pirates were "dry" and exceptions to the usual run of their kind, who preferred rum or brandy.

At last in September 1698 Kidd set sail from Madagascar in the *Quedagh Merchant* loaded with a rich hoard of merchandise goods, jewels, gold and pieces of eight.

CAPTAIN KIDD HANGING IN CHAINS

The next land they touched at was Anguilla in the West Indies, where Kidd sent some men on shore who brought back the unpleasant tidings that Kidd and all his crew had been proclaimed pirates. This piece of news, according to Kidd, caused "great consternation" amongst his crew. He at once left for New York in a small vessel, the *Antonio,* and made for New England, leaving the *Quedagh Merchant* at Hispaniola, with orders to wait there till he returned.

If Kidd imagined that he could get round Bellomont to pardon him, he made a very great mistake. The scandal had become too hot and Kidd was arrested the moment he set foot on shore. His trial took place at the Old Bailey in 1701. He was found guilty on both charges of murder and piracy, and on May 23rd was hanged at Execution Dock.

Many ballads were written to celebrate the deeds and death of Kidd; a few verses of one of these are included here.

THE BALLAD OF CAPTAIN KIDD *

* It is due to the kindness of Mr. J. C. L. Clark, of Lancaster, Massachusetts, that

My name was William Kidd, when I sailed, when I sailed
My name was William Kidd, when I sailed,
My name was William Kidd,
God's laws I did forbid
And so wickedly I did, when I sailed.

I'd a Bible in my hand when I sailed, when I sailed,
I'd a Bible in my hand when I sailed,
I'd a Bible in my hand
By my father's great command,
And sunk it in the sand when I sailed.

I spyed the ships of France as I sailed, as I sailed,
I spyed the ships of France as I sailed,
I spyed the ships of France
To them I did advance
And took them all by chance, as I sailed.

I'd ninety bars of gold, as I sailed, as I sailed,
I'd ninety bars of gold, as I sailed,
I'd ninety bars of gold
And dollars manifold
With riches uncontrolled as I sailed.

Recently a quantity of fresh evidence relating to Kidd's activities in the Red Sea has been discovered by Mr. Basil Lubbock in an old sailor's log in his possession. It proves that Kidd committed piracy earlier than had hitherto been known. Through Mr. Lubbock's kindness I am able to reproduce several lengthy extracts from this log, as Appendix V, the extraordinary spelling of the narrator, Edward Barlow, being left unaltered.

We have spoken of two pirates in particular, Avery and Kidd, as men of mark in their profession, but there were others equally gifted who never caught the eye of the public to the

I am able to give the notation of the Ballad of Captain Kidd. He procured it from an old Civil War veteran, who remembered the song being sung in his childhood.

same degree. The ordinary pirate, as has already been observed, did not seek notoriety; he was satisfied if he could get his plunder and retire into oblivion to spend his gains in his own way, and had no desire to hear the world ringing with his exploits. Consequently we should know very little of these men's lives and deeds were it not for a certain Captain Charles Johnson, who wrote a book about them. It must be borne in mind that the end of the seventeenth and the beginning of the eighteenth centuries, the period of Johnson's life, marked what was perhaps the highest pitch to which pure piracy ever attained; that is to say, the pirate then most nearly corresponded to the popular conception of what a pirate should be.

Johnson's famous book first appeared in 1724 and was published by Ch. Rivington, at the Bible and Crown in St. Paul's Churchyard. In 1890 Rivington's business was purchased by the publishers of this book, and his sign, a Crown above a Bible, is still in the firm's possession.

The title page contains over two hundred words, but leaving out Captain Johnson's asides and comments it runs as follows:

> A General History of the Robberies and Murders of the most notorious Pyrates and also their Policies, Discipline and Government from their first Rise and Settlement in the Island of Providence in 1717 to the present Year 1724.

No facts concerning the author have ever come to light. Whoever he was he certainly possessed an intimate knowledge of the doings of the pirates. It used to be said that his history was made up more of fairy tales than fact, but of late years evidence has proved Johnson to be accurate, and there is no doubt that he is on the whole to be believed. There is a strong assumption that the author himself was, or had been, a pirate, in which case he no doubt considered it wise to shelter himself behind a nom-de-plume.

There was a Captain Charles Johnson, R.N., who was employed by Sir Thomas Lynch to search for the pirate Hamlin of *La Trompeuse* and other Jamaican pirates in 1682. If Johnson was then only twenty-six years old, which is unlikely, he would have been sixty-eight when the "History" was published in 1724, so that although the supposition is not impossible, the evidence that this was the missing author is extremely slender.

Copies of the "History of the Pyrates" were until recently very hard to get, the early editions having become very scarce, but several reprints have appeared during the last few years.

It is impossible to give here even a summary of the lives of all Johnson's heroes. Two will have to suffice, one, Roberts, because he seems to attain most nearly to the popular pirate of fiction and the other, Misson, because he was, in his character and aims, unique.

The first was Captain Bartholomew Roberts who, like so many of the pirates, was a Welshman, being born near Haverfordwest in Pembrokeshire.*

He was remarkable, even among his remarkable companions, for several things. First of all, he only drank tea, thus being almost the only recorded teetotaller known to the fraternity. Also he was a strict disciplinarian and on board his ships all lights had to be out by eight P.M. Any of the crew who wished to continue drinking after that hour had to do so upon the open deck. But try as he would this ardent apostle of abstemiousness was unable to put down drinking entirely.

If Roberts had lived today, he would probably have been a leading light on the council of a local vigilance society. He would allow no women aboard his ships; in fact he made a law by which any man who brought a woman on board disguised as a man was to suffer death. Nor did he permit games of cards or dice to be played for money, as he strongly disapproved of gambling. Being a strict Sabbatarian, he allowed the musicians to have a rest on the seventh day. This was as well, for the post of musician on a pirate ship was no sinecure, since every pirate had the right to demand a tune at any hour of the day or night. He used to place a guard to protect all his women prisoners and it is sadly suspicious that there was always the greatest competition amongst the worst characters in the ship to be appointed sentry over a good-looking woman

* "Pirates' Who's Who," Dulau, London.

prisoner. No fighting was permitted amongst his crew on board ship. All quarrels had to be settled on shore, the duellists standing back to back armed with pistol and cutlass, pirate fashion.

Bartholomew dressed for action, surprisingly, was the very beau of pirates. A tall dark man, he used to wear a rich damask waistcoat and breeches, a red feather in his cap, a gold chain round his neck with a large diamond cross dangling from it, a sword in his hand and two pairs of pistols hanging at the end of a silk sling flung over his shoulders.

We first hear of him sailing from London in November 1719, as master of a slaver, the *Princess,* bound for the coast of Guinea to pick up an honest cargo of "black ivory" at Anamaboe. Here his ship was taken by another Welshman, the pirate Howel Davis. There being no alternative, Roberts joined the pirates, and very soon was as good at the game as any of them.

On the death in action of Captain Davis a council was held to fill the vacant post of commander. There were several candidates, all "brisk and lively" men distinguished by the title of "Lords," such as Sympson, Ashplant, Antis and others. One of these "Lords" named Dennis nominated Roberts in a speech containing an interesting warning and an equally interesting explanation: "Should a captain be so saucy as to exceed Prescription at any time, why down with him ! it will be a Caution after he is dead to his successors of what fatal Consequences any sort of assuming may be." Having expressed this word of warning "my Lord Dennis" continued: "However it is my Advice, that, *while we are sober,* we pitch upon a Man of Courage and skilled in Navigation, one who by his Council and Bravery seems best able to defend the Commonwealth and ward us from the Dangers and Tempests of an instable Element, and the fatal Consequence of Anarchy; and such a one I take Roberts to be. A Fellow, I think, in all Respects worthy of your Esteem and Favour."

This proposal was acclaimed with but one dissenting voice, that of "Lord" Sympson, who had hopes of being elected himself and who sullenly left the meeting grumbling "he did not care who they chose captain so it was not a papist," which Roberts was not. So the newcomer was elected, after being a pirate for only six weeks; thus was true merit quickly recognised and rewarded.

The new commander replied in a short speech "that since he had dipped his hands in muddy water and must be a pyrate, it was better being a commander than a common man"; not perhaps a tactful or graceful way of expressing his thanks, but one which was no doubt appreciated by his audience.

Roberts soon shewed the crew the sort of captain they had by seizing and razing a neighbouring fort, bombarding the town and setting on fire two Portuguese ships, all in revenge for the perfectly justifiable killing of the late Captain Davis at this place.

He then crossed the South Atlantic, arriving at the bay of Bahia in Brazil, where he discovered forty-two Portuguese ships ready laden and on the point of sailing for Lisbon. Roberts, with the most astounding boldness, sailed right in amongst them until he found the deepest laden, which he attacked, boarded and carried off. This prize, amongst other merchandise, contained forty thousand moidors and a cross of diamonds designed for the King of Portugal.

From Brazil Roberts sailed to the West Indies, devastating the commerce of Jamaica and Barbados. When things grew too hot there, he went north to Newfoundland and played havoc with the English and French fishing fleets and settlements.

On two occasions Roberts had been very roughly handled, once by a ship from Barbados, and once by the inhabitants of Martinique; so when he designed his new flag, he portrayed on it a huge figure of himself, sword in hand, standing upon two skulls under which were the letters A.B.H. and A.M.H. signifying A Barbadian's Head and A Martiniquian's Head. Ever afterwards, whenever an inhabitant of either of these islands was so unfortunate as to fall into Roberts's clutches, he paid the penalty with his life.

In April 1721 Roberts was back again on the Guinea coast, burning and plundering. Amongst the prisoners he took out

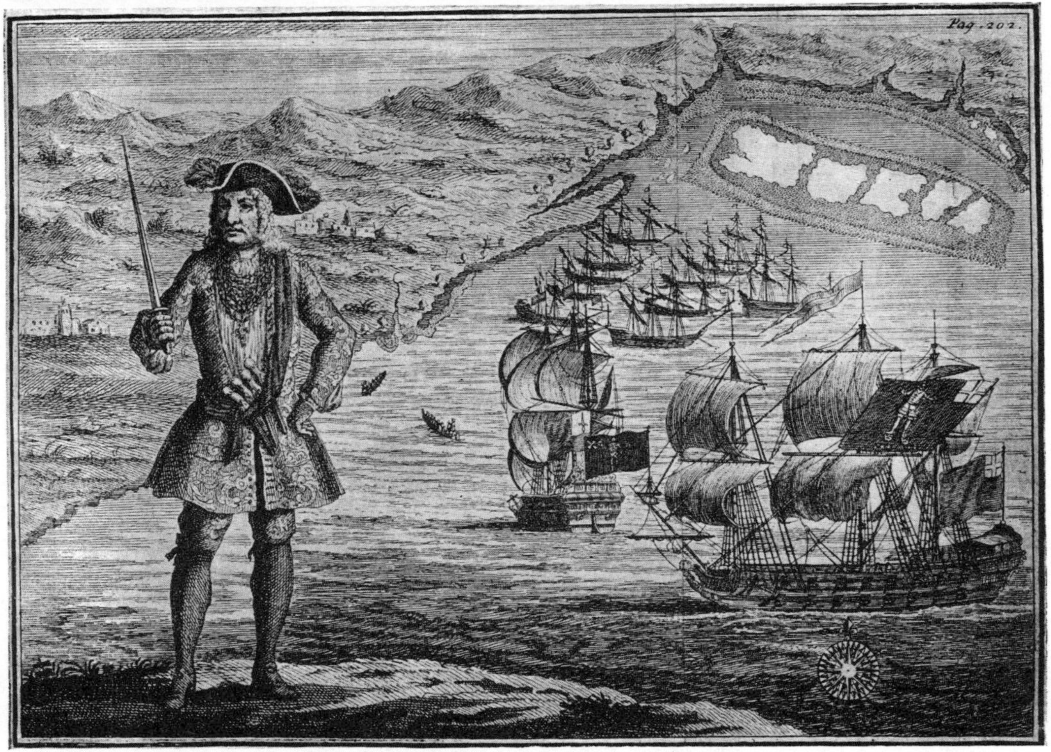

CAPTAIN BARTHOLOMEW ROBERTS, WITH HIS TWO SHIPS, *THE ROYAL FORTUNE* AND *RANGER,* ON THE COAST OF GUINEA

of one of his prizes was a clergyman. Now the captain dearly wished to carry a chaplain on board his ship to minister to the spiritual welfare of his crew and tried all he could to persuade the parson to sign on, assuring him that his only duties should be to say prayers and make punch. But the prelate begged to be excused and was at length allowed to go with all his belongings, except three prayer books and a corkscrew — articles sorely needed aboard the *Royal Fortune.*

The end of Roberts's career was now in sight and none too soon, for he had already taken four hundred ships, a record, so far as is known, held by no other pirate.

A king's ship, the *Swallow* (Captain Chaloner Ogle), discovered Roberts's two ships at Parrot Island; pretending to flee, it was followed out to sea by one of them. A fight took place and after two hours the pirate ship struck, flinging overboard her black flag "that it might not rise in Judgment over them." In a few days' time the *Swallow* returned to Parrot Island to look for Roberts in the *Royal Fortune.*

It was in the morning and Roberts was enjoying a breakfast of salamagundi, a red-hot West Indian pickle, when the first news was brought him of the approach of the *Swallow,* but he refused to be disturbed. Presently hearing that the man-of-war was about to attack, Roberts hurried up on deck, ordered the cables to be cut and sailed out to sea. This was on February 10th, 1722. A furious cannonade began, but unluckily most of the pirate crew, in spite of the early hour and their captain's example, were drunk already and incapable of a strong resistance. At the beginning of the engagement Roberts was killed by a grape shot which struck him in the throat. His body fully dressed, with his arms and ornaments, was thrown overboard according to his own instructions during his lifetime. He was thus saved the fate of his crew, who were all hanged at Cape Coast Castle.

Charles Johnson's "History" is a rich mine of pirate lore. Though his banditti appeared to have few morals and next to no discipline, yet they loved to draw up fine sounding articles or rules for their own conduct.

Below is a list of those drawn up by Captain John Phillips,

commander of the *Revenge,* late "fish-splitter" from Newfoundland. Their democratic nature and lofty tone are especially to be noted:

1. Every man shall obey civil Command; the Captain shall have one full share and a half in all Prizes; the Master, Carpenter, Boatswain and Gunner shall have one Share and quarter.
2. If any man shall offer to run away, or keep any Secret from the Company, he shall be marroon'd with one Bottle of Powder, one Bottle of Water, one small Arm and shot.
3. If any Man shall steel any Thing in the Company, or game, to the Value of a Piece of Eight, he shall be Marroon'd or shot.
4. If at any Time we should meet another Marrooner (that is Pyrate) that Man that shall sign his Articles without the Consent of our Company, shall suffer such Punishment as the Captain and Company shall think fit.
5. That Man that shall strike another whilst these Articles are in force, shall receive Moses's Law (that is 40 stripes lacking one) on the bare Back.
6. That Man that shall snap his Arms, or smoak Tobacco in the Hold, without a cap to his Pipe, or carry a Candle lighted without a Lanthorn, shall suffer the same Punishment as in the former Article.
7. That Man that shall not keep his Arms clean, fit for an Engagement, or neglect his Business, shall be cut off from his Share, and suffer such other Punishment as the Captain and the Company shall think fit.
8. If any Man shall lose a Joint in time of an Engagement he shall have 400 Pieces of Eight; if a limb 800.
9. If at any time you meet with a prudent Woman, that Man that offers to meddle with her, without her Consent, shall suffer present Death.

Such articles having been duly written out and agreed by the company, each member was required to swear to them with his hand upon the Bible. Unfortunately, in the case of Captain Phillips, no Bible could be found aboard the *Revenge* so the oath had to be taken on a hatchet as being the next best thing.

Once the precious articles had been settled, to the accompaniment of much drinking of rum punch, the important

A MOCK TRIAL

business of choosing a flag was discussed, one which "would strike terror upon all beholders." Sometimes the Jolly Roger, consisting of a human skull and two crossed thighbones was chosen, though many pirate crews preferred a plain black or red flag. Some captains fancied something more elaborate, as a "Human anatomy"; that is, a skeleton, holding a rummer, or glass of punch, in one bony hand, and a sword in the other.

When the pirates were not busy getting money at sea or dissipating it on shore they were not unlikely to be found engaging in innocent pastimes. Sometimes they even went in for dancing or play-acting, but above all other amusements they preferred a mock-trial at which each pirate took turn at being judge and prisoner. It was a grim form of pleasantry, since many of the players would in the end stand trial for their lives before a real judge in a real court of law. Johnson gives an account of one such mock-trial which he got from an eye-witness. If it was invented, the inventor must have been the creator of Shallow himself, who had been dead for a hundred years.

The Court and Criminals being both appointed, and also Council to plead, the Judge got up a Tree and had a dirty Taurpaulin hung over his shoulder; this was done by Way of Robe, with a Thrum cap on his Head, and a large Pair of Spectacles upon his Nose. Thus equipp'd he settled himself in his Place; and abundance of Officers attending him below with Crows, Handspikes, etc., instead of Wands, Tipstaves, and such like— The Criminals were brought out, making a thousand sour faces; and one who acted as Attorney-General opened the Charge against them; their Speeches were very laconick, and their whole Proceedings concise. We shall give it by Way of Dialogue.

Attor. Gen.: An't please Your Lordship, and you Gentlemen of the Jury, here is a Fellow before you that is a sad Dog, a sad, sad Dog; and I humbly hope your Lordship will order him to be hang'd out of the Way immediately— He has committed Pyracy upon the High Seas, and we shall prove, an't please your Lordship, that this Fellow, this sad Dog before you, has escaped a thousand Storms, nay, has got safe ashore when the Ship has been cast away, which was a certain Sign he was not born to be drown'd; yet not having the Fear of hanging before his Eyes, he went on robbing and ravishing Man, Woman and Child, plundering Ships cargoes fore and aft, burning and sinking Ship, Bark and Boat, as if the Devil had been in him. But this is not all, my Lord, he has committed worse Villanies than all these, for we shall prove, that he has been guilty of drinking Small-Beer; and your Lordship knows, there never was a sober Fellow but what was a Rogue. My Lord, I should have spoken much finer than I do now, but that as your Lordship knows our Rum is all out, and how should a Man speak good Law that has not drunk a Dram— However, I hope your Lordship will order the Fellow to be hang'd.

Judge: Heark'ee me, Sirrah—you lousy, pittiful, ill-look'd Dog; what have you to say why you should not be tuck'd up immediately and set a sun-drying like a Scare-crow?— Are you guilty or not guilty?

Pris: Not guilty, an't please your Worship.

Judge: Not guilty! say so again, Sirrah, and I'll have you hang'd without any Trial.

Pris: An't please your Worship's Honour, my Lord, I am as honest a poor Fellow as ever went between stem and stern of a Ship, and can hand, reef, steer and clap two ends of a Rope together, as well as e'er a He that ever cross'd salt Water; but I was taken by one George Bradley (the name of him that sat as Judge) a notorious Pyrate, a sad Rogue as ever was unhang'd, and he forc'd me, an't please your Honour.

Judge: Answer me, Sirrah— How will you be try'd?

Pris: By God and my Country.

Judge: The Devil you will— Why then, Gentlemen of the Jury, I think we have nothing to do but to proceed to Judgment.

Attor. Gen.: Right, my Lord; for if the Fellow should be suffered to speak, he may clear himself and that's an Affront to the Court.

Pris: Pray, my Lord, I hope your Lordship will consider. . .

Judge: Consider!— How dare you talk of considering?— Sirrah, Sirrah, I never considered in all my Life— I'll make it Treason to consider.

Pris: But, I hope your Lordship will hear some reason!

Judge: D'ye hear how the Scoundrel prates?— What I'd have you to know, Raskal, we don't sit here to hear Reason—we go according to Law— Is our Dinner ready?

Attor. Gen.: Yes, my Lord.

Judge: Then heark'ee, you Raskal at the Bar; hear me, Sirrah, hear me— You must suffer, for three reasons; first, because it is not fit I should sit here as Judge and no Body be hanged. Secondly, you must be hanged, because you have a damn'd hanging Look— and thirdly, you must be hanged, because I am hungry for know, Sirrah, that 'tis a Custom, that whenever the Judge's Dinner is ready before the Tryal is over, the Prisoner is to be hanged of Course— There's Law for you, ye Dog,—So take him away, Gaoler.

They were an odd mixture of human trash, those pirates of Johnson's. None more strange than Major Stede Bonnet, rich landowner of Barbados, whose neighbours were scandalised when they knew he had gone off "a pirating." But some were more sorry than angry when they learnt "that this Humour of going a Pirating proceeded from a Disorder in his Mind, which has been but too visible in him some time before this wicked Undertaking and which is said to have been occasioned by some Discomfort he found in a married State, be that as it will, the Major was but ill qualified for the Business, as not understanding maritime Affairs."

Needless to say the notorious Edward Teach, otherwise Blackbeard, received well-deserved notice from the pirate historian. It has always been believed that Teach was a Bristol man, but according to the anonymous author, probably Charles Leslie, of "Thirteen Letters from a Gentleman to his Friend," published in 1740, it appears that Teach was a native of Jamaica. The account of him runs as follows:

At this time the famous Edward Teach, commonly known by the Name of Blackbeard, infested the American Seas. He was one of a most bloody Disposition, and cruel to Brutality. His Name became a Terror; and some Governors being remiss in pursuing him, he almost put a stop to the Trade of several of the Northern Colonies. He was born in Jamaica, of very creditable Parents; his Mother is alive in Spanish Town to this Day, and his Brother is at present Captain of the Train of Artillery. He was attacked by a Lieutenant of a man of War (Robert Maynard, H.M. Sloop *Pearl*) and was killed, after a very obstinate and bloody Fight. He took a Glass, and drank Damnation to them that gave or asked Quarter. His Head was carried to Virginia, and there fixed on a Pole.

Teach kept a journal, of which unfortunately but two fragments survive, yet these have a distinct smack of Robert Louis Stevenson about them. They run:

1718. Rum all out. Our Company somewhat sober — A damn'd Confusion amongst us! Rogues a plotting — great Talk of Separation — so I look'd sharp for a Prize.

(Later) Took one with a great deal of Liquor on Board, so kept the Company hot, damned hot, then all things went well again.

New England was at this time the chief emporium for the traffic in pirate plunder, and goods captured off the American coast or in the West Indies and the Indian Ocean were brought there for sale. When too far from the kindly ports of America, the pirates had to find some safe refuge where they could careen their ships, repair their rigging and supply themselves with food and water. The ideal island which exactly filled all these requirements was Madagascar. It was well away from the track of the King of England's or other interfering potentate's warships. The natives were on the whole friendly. Last but not least it was a good centre for working the Red Sea and the Malabar coast, rich fields for the capture of vessels, particularly Indian or "Moorish" coasting ships, also for snapping up an occasional East Indiaman. These Madagascar pirates are dealt with by Johnson in the second volume of his "General History," which appeared in 1726.

The rogues he writes about in this later volume are as amazing a collection of the flotsam and jetsam of the seas as those in the first. One only will be told of here and he is chosen as being in many ways a unique pirate. How much of the story is true cannot be known. Every other account of a pirate's life written by Johnson is in the main true, but it must be confessed that no evidence so far has been found to corroborate his account of the amazing Misson.*

This extraordinary character came of an old French family of Provence. He was the youngest of a large family and received a good education. At the age of fifteen he had already

* "Pirates' Who's Who," Dulau.

shown unusual distinction in the subjects of humanity and logic and had passed quite tolerably in mathematics. Deciding to carve a fortune for himself with his sword, he was sent to the Academy of Angiers for a year. At the conclusion of his military studies his father would have bought him a commission in a regiment of musketeers but young Misson had been reading books of travel and begged so earnestly to be allowed to go to sea that his father got him admitted as a volunteer on the French man-of-war *Victoire,* commanded by Monsieur Fourbin, which he joined at Marseilles. During its cruise in the Mediterranean the young volunteer showed great keenness in his duties and lost no opportunity of learning all he could about navigation and the construction of ships, even parting with his pocket money to receive special instruction from the boatswain and the carpenter.

When they arrived at Naples, Misson received permission from the Captain to visit Rome, a visit which eventually altered his whole career.

While in Rome the young sailor met a Dominican priest, a Signor Caraccioli, who held most unclerical views about the priesthood; indeed his ideas on life in general were, to say the least, unorthodox. A great friendship was struck up between these two, which at length led the priest to throw off his habit and join the crew of the *Victoire.* Two days out from port they met and fought a desperate hand-to-hand engagement with a Sallee pirate, in which the ex-priest and Misson both distinguished themselves by their bravery.

Misson's next voyage was in a privateer, the *Triumph.* Meeting one day an English ship, the *Mayflower,* between Guernsey and Start Point, he and his companions defeated the merchantman after a gallant resistance. Rejoining the *Victoire,* Misson sailed from Rochelle to the West Indies.

During the whole voyage Caraccioli lost no opportunity of preaching to young Misson the gospel of atheism and communism, and with such success that the willing convert soon held views as extreme as those of his teacher. These two apostles now began to talk to the crew and their views, particularly on the rights of private property, were presently shared by almost all on board. A fortunate event occurred just then to help the new "cause." An engagement took place off the island of Martinique with an English man-of-war, the *Winchester,* which ended with the English vessel blowing up. In the course of the action Captain Fourbin was killed and with his death the new era set in. It began, as might be expected, in an outpouring of oratory.

First of all Signor Caraccioli stepped forward and made a long and eloquent address to Misson, inviting him on his own authority to become Captain of the *Victoire.* He called upon him to follow the example of Alexander the Great and Kings Henry IV and VII of England. He reminded him how Mahomet, with but a few camel-drivers, founded the Ottoman Empire, and how Darius with a handful of companions gained possession of Persia. Inflamed by this harangue, young Misson accepted the nomination in his first but, as events showed, far from his last speech. The result proved a triumph for oratory, since the excited French sailors answered it with shouts of "Vive le Capitaine Misson et son Lieutenant le Sçavant Caraccioli."

Misson, returning thanks in a few graceful words, promised to do his utmost, as their commander, for the infant marine republic. The officers then retired to the great cabin, where a friendly discussion took place about their new arrangements. The first question to arise was the choice of suitable colours to sail under. The newly elected boatswain, Mathew le Tondu, a brave but simple mariner, recommended a black flag as being the most terrifying. This brought down a full blast of eloquence from Caraccioli, the new lieutenant, who objected that "they were no pirates but men who were resolved to affect the Liberty which God and Nature gave them" and become "guardians of the People's Rights and Liberties," until he gradually became worked up and gave the wretched boatswain, who must have regretted his unfortunate suggestion, a heated lecture on the soul, on shaking "the Yoak of Tyranny" off their necks, on "oppression and Poverty" and the miseries of life under these conditions as compared with those of "Pomp and Dignity." Finally he showed that their policy was not to be one of piracy, for pirates were men of no principle and led dissolute lives, but *their* lives were to be brave, just and innocent, and *their* cause the cause of Liberty; and therefore instead of a black flag, they should sail under a white ensign with the motto "For God and Liberty" embroidered upon it.

The simple sailors, debarred from these councils, had gathered outside the cabin, where they overheard this speech. At its conclusion, carried away by enthusiasm, they sent up loud cries of "Liberty, Liberty! We are free men! Vive the brave Captain Misson and the noble Lieutenant Caraccioli!" And so off Martinique the new republic was baptised in the same torrent of oratory that launched the Revolution in Paris half a century later.

The first prize taken by these pirates under the white flag was an English sloop commanded by one Captain Thomas Butler, only one day's sail out from St. Kitts. After helping themselves to a couple of puncheons of rum and a few other articles, but without doing any unkindness to the crew, not even stripping them of their clothing, as was the usual custom of pirates on such occasions, they let them go, greatly to the surprise of Captain Butler, who handsomely admitted that he had never before met with so much "candour" in any similar situation. To express his gratitude further, he ordered his crew to man ship and at parting called for three rousing British cheers for the virtuous pirate and his men, which were given with hearty goodwill.

Sailing to the coast of Africa, Misson took a Dutch ship, the *Nieuwstadt,* of Amsterdam. The cargo was found to consist of gold dust and seventeen negro slaves. In the latter Captain Misson recognised a good text for one of his little sermons to seamen, so calling all hands on deck, he made the following observations on the vile trade of slavery, telling his men that:

"The Trading for those of our own Species cou'd never be agreeable to the Eyes of divine Justice. No Man had Power of the Liberty of another and while those who profess a more enlightened knowledge of the Deity sold Men like Beasts, they proved that their Religion was no more than Grimace and that they differ'd from the Barbarians in Name only, since their Practice was in nothing more humane."

Pausing a moment to take breath, the good Captain continued: "For his Part and he hop'd he spoke the Sentiments of all his brave Companions, he had not exempted his Neck from the galling Yoak of Slavery (a metaphor he stole from Caraccioli) and asserted his own Liberty to enslave others. However much these Men were distinguished from the Europeans by the Colour, Customs and religious Rites, they were the Work of the same omnipotent Being, and endued with equal Reason."

Raising his voice to a higher pitch, Misson then declared that "he desired they might be treated like Freemen (for he would banish even the Name of Slavery from among them) and he divided them into Messes, to the end they might the sooner learn their language, be sensible of the Obligations they had of them, and more capable and Zealous to defend that Liberty they owed to their Justice and Humanity."

Naturally this speech met with instant and general applause, and once again the good ship *Victoire* rang with cries of "Vive le Capitaine Misson." The negroes were freed from their irons and dressed up in the clothes of their late Dutch masters, and it is edifying to read that "by their Gesticulation, they showed they were gratefully sensible of their being delivered from their chains."

But a sad cloud was creeping insidiously over the fair reputation of these super-pirates. Out of the last ship they had captured, a number of the Dutch sailors had volunteered to serve under Misson and had been taken on board as members of the crew. Hitherto no swear-word was ever heard, no loose or profane expression had pained the ears of Captain Misson or his ex-priest lieutenant, but the Dutch mariners now began to initiate the crew into ways of profanity and drunkenness. This coming to the Captain's notice, he thought best to nip these weeds in the bud; so calling both French and Dutch upon deck and desiring the Dutch captain to translate his remarks into the Dutch language, he began: "Before he had the Misfortune of having them on Board, his Ears were never grated with hearing the Name of the great Creator profaned, tho' he, to his Sorrow, had often since heard his own Men guilty of that Sin, which administer'd neither Profit nor pleasure and might draw upon them a severe Punishment."

He reminded his listeners "that we so easily took Impression from our Company, that the Spanish Proverb says 'Let a Hermit and a Thief live together the Thief wou'd become Hermit, or the Hermit thief,' that he saw this verified in his ship, for he cou'd attribute the Oaths and Curses he had heard amongst his brave Companions to nothing but the odious Example of the Dutch. That this was not the only Vice they had introduced, for before they were on Board, his Men were Men, but he found by their beastly Pattern they were degenerated into Brutes, by drowning that only Faculty, which distinguishes between man and Beast, Reason."

Warming up to his work Captain Misson roared out how "he could not see them run into these odious Vices," referred to "the post by which they had honoured him, which obliged him to have a watchful Eye over their general Interest." He then "gave the Dutch Notice, that the first whom he catch'd either with an Oath in his Mouth or Liquor in his Head, should be brought to the Geers, whipped and pickled, for an Example to the rest of his Nation."

Then, dropping his voice and turning towards the French sailors he continued, "As to his Friends, his Companions, his Children, those gallant, those generous, noble and heroick Souls he had the Honour to command, he entreated them to allow a small Time for Reflection, and to consider how little Pleasure and how much Danger might flow from imitating the Vices of their Enemies; and that they would among themselves make a Law for the Suppression of what would otherwise estrange them from the Source of Life, and consequently leave them destitute of his Protection."

This speech had the desired effect and ever afterwards, when any one of the crew had reason to mention the name of their Captain, he always put the epithet "Good" before it.

These chaste pirates soon took and plundered many rich

merchant ships, but always in the most gentlemanly manner, so that none of the victims failed to be "not a little surprised at the Regularity, Tranquillity and Humanity of these new-fashioned Pyrates." From out of one of these prizes, an English vessel, they took sixty thousand pounds, but during the engagement the Captain was killed. Poor Misson was broken hearted over this accident. To show his regret he had the body buried on shore and, finding that one of his men was by trade a stone-cutter, raised a monument over the grave with the inscription "Here lies a gallant English Man." At the conclusion of a very moving burial service he paid a final tribute by "a triple Discharge of 50 small Arms and fired Minute Guns."

The *Victoire* was now headed for the island of Johanna in the Indian Ocean, which became for many years the home of Misson and his men. Here they settled down, the Captain marrying the sister of the local dusky queen, and Caraccioli leading to the altar her niece, while many of the crew were joined in holy wedlock to one or more ladies of humbler station.

Already Misson has received more space than he is entitled to in a work of this kind, but his career was so full of charming and surprising incidents that one is tempted to continue to undue length. Let it suffice to say that for some years Misson went on making speeches and robbing ships, and now and again, when unavoidably driven to it, reluctantly slaughtering his enemies.

Finally he left Johanna and took his followers to a secluded bay in Madagascar, where, on landing, he made another little speech, telling his faithful hearers that here they might settle down and build a town, that here in fact "they might have some Place to call their own; and a Receptacle when Age or Wounds had rendered them incapable of Hardship, where they might enjoy the Fruits of their Labour, and go to their Graves in Peace."

This ideal colony, which they named Libertatia, was run on strictly socialistic lines, for no one owned any individual property, all money was kept in a common treasury and no hedges bounded one man's plot of land from another's. Docks were made and fortifications set up. Soon Misson had two ships built, the *Childhood* and the *Liberty,* which were sent on a voyage round the island to map out and chart the coast and to train the released slaves to be efficient sailors. A session house was built, and a form of government set up. At the first meeting of the Assembly Misson was elected Lord Conservator, as they called the president, for a term of three years; during that period he was to have "all the Ensigns of Royalty to attend him." Captain Tew, an English pirate whom Kidd had pursued to his own undoing, was elected Admiral of the Fleet of Libertatia and Caraccioli became Secretary of State, while the Council was formed of the ablest amongst the pirates, without distinction of race or colour. The difficulty of language, as French, English, Portuguese and Dutch were spoken equally, was overcome by the invention of a new language, a sort of Esperanto, which was built up of words from all four.

For many years this pirate Utopia flourished, but at length misfortunes came, one on top of the other, and a sudden and unexpected attack by the hitherto friendly natives finally drove Misson and a few survivors to seek safety at sea. Overtaken by a hurricane, their vessel foundered and Misson and all his crew were drowned. Thus ended an era of what might be styled "piracy without tears."

He was the mildest-manner'd man
That ever scuttled ship or cut a throat.
—Byron

A firsthand account of Madagascar pirates has come down to us in the pages of a rare book, "Madagascar or Robert Drury's Journal," published in 1729. The author was wrecked on the island and remained there a prisoner for fifteen years, living as a native. One day he visited one of the pirate settlements and gave the following description of what he saw:

One of these men was a Dutchman, named John Pro, who spoke good English. He was dressed in a short coat with broad plate buttons and other things agreeable, but without shoes or stockings.

In his sash stuck a brace of pistols and he had one in his right hand. The other man was dressed in an English manner, with two pistols in his sash and one in his hand, like his companion. John Pro lived in a very handsome manner. His house was furnished with pewter dishes etc. a standing bed with curtains and other things of that nature except chairs, but a chest or two served for that purpose well enough. He had one house on purpose for his cook-room and cook-slave's lodging, store house and summer house; all these were enclosed in a palisade, as the great men's houses are in this country, for he was rich and had many castles and slaves. His wealth had come principally while cruising among the Moors, from whom his ship had several times taken great riches, and used to carry it to St. Mary's. But their ship growing old and crazy, they being also vastly rich, they removed to Madagascar, made one Thomas Collins, a carpenter, their Governor, and built a small fort, defending it with their ship's guns. They had now lived without pirating for nine years.

Before passing on to other branches and practitioners of the craft some notice must be taken of two women-pirates of whose misdeeds Charles Johnson had much to say. Nowadays, when what used to be called the "tender sex" has invaded almost every profession except the church, it may not seem strange that women should have willingly entered upon such a rough and manly trade as that of piracy. But in the eighteenth century the home was still considered the proper place for women and much scandal resulted over the fact that travellers at sea were liable to have their throats cut by a woman.

Needless to say both Anne Bonney and Mary Read were very fair to look upon. The former, an Irish lass, was the illegitimate daughter of a Cork attorney, and at a tender age went with her father to Carolina. There she grew up into a strapping, boisterous girl, of a "fierce and courageous temper" which more than once led her into sad scrapes, as when she slew her English servant-maid with a case knife. But apart from such occasional outbursts of temper she was a good and dutiful daughter.

Anne, after several love-affairs, entered into a clandestine marriage with a sailor. When her father heard of it, he turned

ANNE BONNY

her out, at which the sailor ran away to sea and was never heard of again. But a more gallant lover soon hove in sight, the handsome, rich, dare-devil pirate Captain John Rackam, known up and down the coast as "Calico Jack." Jack's methods of courting a woman or taking a ship were similar — no time wasted, straight up alongside, every gun brought to play and the prize boarded.

Anne was at once swept off her feet by her picturesque and impetuous lover and agreed to go to sea with him disguised in sailor's clothes. The honeymoon was spent at sea, until certain tender news was conveyed to Rackam by his bride, when he at once made for Cuba, landing Anne at a small cove where he had a home and friends who promised to take care of her. In due time Anne was back in the pirate ship, as active as any with cutlass and marlinspike, always one of the first to board a prize. These happy days were numbered, however, for while cruising near Jamaica in October 1720 the pirates were surprised by the sudden arrival of an armed sloop, which had been sent out by the Governor of that island to capture Rackam and his crew. A fight followed in which the pirates behaved in a most cowardly way and were soon driven below decks, all but Anne Bonney and her friend Mary Read (of whom more anon), who fought gallantly until taken prisoner, the while reviling their male companions for their cowardly conduct. The prisoners were carried to Jamaica, tried for piracy at St. Jago de la Vega, and convicted on November 28th, 1720.

Anne pleaded to have her execution postponed because of the condition of her health, which was granted. Though she never seems to have been hanged, her ultimate fate is unknown.

On the day that her lover, "Calico Jack," was executed, he obtained, by special favour, permission to see Anne, but must have derived little comfort from this farewell interview, for all he got in the way of sympathy from his lady-love were the words: "she was sorry to see him there, but if he had fought like a Man, he need not have been hang'd like a Dog."

Mention has been made of Mary Read, who was condemned to death at the same time as Anne Bonney. Her early life was even more romantic than Anne's, and Johnson the historian evidently feared that doubts might be raised in the mind of his reader as to the strict truth of his statements. "The odd Incidents," he observes, "of their rambling Lives are such, that some may be tempted to think the whole Story no better than a Novel or Romance; but since it is supported by many thousand witnesses, I mean the People of Jamaica, who were present at their Tryals, and heard the Story of their Lives, upon the first Discovery of their Sex, the Truth of it can be no more contested, than that there were such Men in the World as Roberts and Black-beard, who were Pyrates." With any lurking doubts thus dispelled let us enquire into the life and actions of Mistress Mary Read.

Little is known of her origin, beyond the fact that her mother was a "young and airy widow." For various good reasons, little Mary was brought up as a boy and at the age of thirteen was engaged as a "footboy" by a French lady. But Mary soon tired of a service so unexciting, and engaged herself on board a man-of-war. She soon tired of this life too and enlisted as a common soldier in a regiment of foot in Flanders, where she saw active service and showed considerable personal gallantry. But once again she yearned for change and quitted the infantry for a regiment of horse. One of her companions in this regiment was a Flemish trooper with whom Mary fell deeply in love and at last "disclosed to him the secret of her sex." The trooper, a man of honour, insisted she should change her uniform for womanly attire and marry him. The wedding of the two troopers "made a great noise" and was attended by several of the officers. The bridegroom was given his discharge and the happy couple set up house at a tavern at Breda called the "Three Horseshoes," which stands to this day.

The husband died and the widow, once more donning male attire, enlisted in another regiment in Holland, but being unable to settle down again to military life she soon deserted and shipped herself as a sailor in a vessel bound for the West Indies, which was captured on its way out by Captain Rackam, the pirate. With others Mary volunteered to join the pirates and signed their articles, although without disclosing her sex.

MARY READ

Her career of piracy might have ended soon, for Captain Woodes Rogers had lately been sent out to New Providence Island, Bahamas, to offer a Royal pardon to all pirates who would agree to mend their ways, which Rackam and his crew accepted. But it was difficult for a man, or woman, who had once played the game of piracy to settle down to an honest life, and soon Rackam was off again with Mary amongst his crew. They took many ships, mostly from Jamaica, in one of which was "a young fellow of engaging behaviour" who at once attracted the attention of Mary, although she kept her secret to herself. One day this young sailor fell out with another of the pirates. As the ship lay at anchor off an island, it was agreed to go ashore to fight it out, according to the pirate rules. Poor Mary's feelings may well be imagined, and well might she "apprehend the Fellow might be too hard for him, for when Love once enters into the Breast, it stirs the Heart up to the most noble Actions." What Mary did was to pick a quarrel with the bully and arrange to fight him at once and she was so handy with her pistol and sword that she killed him on the spot.

After this Mary allowed the secret of her sex, hitherto so jealously guarded, to be revealed to the "young fellow of engaging behaviour" and "straight away they plighted their Troth to each other, which Mary Read said, she look'd upon to be as good a Marriage in Conscience, as if it had been done by a Minister in Church."

When, not long after, Mary stood beside Anne Bonney and the other prisoners in the dock at St. Jago de la Vega, the court was in favour of discharging her and would have done so but for one damning piece of evidence. It was proved that once on being asked by Rackam what pleasure she could find in a life continually in danger of death by fire, sword or else by hanging, she had replied "that as to hanging, she thought it no great Hardship, for, were it not for that, every cowardly Fellow would turn Pyrate and so infest the Seas, that Men of Courage must starve."

The court thereupon decided that no exception could be made in her case and she was condemned to death.

With pitch and tar her hands were hard
Tho' once like velvet soft,
She weighed the anchor, heav'd the lead
*And boldly went aloft.**

By the beginning of the eighteenth century piracy in North America had become a great trade, with depôts and agents in most of the harbours and ports from Salem in the north to Charleston in South Carolina. Willing volunteers were to be found at most of these ports, the favourite recruiting ground, as before, being Newfoundland. To this island there came each season hundreds of fishing boats, bringing numbers of poor men from the West of England who received low wages from the contractors and had to pay their own passages home at the end of the fishing season. Their work, fishing, or else the splitting and drying of the cod on shore, was very hard, and their only relaxation the drinking of black-strap, a villainous concoction of rum, molasses and chowder beer. This black-strap cost money, as did also the bare necessities of life, so that when the time came to return to England, many men had not enough money left to pay their passages. It was such unfortunates as these that the pirates looked to for manning their ships on the principle that beggars cannot be choosers.

The Gulf of Florida swarmed with these pirates, who could always find refuge in the West Indies and the Spanish Main. Their vessels sailed regularly from New York, Newport and Philadelphia, at which latter port it was said they "not only wink at but embrace pirates, ships and men." It was not only the merchants who were in league with them: not a few of the Colonial Governors were known to receive presents or bribes, which caused them to look the other way when plunder was being brought ashore.

In any case the authorities had few inducements to take strong measures with the pirates. As we have seen, the latter were far from being looked on askance by the colonials, who did a most profitable and thriving trade in buying stolen goods at low prices. If a strong and honest governor tried to carry

* (Anon) "Pirates' Own Book."

out his duties, all kinds of difficulties were put in his way. Even if he did arrest a pirate, there was no means of trying or punishing him in any of the colonies, and he had to be transported with the witnesses to England, to be tried there by the Court of Admiralty, a long, expensive and tedious process. So it was not to be wondered at that the authorities usually remained blind to what was going on under their very noses.

A report written by Edward Randolph, Surveyor-General of Customs in the American colonies, throws considerable light on the ways of pirates on the New England coast. The document * is headed "A discours about Pyrates with proper Remedies to Suppress them," and was one of many such reports sent home to England by the indefatigable Randolph. It is dated 1695. After dwelling on the state of piracy, and how pirates were accustomed to plunder Spanish ships and bring to New England "great quantities of silver in coin and Bullion, with Rich Copes, Church plate and other Riches," it states that "many of these freebooters have taken to sailing to the Red Sea, where they take from the Moors all they have, without Resistance, and bring it to some one of the Plantations in this Continent of America or Islands adjacent, where they are received and harboured and from whence also they fit out their vessells to the same places."

The writer then goes on to give particulars of "the chief places where Pyrates Resort and are Harboured" and pours a strong light on the relations that existed between the outlaws and the officials in the Bahamas and of the various colonies. It is obvious that the corruption had gone so deep and extended so wide as to be a public scandal, for Randolph is able to cite the exact amounts of tribute monies paid in various instances. He concludes with several strong recommendations, including a more careful selection of governors, the pursuit of the pirates to their lairs, the pardon of the principal ones, and the forfeiture of all former pirate property now in the hands of officials. It is an interesting document of the time and has never before been printed. It will be found as Appendix VI.

But the evil was too deep seated, too much influence lay be-

* MS in the possession of the author.

hind it, for such recommendations to have any effect as yet. The magistrates got their money, the public its cheap goods. Even when occasionally a pirate was caught the magistrates still got their money and the public at least got a first class show, as will appear from the story of John Quelch. There are a number of stories extant to show what a Roman holiday a pirate hanging provided for all classes of the New England ports, but none is quite so complete in detail as this.

It was in July 1703 that a smart brigantine, the *Charles,* newly built and fitted out as a privateer by some of the leading citizens of Boston, received a commission from the Governor of Massachusetts, Joseph Dudley, to prey upon French shipping off the coast of Acadia * and Newfoundland.

While riding at anchor off Marblehead, in Massachusetts, a mutiny of the crew took place; the captain was thrown overboard and the *Charles* set sail under the command of the leader of the mutiny, John Quelch. Three months later the pirates were off the coast of Brazil flying as flag the "Old Roger," which was ornamented by "an Anatomy with an Hourglass in one hand, and a dart in the Heart with three drops of Blood proceeding from it in the other," and in a short while they had captured nine Portuguese vessels, which they plundered of rich booty which included a hundredweight of gold dust, gold and silver coins to the value of over one thousand pounds, ammunition, small arms and a great quantity of fine fabrics, provisions and rum.† Having in a few months made a fortune for himself and his crew Quelch steered for home.

Why Quelch should have chosen to return to Marblehead of all places is not clear. The whole country-side had been roused by the mutiny and his attacks on the ships of a friendly nation, and scarcely had he set foot on shore when an information was filed against him by the Attorney-General. His crew, which had dispersed with its share of the spoils, was soon rounded up, and at the end of ten days twenty-five of the pirates, including Quelch, were in gaol at Boston. Quantities

* Nova Scotia.

† These particulars of the career of John Quelch are largely taken from "The Pirates of New England Coast," Dow & Edwards, 1923.

of gold and silver which had been sold to various persons in adjacent parts of the colony, were also retrieved and sequestrated at Boston.

The twenty-five were arraigned before the court of the Admiralty on June 9th, 1704 (since 1701 such trials could be held outside England under an Act of William III). Had Quelch confined his attentions to French ships it is possible that the commission he carried, though acquired by mutiny, might have saved him, but the evidence of his having plundered and murdered the friends and allies of his Queen was too overwhelming. In addition various of his men turned Queen's evidence and swore that he had killed the captain of a Portuguese ship. Sentence of death was passed on Quelch and twenty-one of his crew, though in the following July thirteen of the latter were pardoned on condition that they entered the Queen's service.

Almost every hour between the passing of the sentence and the carrying out of the execution was devoted to the spiritual salvation of the condemned. "The Ministers of the Town had used more than ordinary Endeavours to Instruct the Prisoners, and bring them to Repentance. There were Sermons Preached in their hearing Every Day; and Prayers daily made with them, and they were Catechised; and they had many occasional Exhortations, and nothing was left that could be done for their Good." *

The Reverend Cotton Mather, who appears to have revelled in such distressing scenes, preached a sermon which he afterwards had printed, entitled "A Discourse occasioned by a Tragical Spectacle in a Number of Miserables under sentence of Death for Piracy," which began: "We have told you often, we have told you weeping, that you have by sin undone yourselves; That you were born Sinners, That you have lived Sinners, That your Sins have been many and mighty, and that the Sins for which you are now to Dy are of no common aggravation. . ."

Friday, June 20th, was a day of high holiday at Boston for on that day the prisoners passed in procession from the prison to the wharf, the route being lined many deep by gaping Bos-

* Jameson, "Privateering and Piracy in the Colonial Period."

tonians. The Silver Oar, the emblem of the court of Admiralty, was carried in front, followed by the constables of the town, the Provost Marshal, his officers and two ministers, one of whom, needless to say, was the Reverend Cotton Mather. Behind these walked the prisoners, guarded by forty musketeers.

On reaching the wharf the prisoners were taken in boats and rowed across the harbour to the gallows which had been erected on a small island called Nix's Mate. Arrived at the place of execution, the wretched prisoners were lined up on the gallows while they underwent a last and prolonged haranguing by the Reverend Cotton Mather. This over, the divine called upon the malefactors and the surrounding sightseers to kneel down while he prayed aloud at enormous length. No word of hope or comfort was to be found in the prayer, in which the speaker worked himself up into such heights of oratory as: "And now, we fly, we fly to *Sovereign Grace.* Oh ! that the Poor men, which are immediately to appear before the awful Tribunal of God, may first by *Sovereign Grace* have produced upon their Souls those Marks of thy Favour, without which t'is a dreadful Thing to appear before that awful Tribunal. Oh ! Great God, Let thy *Sovereign Grace* operate on this fearful occasion !"

The time for the end at last drew near, when by an old established custom the prisoners were allowed and expected to address the multitude. Captain Quelch was a disappointment to the ministers, for instead of repeating the usual platitudes about regret for past wickedness and warning his hearers to take heed by his bad example he "seem'd to brave it out too much . . . also when on the Stage he pulled off his Hat, and bowed to the Spectators, and not Concerned, nor behaving himself so much like a Dying man as some would have done."

One onlooker, who afterwards wrote a description of the scene, noticed that "the Ministers had, on the way to his Execution, much desired him to Glorify God at his Death, by bearing a due Testimony against the Sins that had ruined him," so that they must have been disappointed when Quelch called out: "Gentlemen, 'Tis but little I have to speak; what I have to say is this, I desire to be informed for what I am here. I am Condemned only upon Circumstances. I forgive all the World, so the Lord be merciful to my Soul." The good effect of these last words were somewhat spoiled by the speaker's adding a pointed economic warning: "They should also take care how they brought Money into New England, to be Hanged for it !"

All the other prisoners spoke in a spirit of humbleness and hoped to be forgiven their sins except one, an Irishman, Peter Roach, who "seem'd little concerned, and said but little or nothing at all."

Judge Sewall, who kept a diary,* remarks on the great crowds which assembled:

When I came to see how the River was cover'd with People, I was amazed. Some say that there were 100 Boats. 150 Boats and Canoes saith Cousin Moodey of York. Mr. Cotton Mather came with Capt. Quelch and the others for execution from the Prison to Scarlit's Wharf, and from thence in the Boat to the place of Execution about midway between Hanson's point and Broughton's Warehouse. When the scaffold was hoisted to a due height, the seven Malefactors went up: Mr. Mather prayed for them, standing upon the Boat. Ropes were all fasten'd to the Gallows. When the Scaffold was let to sink there was such a Screech of the Women that my wife heard it sitting in her Entry next the Orchard, and was much surprised at it; yet the wind was sou-west, our house a full mile from the place.

Justice having been so satisfactorily served there remained only the generous disbursements of the pirates' plunder to be made. So far as the sentences go, the trial has been characterized as "one of the clearest cases of judicial murder done in our American annals." † But amongst those who received a share of the loot were Judge Sewall who got £25. 7.0, the Attorney-General who received £36. 0. 0, while the lawyer who defended the prisoners was paid £20. 0. 0. The Sheriff was no doubt satisfied with his £5. 0. 0, while the executioner

* Jameson, "Privateering and Piracy in the Colonial Period."
† Dow & Edwards, "Pirates of the New England Coast," 1630–1730.

received £2. 0. 0 "for erecting the gibbet." By the time everybody, including Cotton Mather, had taken his share, the sum of £726. 19. 4 had been spent out of the money stolen from the Portuguese.

It was two years before the officials of the Province were ready to hand over to the Crown what remained of the "coyn'd, Bar & Dust Gold imported by Capt. John Quelch." This, on being weighed by the Boston goldsmith, was found to come to 788 ounces, and after being placed in five leather bags was sent in H.M.S. *Guernsey* to the "Lord High Treasurer of England for her Majesty's use." There is no evidence that one shilling of this ever returned to the pockets of the Portuguese owners.

EACH English monarch in turn issued threats, bribes and proclamations to frighten or seduce the pirates, but with no success. The wars of the eighteenth century merely served to increase the privateers of all nations and, as the Reverend Cotton Mather said, "The Privateering stroke so easily degenerates into the Piratical." Hard on these conflicts came the American Revolution and a radical alteration in the political complexion of the West of Europe, with its consequent enfeeblement of law and order.

CHAPTER III

THE NINETEENTH CENTURY

THROUGHOUT the seven years of the American Revolution, from 1775 to 1782, privateers swarmed in the West Indies. Most of these, whether British, French, Spanish or American, carried more or less legitimate commissions. The serious trouble came later on, during the long struggle between England and France which raged from 1793 to 1815. Then many of the privateers so-called were neutrals, who were more interested in winning prizes and plunder for themselves than in helping either side in their bitter contest. When the war came to a close, thousands of men who had served in these privateer vessels were thrown out of employment, and were just the material of which pirates were made.

These new pirates were worse than any that had existed before. The earlier pirates, with all their black faults and their cruelty, were not without some trace of humanity, and on occasion could fight bravely. These new pirates were cowards without a single redeeming feature. Formed from the scum of the rebel navies of the revolted Spanish colonies and the riff-raff of the West Indies, they were a set of bloodthirsty savages, who never dared attack any but the weak, and had no more regard for innocent lives than a butcher has for his victims. The result is a monotonous list of slaughterings and pilferings from which scarcely one event or a single character stands out to strike a spark from the imagination.

Perhaps the only picturesque villain of the lot is Jean Lafitte, who instituted a reign of terror in the Gulf of Mexico, made himself dictator in Galveston with power to sell letters of marque to his fellow outlaws, had a reward of five thousand dollars offered for his head by the Governor of Louisiana and retaliated by posting an offer of fifty thousand for the Governor's head.

Spain could or would do nothing to overcome the menace to West Indian shipping. During most of the period she was busy with her rebellious South American colonies, who provided many of the pirate crews and the commissions under which the pirate vessels pretended to sail, although these commissions were more often than not forgeries or valueless papers bought from minor officials. Even the effects of the vigorous co-operation of the British and American navies were largely nullified by the Spanish officials in Cuba which derived not inconsiderable benefits from its position as a pirate clearing house.

However Britain and America persisted in the face not only of local indifference but of incredible hardships, yellow fever, days on end without rest in open boats under a tropical sun, constant exposure to disease and attack, and by 1835 they had pretty well cleared the waters of the West Indies and the North Atlantic.

For all practical purposes this era of piracy may be said to have ended with the capture of the *Panda* in 1835. This affair was not only internationally celebrated at the time but is almost a complete text of piracy as it existed off the coast of North America in the early nineteenth century. Fortunately an account exists which was written at the time by an eye-witness, one of the crew of the *Mexican,* the vessel whose capture ultimately led to the hanging of the *Panda* brigands. It is so striking in its details that it is worth giving *in extenso:* *

I was at Peabody's store house on the morning of the day of sailing and others of the crew came soon after. After waiting quite a while, it was suggested that we go after the cook, Ridgely, who then boarded with a Mrs. Ranson, a coloured woman living in Becket Street, so we set out to find him. He was at home but disinclined to go, as he wished to pass one more Sunday home. However, after some persuading he got ready and we all started out of

* Narrative of John Battis of Salem, one of the crew of the *Mexican,* taken from Ralph D. Paine's "Ships & Sailors of old Salem," Lauriat & Co., Boston, 1923.

the gate together. A black hen was in the yard and as we came out the bird flew upon the fence, and flapping her wings, gave a loud crow. The cook was wild with terror and insisted that something was going to happen; that such a sign meant harm and he ran about in search of a stone to knock out the brains of the offending biped. The poor donkey did not succeed in his murderous design, but followed us grumbling.

At about ten o'clock we mustered all present and accounted for, and commenced to carry the specie, with which we were to purchase our return cargo, on board the brig. We carried aboard twenty thousand dollars in silver, in ten boxes of two thousand dollars each; we also had about one hundred bags of saltpetre and one hundred chests of tea. The silver was stored in the "run" under the cabin floor, and there was not a man aboard but knew where the money was stored. At last everything being ready we hove anchor and stood out to sea in the face of a southeast wind. As soon as we got outside and stowed anchor we cleared ship and the captain called all hands and divided the crew into watches. I was in the first mate's watch and young Thomas Fuller * was in the captain's watch.

On account of the several acts of piracy previously committed on Salem ships, Captain Butman undoubtedly feared, or perhaps had a premonition of a later happening to his vessel, for the next day while I was at work on the main rigging, I heard the captain and first mate talking about pirates. The captain said he would fight a long while before he'd give his money up. They had a long talk together, and he seemed to be very much worried. I think it was the next day after this conversation between Captain Butman and Mr. Reed that I was at the wheel steering when the captain came and spoke to me. He asked me how I felt about leaving home, and I replied that I felt the same as ever, "all right." I learned afterwards that he put this question to the rest of the crew.

We sailed along without anything occurring worthy of note until the night of the nineteenth of September (1832). After supper we were all sitting together during the dog-watch (this being between six and eight o'clock P.M.) when all seemed bent on telling pirate yarns, and of course got more or less excited. I went below at twelve o'clock and at four next morning my watch was called. Upon coming on deck the first mate came forward and said that we must keep a sharp look out as there was a vessel 'round,

* Captain Thomas Fuller, the last survivor of the *Mexican,* died at Salem in December 1906 in his ninety-fourth year.

and that she had crossed our stern and gone to the leeward. I took a seat between the knight-heads and had been sitting there but a few minutes when a vessel crossed our bows and went to the windward of us.

We were going at a pretty good rate at the time I sang out and the mate came forward with a glass, but he could not make her out. I told him he would see her to the windward at daylight. At dawn we discovered a top-sail schooner about five miles off our weather quarter, standing on the wind on the same tack as we were. The wind was light, at south southwest, and we were standing about southeast. At seven o'clock the captain came on deck and this was the first we knew of the schooner being about us.

I was at the wheel when the captain came out of the cabin; he looked toward the schooner, and as soon as he perceived her he reached and took his glass and went onto the main top. He came down and closing the glass said: "That is the very man I have been looking for. I can count thirty men on his deck." He also said that he saw one man on her fore-topgallant yard, looking out, and that he was very suspicious of her. He then ordered us to set all sail (as the schooner didn't seem to sail very fast) thinking we might get away from her.

While I was up loosing the main-royal I sat on the yard, and let them hoist me up to the truck so that I could have a good look around. I saw another vessel, a brig, to the eastward of us and reported it. The schooner had in the meantime sailed very fast, for when I started to come down she was off our beam. From all appearances and her manner of sailing we concluded afterwards that she had a drag out. We then went to breakfast, the schooner kept ahead of us and appeared to be after the other vessel. Then the captain altered the brig's course, tacking to the westward, keeping a little off from the wind to make good way through the water to get clear of her if possible. After breakfast when we came on deck the schooner was coming down on us under a full press of sail. I noticed two kegs of powder alongside our two short carronades, the only guns we had. Our means of defence, however, proved utterly worthless as the shot was a number of sizes too large for the guns.

A few moments before this the schooner had fired a shot at us to heave to, which Captain Butman was on the point of doing as I came on deck. The schooner then hoisted patriotic colors (Columbian flag), backed her main topsail and laid to about half a mile to the windward. She was a long low straight topsail schooner of about one hundred and fifty tons burthen, painted black wth a narrow white streak, a large figure-head with a horn of plenty painted white; masts raked aft, and a large main topsail, a regular Baltimore clipper. We could not see any name. She carried thirty or more men, with a long thirty-two pound swivel amidships, with four brass guns, two on each side.

A hail came in English from the schooner, asking us where we were from and where bound and what our cargo was. Captain Butman replied, "Tea and saltpetre." The same voice from the schooner then hailed us for the captain to lower a boat and come alongside and bring him his papers. The boat was got ready and Captain Butman and four men — Jack Ardissone, Thomas Fuller, Benjamin Larcom and Fred Trask — got in and pulled to the schooner. When they parted Captain Butman shook hands with the mate, Mr. Reed, and told him to do the best he could if he never saw him again.

The *Mexican's* boat pulled up to the gangway of the schooner but they ordered it to go to the forechains where five of the pirates jumped into our boat, not permitting any of our men to go on board the schooner and pushed off, ordering the captain back to the brig. They were armed with pistols in their belts and long knives up their sleeves. While at the schooner's side, after getting into our boat, one of the pirates asked their captain in Spanish what they should do with us, and his answer was: "Dead cats don't mew — have her thoroughly searched and bring aboard all you can — you know what to do with them."

The orders of the captain of the schooner being in Spanish were understood by only one of the *Mexican's* crew then in the boat, namely Ardissone, who burst into tears and in broken English declared that all was over with them.

Our boat returned to the brig and Captain Butman and the five pirates came on board; two of them went down in the cabin with us and the other three loafed around the deck. Our first mate came up from the cabin and told us to muster aft and get the money up. Larcomb and I, being near the companion-way, started to go down into the cabin when we met the boatswain of the pirate coming up, who gave the signal for attack.

The three pirates on deck sprang on Larcomb and myself, striking at us with the long knives across our heads. A Scotch cap I happened to have on with a large cotton handkerchief inside, saved me from a severe wounding as both were cut through and through. Our mate, Mr. Reed, here interfered and attempted to stop them from assaulting us whereupon they turned on him.

We then went down into the cabin and in to the run; there were eight of us in all; six of our men then went back into the cabin, and the steward and myself were ordered to pass the money up which we did, to the cabin floor, and our crew then took it and carried it on deck.

In the meantime the pirate officer in charge (the third mate) had hailed the schooner and told them they had found what they were looking for. The schooner then sent a launch containing sixteen men, which came alongside and they boarded us. They made the crew pass the boxes of money down into the boat, and it was then conveyed on board the pirate. The launch came back with about a dozen more men, and the search began in earnest. Nine of them rushed down into the cabin where the captain, Jack Ardissone, and myself were standing. They beat the captain with the long knives and battered a speaking trumpet to pieces on his head and shoulders. Seeing we could do nothing, I made a break to reach the deck by jumping out of the cabin window, thinking I could get there by grasping hold of the boat's davits and pulling myself on deck. Jack Ardissone, divining my movement, caught my foot as I was jumping and saved me, or I should probably have missed my calculation and gone overboard. Jack and I then ran and the pirates after both of us, leaving the captain whom they continued to beat and abuse, demanding more money. We ran into the steerage. Jack, not calculating the break of the deck soon went over into the hold, and I on top of him. For some reason the pirates gave up the chase before they reached the break between the decks, or they would have gone down with us. By the fall Jack broke two of his ribs. Under deck we had a clean sweep, there being no cargo, so we could go from one end of the vessel to the other.

The crew then got together in the forecastle and stayed there. We hadn't been there long before the mate, Mr. Reed, came rushing down, chased by the boatswain of the pirate, demanding his money. The mate then told Larcomb to go and get his money, which he had previously given Larcomb to stow away for him in some safe place; there were two hundred dollars in specie, and Larcomb had put it under the wood in the hold. Larcomb went and got it, brought it up and gave it to the pirate, who untied the bag, took a handful out, retied the bag, and went up on deck and

WALKING THE PLANK

threw the handful of money overboard, so that those on the schooner could see that they had found more money.

Then the pirates went to Captain Butman and told him that if they found any more money which they hadn't surrendered they would cut all our throats. I must have followed them into the cabin, for I heard them tell the captain this. Previous to this, we of the crew found that we had about fifty dollars, which we secured by putting into the pickle keg, and this was secretly placed in the breast-work forward. On hearing this threat made to the captain I ran back and informed the crew what I had heard, and we took the money out of my keg and dropped it down the air-streak, which is the space between the inside and outside planking. It went way down into the keelson. Our carpenter afterwards located its exact position and recovered every cent of it. Strange to say the first thing they searched on coming below was the pickle keg. The search of our effects by the pirates was pretty thorough, and they took all new clothes, tobacco, etc. In the cabin they searched the captain's chest, but failed to get at seven hundred dollars which he had concealed in the false bottom; they had previously taken from him several dollars which he had in his pocket, and his gold watch, and had also relieved the mate of his watch.

About noon it appeared to be very quiet on deck, we having been between decks ever since the real searching party came on board. We all agreed not to go on deck again and to make resistance with sticks of wood if they attempted to come down, determined to sell our lives as dearly as possible. Being somewhat curious, I thought I'd peep up and see what they were doing; as I did so a cocked pistol was pressed to my head and I was ordered to come on deck and went, expecting to be thrown overboard. One took me by the collar and held me out at arm's length to plunge a knife into me. I looked him right in the eye and he dropped the knife and ordered me to get the doors of the forecastle which were below. I went down and got them, but they did not seem to understand how they were to be used, and they made me come up and ship them. There were three of them and as I was letting the last one in I caught the gleam of a cutlass being drawn, so taking the top of the door on my stomach, I turned a quick somersault and went down head first into the forecastle. The cutlass came down, but did not find me; it went into the companionway quite a depth. Then they hauled the slide over and fastened it, and we were all locked below.

They fastened the after companionway leading down into the

cabin, locking our officers below as well. From noises that came from overhead, we were convinced that the pirates had begun a work of destruction. All running rigging, including tiller ropes, were cut, sails slashed into ribbons, spars cut loose, ship's instruments and all movable articles on which they could lay their hands were demolished, the yards were tumbled down and we could hear the main boom swinging from side to side. They then, as appears from later developments, filled the caboose or cook's galley, with combustibles, consisting of tar, tarred rope yarn, oakum etc., setting fire to the same, and lowered the dismantled mainsail so that it rested on top of the caboose. In this horrible suspense we waited for an hour or more when all became quiet save the wash of the sea against the brig. All this time the crew had been cooped up in the darkness of the forecastle, of course unable to speculate as to what would be the next move of the enemy, or how soon death would come to each and all of us.

Finally about three o'clock in the afternoon, Thomas Fuller came running forward and informed us that the pirates were leaving the ship. One after another of the crew made their way to the cabin and on peering out of the two small stern windows saw the pirates pulling for the schooner. Captain Butman was at this time standing on the cabin table, looking out from a small skylight, the one means of egress the pirates had neglected to fasten. We told him that from the odor of smoke, we believed they had fired the brig. He said he knew it and ordered us to remain quiet. He then stepped down from the table and for several moments knelt in prayer, after which he calmly told us to go forward and he would call us when he wanted us.

We had not been in the forecastle long before he called us back, and directed that we get all the buckets under deck and fill them with water from the casks in the hold. On our return he again opened the skylight and drew himself up on deck. We then handed him a small bucket of water, and he crept along the rail in the direction of the caboose, keeping well under the rail in order to escape observation from the schooner. The fire was just breaking through the top of the caboose when he arrived in time to throw several handfuls of water on top so as to keep it under. This he continued to do for a long while, not daring to extinguish it immediately lest the pirates should notice the absence of smoke and know that their plan for our destruction had been frustrated. When the fire had been reduced to a reasonable degree of safety he came and opened the aft companionway and let us all up. The schooner being a fast sailor was in the distance about hull down. The fire in the caboose was allowed to burn in a smouldering condition for perhaps a half-hour or more, keeping up a dense smoke. By this time the pirate schooner was well nigh out of sight, or nearly topsails under, to the Eastward. On looking about us, we found the *Mexican* in a bad plight, all sails halyards and running gear were cut, headsails dragging in the water, and on account of the tiller ropes being cut loose, the brig was rolling about in the trough of the sea. We at once set to work repairing damages as speedily as possible and before dark had bent new sails and repaired our running gear to a great extent.

Fortunately through the shrewdness and foresight of Captain Butman, our most valuable ship instruments, compass, quadrant, sextant, etc., had escaped destruction. It seems that immediately on discovering the true character of the stranger, he had placed them in the steerage and covered them with a quantity of oakum. This the pirates somehow overlooked in their search, although they passed and repassed it continually during their visit. The brig was then put before the wind, steering north, and as by the intervention of Divine Providence, a strong wind came up, which before dark developed into a heavy squall with thunder and lightning, so we let the brig go before the fury of the wind, not taking in a stitch of canvas. We steered North until next morning, when the brig's course was altered, and we stood due West, tacking off and on several courses for a day or two, when finally a homeward course was taken which was kept up until we reached Salem October 12th 1832.

But this was not the end of the *Mexican* affair. The second part of the story was unfolded at the trial of the pirates of the *Panda,* which took place at Boston three years later.

It was then discovered what a lucky escape the crew of the *Mexican* had. After she had been set on fire and the pirate schooner was bearing away, Captain Gibert learnt for the first time that his orders to butcher all the crew had been disobeyed and he cursed and swore and threatened to turn back and make sure that no survivors should be left to tell the tale.

A hue and cry was raised and in the end the *Panda* was run to ground in the River Nazareth on the west coast of Africa, where she was discovered and recognised by Captain Trotter in H.M.S. *Curlew* whose duty it was to patrol that coast for slavers. Trotter attacked the *Panda* and took her but most of the pirates escaped to shore, though twelve of them were captured by a native chief and brought back prisoners to the English ship. They were at once ironed and despatched to England and from there were sent in another warship, the brig *Savage,* to the United States, reaching Salem in 1834.

The trial at Boston created the greatest excitement. It was not every day that twelve pirates, in chains, were to be stared at.

The trial opened on November 11th and lasted for sixteen days, when the jury found Gibert, De Soto, Ruiz and four seamen guilty but in the case of De Soto added a strong recommendation to mercy for "his generous, noble and self-sacrificing conduct" in saving the lives of seventy persons of the ship *Minerva.*

This had happened in 1831, when De Soto was master of a ship on a voyage home from Philadelphia to Havana. One day, while passing the Bahama reefs, he observed a ship ashore, with her masts and yards crowded with people. At great risk to himself and his vessel, De Soto rescued seventy-two persons, whom he took to Havana. An insurance company in Philadelphia, as a token of their appreciation of his bravery and self-sacrifice, presented him with a silver cup. For this act of heroism De Soto escaped the death penalty and was subsequently pardoned by President Andrew Jackson. The carpenter Ruiz was also reprieved on the score of insanity.

To end the story of the *Panda* and the *Mexican* we will quote from a local Boston paper, published on the day of the execution:

> Five of the pirates were executed this morning at half past ten. They were accompanied to the gallows by a Spanish priest, but none of them made any confession or expressed any contrition. They all protested their innocence to the last. Last night Captain Gibert was discovered with a piece of glass with which he intended to commit suicide. And one of the men (Boyga) cut his throat with a piece of tin, and was so much weakened by loss of blood that he was supported to the gallows, and seated in a chair on the drop when it fell. It would seem from their conduct that they retained hopes of pardon to the last moment.

With the hanging of the crew of the *Panda,* piracy as a real menace to the shipping in American waters may be said to have ended. For some years longer a few miscreants hung about Cuba and some of the out of the way West Indian islands, but the damage they did was negligible. With the continuation of peace and the gradual settled stability of the new republics it no longer paid to run the risk of piracy on the high seas.

Before passing on to other matters some mention should be made of another trial for piracy which created a great stir at the time.

The story opens in April 1821 when Aaron Smith signed on as first mate in the *Zephyr,* Captain Lumsden, bound from Kingston, Jamaica, for England. On June 29th they sailed with a cargo and seven passengers. It was soon apparent to Smith that his captain was both ignorant and obstinate, for although it was known that the safest route was by the windward passage he insisted on taking the leeward passage because it was the shorter, in spite of the well-known risk of pirates.

When they were five days out and opposite Cape Antonio, southern Cuba, a suspicious looking schooner was sighted bearing down on the *Zephyr.* As she overhauled them her decks were seen to be crowded with men. Resistance or escape being impossible Captain Lumsden at once surrendered and the English ship was soon plundered. When everything of value had been taken, the *Zephyr* was allowed to go with all her crew except Aaron Smith, whom the pirates kept to act as navigator, ordering him to steer to Rio Medias in Cuba.

At two o'clock the same afternoon they arrived at the harbour, when Smith "perceived a number of boats and canoes pulling towards the corsair; and the captain told me that he expected a great deal of company from the shore, and among others, two or three magistrates and their families and some priests, observing also that I should see several pretty Spanish girls. I remarked that I wondered he was not afraid of the magistrates. He laughed and said I did not know the Spanish character. Presents of coffee and other little things, said he, will always ensure their friendship; and from them I receive intelligence of all that occurs at Havana and know every hostile measure time enough to guard against it."

When the canoes and boats arrived alongside, two magistrates, a priest and several ladies and gentlemen came aboard and were received "in great pomp by the captain, whom they congratulated on his success." Smith was politely introduced by the captain to his guests, as his latest recruit and navigating officer, and the party descended into the cabin to drink the captain's health. One of the ladies proposed a dance, which was at once acceded to by the hospitable captain. Another of the young ladies, the daughter of a magistrate, to his great annoyance, chose Smith to be her partner. He "declined the honour rather abruptly, but the young lady, notwithstanding my apparent rudeness, pressed me to know the cause of my refusal. I told her candidly, that my thoughts were too much occupied with my melancholy situation and the misery it would occasion my wife and family, to take interest in the amusement." As a matter of fact Smith was single (though, as will appear, not unfettered), but had already pleaded to be allowed to go home in the *Zephyr* on the grounds that he had a wife and family in England. The young woman appears not to have been altogether unsophisticated, for she replied with an air of pretty naïveté: "You cannot be a married man, for I have been told that when people are married, they always endeavour to conceal it."

The young Spanish lady and the Englishman now retired to a corner to hold a long and confidential conversation on the subjects of gallantry, honour and depression of the spirits. He learned that her Christian name was Serafina but apparently never discovered her surname. She assured him that she pitied him and felt so deeply interested on his behalf that she would see if she could persuade her father, the magistrate, to procure his release.

As the evening progressed it is obvious that Smith's gloom was taking on the rosy tinge of romance. He tells us that Serafina "was young and evidently unacquainted with the world, and therefore ignorant of the artifices practised in it."

When a man begins to feel that, he is in a dangerous state. She was "unembarrassed in her manners and there was an openness and frankness in all that she said or did, that *under any other circumstances* might perhaps have had a more powerful influence." Her features were "regular and pretty, but not handsome, and her eyes sparkling, animated and full of intelligence. She was a brunette, and her whole appearance was of that description which interests the beholder almost at first sight. In her disposition she was kind, benevolent and humane, and possessed strong and warm feelings which were very manifest when she was interested in anything."

After dancing a little while, Serafina "pleaded indisposition and sat down" and asked Aaron many questions about the grandeur and richness of London until "the very great degree of feeling and interest that she betrayed on my account led me to flatter myself that I had made some tender impressions on her heart." But the tête-à-tête was rudely interrupted by the captain who came up and "ordered me to lead the young lady out immediately—a mandate that I did not dare to disobey."

In the early hours of morning the party began to break up and the captain produced presents for all his guests. The first was a trunk of linen and silk belonging to Aaron, which was presented to the priest "who was highly pleased and told the captain he might be assured of his prayers, and indeed ought to attribute his present success to the intercessions which he had made with the Virgin." No guest left the schooner without a gift—taken out of the *Zephyr*—and all returned to shore happy and contented.

At midday more boats came off bringing numbers of Cubans who had come to buy the plunder, and amongst the first to step on board were Serafina and her father. Leading Aaron to one side she told him that her mother was most anxious to meet him and that she would try to arrange for him to be allowed ashore. In return for this kindness Aaron confessed that he was not a married man, but still fancy free: "at which confession she appeared highly pleased."

The sale then began, and Smith was placed in charge of the steelyards, to weigh out the coffee to the purchasers. As neither the captain nor any of his crew understood arithmetic Smith had to make out the bills, and when all the accounts were settled and paid, a large dinner party was held. The captain, who spoke a little English, whispered to Smith that he was to make a strong mixture of spirits which would rapidly intoxicate, to produce it after dinner as an English cordial; when this had its effect on the guests he would hold an auction of the wearing apparel he had taken out of the *Zephyr*.

Smith played his part well by handing round glasses containing a mixture of wine, rum, gin, brandy and porter which the guests pronounced excellent. The result was everything the captain had hoped for. The bidding was wild, and enormous sums were paid for the most trifling articles.

While the whole company aboard was sleeping off the effects of the English cordial the lovers, for that they had now become, enjoyed a tender conversation which ended in mutual promises that if ever the opportunity came they would elope and marry.

Up to this point it would seem that many worse fates might befall a young man than to fall into the hands of Cuban pirates, but the other side of the picture now appeared.

During the next two days, while the pirates cruised in search of further prizes, a mutiny was suspected amongst some of the crew and was stamped out by the most barbaric cruelty. On the third day out a sail was sighted; this proved to be a Dutch vessel, which allowed herself to be carried back to Cuba without firing a shot. When they got into harbour news came that the magistrate, Serafina's father, had been shot and wounded by a thief, and an urgent appeal came for Smith to be sent to dress his wounds. The captain, although not at all willing to send Smith, did not like to offend his friend and patron and allowed Aaron to go ashore, under a strong guard. On examination the wound was found to be slight, but the cunning Smith pronounced it serious in order to be allowed to see his Serafina as often as possible.

On the third or fourth visit, when Aaron and Serafina had slipped into another room for a hurried word and embrace, he noticed that "her eyes and her countenance beamed love and joy and I immediately perceived she had some welcome intelligence to communicate. 'I have arranged all,' cried she passionately, throwing herself into my arms, 'the guide is in readiness, and it only remains for us to fix the time and find the opportunity.'"

This happy communication moved him profoundly: "I clasped the dear lovely creature in my arms; I was too agitated to speak and, while I held her to my heart, shed over her tears of joy and gratitude." Serafina was the first to recover her self-possession and "blushing to find herself in that situation, gently disengaged herself from my arms, and advised me to be on my guard, and not let anyone see my emotion."

The practical Serafina had arranged everything. On the second evening Aaron was to come to the house under pretence of performing a surgical operation on her father and she would have two horses and a trustworthy guide in waiting.

Alas, when the evening came, the guide turned out a traitor and the escape had to be postponed until suspicion had subsided.

Meanwhile the pirates were so successful as to bring in several more small prizes in addition to a large English ship. Once more a roaring trade went on with the local inhabitants, but the news had by now reached the ears of the Governor at Havana. A strong force of police was despatched, warning of which was thoughtfully sent to the pirates by one of the magistrates.

The police were very easily squared on arrival and obligingly disappeared. Another Cuban pirate then arrived with the cargoes out of three English vessels and a regular market was opened for stolen plunder. On board another prize, an American vessel, were two passengers, a Spanish officer and his wife. The lady was very ill, partly as a result of the voyage but partly due to her terror of the pirates. Smith, who by now had won for himself quite a reputation as a doctor and was called in to attend all cases of wounds or sickness, was ordered to treat the ailing lady, who was aboard the same vessel as himself. Under his directions the lady was soon restored to health and was most grateful.

Space on board being very limited, the three prisoners, Smith, the Spanish officer (whom Smith considered an ill-mannered brute) and his wife slept in one cabin on mattresses which were laid on the floor. This brought on a misunderstanding which might have led to trouble. The incident will best be told in Aaron Smith's own words:

The officer and his wife had a mattress prepared for them next to mine in the cabin, where they slept that night. To the latter I was very assiduous in my attentions and made up little messes of arrow root and wine, and did all in my power to administer to her comfort. For these attentions she was remarkably grateful, but manifested a degree of warmth in her gratitude that I was fearful would lead to serious consequences. One night, after we had retired to our respective mattresses, I woke about midnight, to find the lady by my side and her arms thrown round my neck fast asleep. I awakened her gently, and respectfully informed her of her mistake. She made no reply but returned to the side of her lawful spouse. I looked upon this as a mere accident arising from the contiguity of our mattresses, and therefore thought no more of it. On the following night, however, I was again roused from my slumbers by her caresses; but on this occasion the consequences were nearly fatal to me. The husband awoke just at the same instant, and missing his wife, and seeing her by my side, vociferated so loudly as to awaken both her and the captain, but I thought it most prudent for myself to counterfeit sleep. At her first awakening the Spanish lady gave a faint scream, but soon recovered her presence of mind and succeeded in pacifying her enraged husband, whom she convinced that the mistake had occurred in her sleep, and that his honour remained uninjured which he the more readily believed from my being apparently asleep.

The situation was still fraught with danger, but the pirate captain walking in to hear what was amiss and having the matter explained to him, he burst into loud laughter, which put all concerned at their ease.

Smith seems to have been one of those lucky, or unlucky, men whom all women adore. After the unfortunate episode of the mattresses he determined that his conduct should be most circumspect, though, sad to relate, he makes no mention of his duty to Serafina. Here again it is best to quote his own words:

Ever since the occurrences of that evening, the Spaniard kept a jealous eye upon his fair partner, and I was equally reserved and cautious in my communications with her. But her own imprudence had nearly rendered all my precautions abortive. I was below in the cabin, mixing some medicine for a sick man, when the lady slipped from her husband and came down. She had no sooner entered the cabin, than she seated herself on my knee and very familiarly putting her arm round my neck, gave me a kiss. The officer, who had followed her almost the instant she left him, entered at the moment and with most furious gesticulation rushed upon deck, and called the captain to inflict summary punishment upon me. The lady, however, stood my friend on this occasion as on the former, and declared that her husband must have been mistaken, as no such thing had occurred. She then explained the cause of being seen on my knee, and said she had slipped in consequence of the motion of the vessel, and I had caught her in my arms, and saved her from falling and seriously hurting herself. As there was a swell and the vessel occasionally gave a lurch, the tale had the air of probability, and the captain declared that punishment was out of the case.

The jealous husband, who had little belief in such a cock and bull story, adopted "a constrained air of satisfaction" and left the cabin muttering something about watching for an opportunity for revenge, but to the great relief of Smith the couple were given their freedom next day and left for Havana.

For several days after this the pirate ship lay at anchor and nothing of importance occurred. Then bad news came in a letter to the captain from the magistrate, warning him to get away quickly. It seemed that so many complaints of his piracies had reached the Governor of Havana that he had decided on strong measures, and was sending one hundred soldiers overland to seize the pirates, while five gunboats awaited them outside the reef if they should try to escape.

The pirates pulled out of the harbour the same night, and by daylight the ship was in a cove a little way off, surrounded by jungle which completely hid her from observation at sea.

As soon as the coast was clear the pirates left their hiding place and proceeded to cruise in search of a prize, picking up a French vessel which they gutted of everything valuable.

One stormy night, when their ship was anchored off the coast and the captain was down in his cabin with a severe attack of fever, the crew got very drunk. Smith seized the opportunity of escape. He put his nautical instruments and some biscuits in a bag, lowered himself into a fisherman's canoe which was moored astern, then cut the painter and let her drift away with the current. When far enough from the ship to be out of hearing, he hoisted sail and steered in the direction of Havana. Sailing the whole of the next day and the following night, he at last landed in Havana harbour, and thought all his troubles were over. But as he was strolling along the main street of the city, whom should he meet face to face but his old enemy the Spanish captain, marching at the head of a file of soldiers. He called to his men to seize the pirate and Smith was dragged off to the Governor's office, where the captain charged him with piracy and with having robbed him of specie to a large amount.

For several days Smith lay in a dark verminous cell in the town jail. At length he was led before a judge and put through a long cross-examination. When this was over he was put into the general prison along with four or five hundred other prisoners of all nations who earned a little money rolling cigars, which Smith also learnt to do during the seven weeks he was kept there awaiting further enquiries. At length he was brought to trial, on the charge lodged by the Spanish captain, but was remanded while the judges deliberated on his case. Then one day one of the judges came and interviewed him in the prison, and with perfect frankness told him that for the sum of one hundred doubloons he might be liberated, but otherwise he would be handed over to the Jamaican government, which had applied for him.

Smith, who had not got a penny, still less a hundred doubloons, explained to the judge that any sort of payment was out of the question. On the following day three English officers from Admiral Sir Charles Rowley's flagship, with a guard of

ESCAPE OF AARON SMITH

Spanish soldiers, conducted him from the prison on board the man-of-war *Sybille*. Here, to his utter astonishment, he was put in irons and taken below like a felon.

After a long voyage the *Sybille* arrived at Deptford where Smith had his irons knocked off and was taken to Newgate prison to await his trial for piracy at the Admiralty Sessions.

The trial, which excited great public interest, began on Friday December 20th, 1823 at the Old Bailey. A large number of witnesses were called and examined, but it was chiefly due to the evidence of one of the fair sex that the jury found in the prisoner's favour. This was a Miss Sophia Knight, "a female of considerable attractions," who on being called "was exceedingly agitated and the prisoner burst into tears as she entered the witness box." She declared she had been intimately acquainted with the prisoner for more than three years. She also said that she expected on his arrival in England to become his wife, at which stage in her evidence the witness broke down and wept. The prisoner, "who appeared deeply affected," wept also. The jury, equally moved, returned a verdict of not guilty.

Whether the loyal Miss Knight married her Aaron, or whether (which is most unlikely) he returned to his Serafina, history does not record.*

* The above account of Aaron Smith's adventures is taken from his book "The Atrocities of the Pirates" from the edition published in 1929 by the Golden Cockerill Press.

BOOK IV

THE PIRATES OF THE EAST

CHAPTER I

THE AFRICAN COAST

THE rise of piracy along the west coast of Africa seems to have occurred at a comparatively late date; at least the records are quite recent. Since the time of Da Gama's expedition in 1498 a steady trade had gone on between Portugal and the East by way of the Cape of Good Hope. The records of piracy on this route are vague until the eighteenth century when the marauders described in Johnson's pirates crossed over to try their luck in these waters when the other shore of the Atlantic was becoming uncomfortably hot for them. But the most famous name associated with the eastern route to the Indies belongs to the nineteenth century — that of Benito de Soto (not to be confused with Bernardo de Soto of *Panda* fame), a native of Corunna, who was first heard of as mate of a Portuguese slaver, the *Defensor de Pedro,* which sailed from Buenos Aires for the Guinea coast in November 1827.

The captain was an officer of the Portuguese Royal Navy, Dom Pedro de Maria de Susa Sarmiento, who had been compelled to take on forty hands in Brazil. Not until too late did he discover that a dozen of them were Cuban pirates.

They had not been long at sea before De Soto began to sound some of his companions and discovered that a good number were quite ready to fall in with his idea of seizing the ship and returning to piracy. The opportunity came in January, when the captain, the first mate and some of the men not in the conspiracy were on shore at Mina on the Guinea coast. Those on board who refused to join the mutiny were turned adrift in a small boat, and all were drowned.

De Soto, altering the name of the ship to the *Black Joke,* then steered for Ascension Island and on February 13th, 1828 sighted the *Morning Star,* Captain Souley, which was returning to England from Ceylon. She had on board, besides a valuable cargo of cinnamon and coffee, a large number of passengers including twenty-five English soldiers who had been invalided home, their wives, and several civilians. The owner was a Quaker named Tindall, who had refused to arm the ship because of his principles.

Although the *Morning Star* was a good sailor the *Black Joke,* an even better one, soon overhauled her and fired a shot across her bows to bring her to. Captain Souley ignored this hint, but when a shower of canister followed he considered it wiser to take notice of it. The pirate then lowered the English ensign which he had been flying and ran up in its place the colours of the Republic of Columbia. De Soto ordered a boat to bring the captain and his papers but, instead, the second mate rowed over with a sailor and three of the soldiers. When the mate and the sailor gained the deck they found De Soto in a towering rage because the *Morning Star* had given him such a long chase, and he ordered them to return at once and bring the captain or his gunners would sink the East Indiaman.

When the captain arrived he was instantly put to death and the others already on board the *Black Joke* were detained, while a Frenchman, St. Cyr Barbazon, was sent across with some men to kill everyone on board the *Morning Star.*

The order was not literally carried out, but only those who took refuge below escaped. In a pandemonium of curses and screams the pirates slashed left and right amongst the unresisting crew and passengers who had remained on deck. The pirates then plundered the ship of money, plate, jewels, nautical instruments and everything else of value, which they sent back to their own vessel. When they had done with killing and looting they sat down in the cabin and ordered the steward to serve them with food and drink. The meal rapidly became an orgy of drunkenness and worse; it was only brought to an end by De Soto bawling out to know why his men did not come back, his angry voice rising above the shrieks of the women who had been forced to enter the cabin and the pounding of the men in the hold in which they had been battened down.

Before leaving Barbazon cut the rigging of the *Morning Star,* sawed down the masts and bored holes in her bottom to make her sink. When the last of the savages had gone and the *Black Joke* was hull-down on the horizon some of the women managed to free the men. They found themselves in a hopeless position. The ship was filling rapidly and they appeared to have missed one form of death only to find another. Fortunately they were able, by constant work at the pumps, to keep the vessel afloat until next morning, when they were rescued by another English ship, also homeward bound.

The incident made a tremendous stir, not only in England but throughout Europe. One result of it was that thereafter all Mr. Tindall's ships were more heavily armed than those of any other merchant.

De Soto continued on his way, taking several ships in the neighbourhood of the Azores and in all cases killing and drowning their crews. Soon the *Black Joke* had become such a menace to all merchant shipping that home coming vessels from India were ordered to collect at St. Helena and from there sail in convoy for mutual protection.

Presently the pirates had so much plunder that they decided to go to Spain to sell it and enjoy themselves. In his native port of Corunna, De Soto procured false papers and with them proceeded to Cadiz, where he expected to find a good market for his plunder. It was dark when the *Black Joke* arrived off the city, so they anchored for the night outside, intending to go into the harbour the next morning, but the wind shifted to the west and suddenly began to blow a heavy gale towards the land. The pirate ship was driven on to the rocks, but with dawn the gale dropped and the crew were able to reach shore safely in their boats.

De Soto, finding his plans upset, formulated a new scheme. He instructed his men in a story, which he hoped would sound well in the ears of the officials at Cadiz, to the effect that they were honest merchantmen whose captain had been drowned, and they now merely begged permission to sell the wreck. Then they entered Cadiz and presented themselves to the officer of the Marine, who received their tale with sympathy. De Soto soon found a merchant who was willing to buy the wreck for one thousand seven hundred and fifty dollars. The contract was duly signed, but the money had not been paid over when some inconsistency in the pirates' account of themselves aroused suspicion and six of them were arrested. De Soto and one of his crew escaped in time and took refuge in the neutral ground that separated Spain from Gibraltar.

As soon as the hue and cry for the fugitives had subsided De Soto managed to enter the garrison in disguise and with a false pass and took up his residence at a small tavern in a narrow lane. Feeling himself to be secure in Gibraltar the pirate cut quite a fine figure, for according to one who knew him then, "he dressed expensively — generally wore a white hat of the best English variety, silk stockings, white trowsers and blue frock coat. His whiskers were large and bushy, and his hair, which was very black, profuse, long and naturally curled, was much in the style of a London preacher of prophetic and anti-poetic notoriety. He was deeply browned by the sun and had the air and gait expressive of his bold, enterprising and desperate mind." *

The first person to have any suspicions about this dashing visitor to Gibraltar was the maid of the tavern, who told her master that she found a dirk beneath the gentleman's pillow each morning when she made his bed. An examination of his room was made, during which were found among other incriminating articles a trunk containing clothes belonging to some of the passengers in the *Morning Star* and a pocket-book in the ill-fated captain's handwriting. De Soto was at once arrested, tried before the Governor, Sir George Don, found guilty and condemned to death.

Up to the day of his execution he persisted in asserting his innocence, but "the awful voice of religion at length subdued

* "Pirates' Own Book."

him" and he made a full confession of his crimes and became penitent. One who was a witness of his execution tells us:

> I believe there never was a more contrite man than he appeared to be; yet there were no drivilling fears upon him—he walked firmly at the tail of the fatal cart, gazing sometimes at his coffin, sometimes at the crucifix which he held in his hand. The symbol of divinity he frequently pressed to his lips, repeated the prayers spoken in his ear by the attendant clergyman, and seemed regardless of everything but the world to come.

When the procession reached the gallows by the waterside the pirate mounted the cart, but finding the halter too high for his neck jumped up on his coffin and placed his head in the noose. Then, as he saw the first turn of the cartwheels, he cried out, "*Adios, todos*—goodbye, everybody," and fell forward.

After passing south of St. Helena there was little risk of meeting pirates until the East Indiamen had rounded the Cape of Good Hope, when they would sail well to the east to avoid another pirate haunt, the island of Madagascar, after which they would be fairly safe until within fifty miles or so of the Malabar coast.

The expedition of Captain Woodes Rogers to New Providence in the Bahamas in 1718 broke up that notorious nest of pirates. Some were hanged and the rest, about two thousand in number, surrendered and received the royal pardon. A few of the hardest cases, however, fled to the east and established new headquarters at Madagascar, soon converting the island into as important a pirate base as the Bahamas had ever been.

By 1721 their depredations on British shipping, particularly that of the East India Company, had become so serious that the English Government sent out a squadron to dislodge them. The choice of the commander could scarcely have been more unfortunate. Commodore Thomas Matthews had the single quality of bravery but apart from that he was "void of common sense, good manners, or knowledge of the world." * Apart from his intellectual deficiencies he was both truculent and

* "Horace Mann to Horace Walpole."

dishonest. On the voyage out in the *Lion,* Matthews called at St. Augustine's Bay, Madagascar, to look for pirates. Observing none at a first glance, instead of waiting for his two other ships, the *Salisbury* and the *Exeter,* to assist him, Matthews went on to Bombay. Before leaving he entrusted to the natives a letter for Captain Cockburn of the *Salisbury,* in which he gave full particulars of the squadron's plans. Scarcely had Matthews left when two notorious pirates, Taylor and La Bouche, arrived, read the letter and immediately sent out a general warning to all the pirates in the vicinity.

On his arrival in Bombay Matthews at once started a violent quarrel with the Governor as to who should fire the first salute. His overbearing conduct offended all the East India Company's officials, and duels between his officers and those of the Bombay Marine were almost of daily occurrence. His arrival should have been most opportune, since plans had been completed for a joint attack by the English and Portuguese on the great pirate Angria at Alibag. The failure of this attack, for which Matthews was largely to blame, will be described in the next chapter.

After this fiasco Matthews devoted himself entirely to private trade and took good care to leave the pirates severely alone. He coasted about for a year, quarrelling with everybody he met, and then decided to return to Madagascar and the duty he had been sent out to perform.

On reaching Carpenter's Bay in Mauritius, Matthews found a message from the pirates, "written on Captain Carpenter's tomb with a piece of charcoal," to say that they had got tired of waiting for him and had gone to Fort Dauphin. "This made us hurry with all speed for that Port," writes Clement Downing, "in hopes to have met with them, it being reported that they were full of Riches, which put Vigour and Courage in the Heart of every Man and Boy in the whole squadron." *

At Bourbon they sold a quantity of arrack, for which the French paid handsomely. Eventually the squadron reached St. Mary's Island, "the Place Capt. Avery resorted to and then fortified the same very strongly, tho' it was much run to Ruin

* Clement Downing, "History of the Indian Wars," 1737.

now, by reason of the Negroes' Neglect and the Pirates not regarding it as formerly."

They found no pirates, but came across the wrecks of several merchant ships which had been run ashore by them, while the beach was strewn with their cargoes; china ware, drugs and spices. In some places the sailors waded up to their knees in cinnamon, cloves and pepper. Presently the local king arrived accompanied by his two daughters, and they were invited on board. "The king offered the Captain his two Daughters as a Present, being what they used to offer amongst the Pyrates; for they thought we were all alike; But tho' the Captain refused this kind offer, the Ladies were accepted by some of our Officers, who paid dear enough for the Honour, for it cost one of them his Life, and the other was well Peper'd."

The King made the English officer swear friendship by drinking each other's healths in a glass of salt water mixed with gunpowder, "it being the Ceremony they had learned from the Pyrates."

Another picturesque visitor to pay them his respects was a white man and a full-blooded pirate, James Plantain, born at Chocolate Hole in Jamaica. He arrived fully armed, with a guard of twenty natives. He owned a large tract of the countryside and was known to the natives as the King of Ranter Bay. From him Matthews received the interesting news that the famous pirate Taylor, for whom he was searching, was hiding in the interior. Instead of arresting Plantain, Matthews did a very good business deal with him in stolen plunder, selling him hats, shoes, stockings and arrack, for which the King of Ranter Bay paid a good price in gold and diamonds.

In spite of his notions as to piracy, John Plantain showed himself an honester man than Matthews. Having paid liberally for the things he had bought, he left the hogsheads of wine and arrack on the beach under a small guard. As soon as his back was turned, Matthews manned his boats, brought off all the liquor he had been paid for, and some of the native guard as well. After which notable achievement he sailed away for Bengal, consoling himself with the thought that he was not like one of "those vile pirates, who, after committing many evil actions, had settled down among a parcel of heathens to indulge themselves in all sorts of vice." *

This James Plantain, after making his fortune at piracy, had returned to Madagascar where he lived in a fortified castle, with a Scotsman and a Dane. His history is told in full by Clement Downing, and only a sketch of his life and activities will be given here.

While still little more than a lad, it had been discovered that "being of a roving Disposition, he could not bear being under any restraint"; this, combined with his love for the sea, caused him very soon to find his proper calling. Starting his piratical career from Rhode Island, young Plantain served his apprenticeship under a good master, Captain John Williams of the *Terrible,* and sailed under him to Guinea. Here they joined up with other pirates and took a number of rich prizes. The pirate captain England was in command of one of the ships, the *Victory,* while the famous Bartholomew Roberts commanded another.

A quarrel sprang up between England's followers and Roberts's as to where they should go next, and in the end they separated. Plantain sailed in the *Fancy* to Madagascar, where the pirates "were very joyfully received by the King." They stopped here a while and then went on to Johanna, where they were surprised to find two Company's ships, the *Cassandra* and *Greenwich,* the former commanded by a Captain Macree and the latter by a Captain Kirby, which had put in for water on the voyage to Bombay: their cargo consisted of money, the yearly investment for Bombay and Surat.

The two Company's captains decided to attack the two pirate ships, and they looked forward to a handsome reward from the Company for the capture of two such notorious pirates as England and Taylor. The cables were cut and the two East Indiamen stood out to sea, but the fight did not begin till next morning, when the wind rose.

The pirates now closed, flying a black flag with skull and cross-bones at the main, a red flag at the fore and the cross of

* J. Biddulph, "Pirates of Malabar," 1907.

St. George at the ensign staff. Macree opened fire but to his surprise and indignation his consort, the *Greenwich,* sailed away and left him to fight alone.

Although Macree had a fine new ship and a crew of first-class fighting men, the odds against him were too great. After three hours' furious bombardment, he saw that his only chance of escape was to run his ship ashore, although, had Kirby stood by him, both the pirates would, without doubt, have been defeated and captured. Already thirteen men on the *Cassandra* had been killed, and twenty-four wounded, including the gallant captain. Those who could swim reached the shore, but several too badly wounded to leave the ship were butchered by the pirates. Macree and his survivors hurried inland and were kindly received by the natives, who refused to surrender them.

After a few days the pirates' wrath abated, partly no doubt because they had captured a fine new ship with seventy-five thousand pounds in hard cash on board, and they invited Macree to a peaceful meeting. When he arrived he was well received by England and most of the pirates, although others, headed by the bloodthirsty Taylor, were for shooting him.

This raised a violent quarrel when all of a sudden a fierce-looking pirate, "with a terrible pair of whiskers and a wooden leg, being stuck round with pistols, like the man in the Almanack with Darts," * spoke up, with many oaths, in favour of sparing Macree, and taking him by the hand swore to make mincemeat of the first man that hurt him, protesting that Macree was an honest fellow, and he had formerly sailed with him.

After a lot of talking and even more punch drinking, it was agreed to give Macree the "Fancy" and let him go, much to the anger of Taylor. After forty-eight days of terrible suffering, almost naked and half starved, Macree and his men reached Bombay.

In the meanwhile the pirates sailed to the Malabar coast,

* The original of Stevenson's one-legged pirate John Silver.

where they captured several big Portuguese and Moorish vessels, which they carried back to Madagascar. Here they were given the letter left by Matthews so they thought it wise to hide themselves for a while.

James Plantain, by now a rich man, decided to retire. He built himself a fort, settled down to rule as King of Ranters Bay and was much beloved by his coloured subjects, who composed and sang songs in his praise. He had a small army of coloured soldiers, with which he made raids on the cattle of the neighbouring kings.

Plantain had "many wives whom he kept in great subjection, and after the English manner, called them Moll, Kate, Sue and Pegg. These Women were dressed in the richest silks, and some of them had Diamond Necklaces." Nevertheless, in spite of this seraglio, the King of Ranter Bay cast a loving and envious eye upon the granddaughter of the King of Messaleage, a neighbouring native potentate. This princess had white blood in her veins, being said to be the daughter of an English pirate, and was named Eleanora Brown, after her father. She had pleasant manners and could speak a little English. Downing, who had met her and Plantain, tells us that the latter, "being desirous of having a Lady of *English* Extraction, sent to the King of Messaleage (whom the Pyrates called Long Dick, or King Dick) to demand his Granddaughter for a Wife."

This request was flatly refused by King Dick, so the infatuated Plantain waged a bloody war on the lady's grandfather, which ended at last in victory for the ex-pirate and dreadful tortures for all his white captives. But disappointment was in store, for "the Lady, on whose account these Wars were begun, prov'd to be with Child by one of the Englishmen which Plantain had murdered. This so enraged Plantain that he ordered King Dick to be put to the same cruel Death as the English and Dutchmen had suffered." However, after burning and plundering the late monarch's dominions, Plantain returned to Ranter Bay, "bringing the lady before mention'd with him, which he accounted the chief Trophy of his Victory, who tho' she was with Child, he accepted of, and was much enamoured of her."

Certainly Eleanora Brown seems to have been above the ordinary pirate's wife of Madagascar for her late father "had taught her the Creed, the Lord's Prayer, and the ten Commandments and gave her an insight into the Christian Faith," all of which must have been a great consolation to James Plantain. On arrival at his fortress "he made a grand Entertainment and gave her the whole Government of his Household Affairs, discharging several of his other Wives." We get a delightful insight into the domestic life of the Plantains when we learn that the Queen of Ranter Bay "would often talk to him concerning Religion, ask him after God, and say her Prayers Night and Morning; on which account, Plantain used to say he had now got a religious wife, but yet took what she said in good part." This benevolent husband dressed his new wife in "the richest Jewels and Diamonds he had, and gave her twenty Girl Slaves to wait on her."

But sterner calls had to be answered, for the King of Ranter Bay aspired to be king of the whole of Madagascar, which, after many fierce and bloody wars, he did actually become. We can well believe that on such an occasion "he made several great and splendid Entertainments to which he invited all the Dutch, French and English on the Island." Amongst the rest was Captain England, "who was at that time very weak, and did not live above a month, and t'was said his Death was occasion'd by the severe Stings of his Conscience for his wicked Course of Life," although our historian hurries to add that "this is a thing that seldom happens to those sort of men."

The new King of Madagascar soon, we learn, grew "weary of his Kingship, and resolved to quit his Territories — and to leave the Natives in quiet possession of their Properties." The truth was that Plantain saw clear evidence of an approaching native rebellion. So he built a sloop and, with one wife, the faithful Nelly, set sail for the Malabar coast, where they were joyfully received by Angria, who on learning "what course of Life Plantain had lived, and what a valiant fighting man he was, entertained him in a Magnificent manner."

This is the last we hear of this odd character; whether he died of disease, drink, or wounds in Angria's service, or whether he lived to return to Chocolate Hole, will probably for ever remain a secret.

CHAPTER II

THE PIRATES OF MALABAR

The west coast of India between Bombay and Cochin, known to sailors as the Malabar coast, produced at the end of the seventeenth century a dynasty of pirates who acquired almost a monopoly of the business, and who made themselves so powerful that for sixty years the strength of the East India Company, even with the intermittent support of the royal navy, was unable to subdue them. The control of the federation rested in the hands of the native Mahratta family of Angria, but their employees were by no means all Indians. Many of the worst of them were Europeans, especially English, attracted to both the Red Sea and the Indian Ocean by stories of the fabulous spoils taken by Avery.

The first of the family of Angria to exercise recognised command was Kanhoji or Conajee, who in about 1698 became admiral of the Maratha navy. Kanhoji had gradually succeeded in making himself independent of his overlords at Poona and became master of the whole coast for some three hundred miles south of Bombay. Along this coast he built a series of forts at Alibag, Severndroog and Vijaydroog, whence he issued forth as a veritable pirate king to wage war on all shipping, but particularly on that of the East India Company.

There came a time when the Company's government at Bombay, equally slow to anger and to action, felt constrained to inform Kanhoji that his acts of piracy on their vessels could not continue unpunished. To this he simply replied that he would give the English cause to remember the name of Kanhoji Angria. He carried out his threat so thoroughly that in 1704 a special emissary was sent to warn him that he could not be permitted to search vessels in Bombay waters, "to which he sent a defiant answer that he had done many benefits to the

English, who had broken faith with him, and henceforth he would seize their vessels wherever he could find them." * The Company was reduced to complaints to the directors at home, to the effect that Kanhoji was able to take any European ship except the largest, that in fact he seized "all along the coast from Surat to Debul . . . all private merchant vessels he meets." †

A few years later Kanhoji had seized and fortified an island within sight of Bombay itself, so that with his fleet of powerful ships, some carrying as many as forty guns and most of them commanded by experienced European seamen, as a rule Hollanders, he became a serious menace to the town. The defences of Bombay were of the most primitive kind — when the directors ordered it to be fortified the Bombay Council excused themselves with the remark: "We know that it is natural to engineers to contrive curiosities that are very expensive" and were content to put up a few martello towers along the shore.

The pirates were now able to arrest any ship they chose as it was entering or leaving the harbour. The Company, frightened, sent a strong fleet of twenty galliots by way of reprisal. The result is told laconically in the official record of the expedition: "9th June. — Returned our gallivats, having by mismanagement of the chief officer lost about 50 men and destroyed one town of Angria's."

When it is considered, however, what riffraff went to make up the officers and men of the Company's underpaid and under-disciplined army, it is wonderful that they ever came off victors at all. The meanness of the Directors is almost unbelievable. They once issued an order forbidding the waste of gunpowder at exercise with the single exception that "sometimes the men must be used to firing, lest in time of action they should start at the noise or the recoil of their arms."

But in 1715 a new and strong Governor of Bombay was appointed, Charles Boone, a man of very different stamp from his weak and venal predecessors, who were interested chiefly in feathering their own nests. His first act was to build a

* J. Biddulph, "Malabar Pirates."

† R. G. Gordon, I.C.S., Bombay.

strong wall right round the settlement. He then constructed ships of war, but found great difficulty in manning them, for the Company paid its sailors such miserable wages that the better of them preferred to take service with Angria. Nevertheless Boone had soon at his disposal a fine fleet of nineteen frigates, yawls, ketches and rowing galleys, with which he might have accomplished the suppression of the pirates but for the incompetence and indiscipline of his subordinates.

When Commodore Matthews arrived at Bombay from Madagascar in 1721 he found that Boone had already arranged a strong coalition with the Portuguese for a joint attack on the Malabar pests. But Matthews's temper irritated the Portuguese commander, the Portuguese themselves bolted and ran after the first shots when attacking Angria at Colaba, and the expedition broke down in bickerings as to who was to blame. Matthews struck the Portuguese commander over the mouth with his cane, which disrupted the alliance on the spot.

This expedition was to have been the crowning event of Boone's governorship. He was now retiring disappointed, yet somehow he had contrived to do more damage to the pirates on both the Malabar and the Red Sea than any of his predecessors, despite the difficulty put in his way by intriguing councillors and insubordinate lieutenants. On January 9th 1722 he sailed for England. As he proceeded down the coast his three ships were attacked by Angria's squadron but he beat it off. When near Anjediva he got in his last blow by surprising the pirates plundering a ship, which he rescued, at the same time capturing one of the pirates' grabs.

Kanhoji Angria died in 1729, leaving five sons to quarrel over his property. The Portuguese allied themselves first to one brother and then to another, but paved the way for their own downfall on the west coast of India by overlooking the winning brother, Tulaji. This son finally established himself firmly as his father's successor and during most of the rest of the century the battle for the control of the Indian waters lay between him and the English, the power of the Dutch and the French beginning to wane as well as that of the Portuguese.

The internecine quarrels of the Mahrattas gave the East

India Company a respite of twenty years. In the meantime they were building and arming their ships on the same lines as men of war, and were able to put up a good fight if need be. Several times when attacked they took the offensive and sank the Indian grabs before the action was concluded.

On the rise of Tulaji Angria however, the old menace was renewed in all its strength. His first enterprise was to attack an English fleet under convoy and carry off five sailing vessels from under the guns of two warships. In 1749 he captured the *Restoration,* the best ship in the Bombay service, after a fight from midday to dark which did little credit to the gunnery and discipline of the British vessel.

Tulaji now reigned supreme up and down the coast from Cutch to Cochin, and but for the assistance of four men of war under Commodore Lisle, sent especially from Madras to protect Bombay, all trade would have been brought to a standstill. Nevertheless Tulaji's swift sailing vessels often followed the convoyed fleets for days, waiting like a pack of wolves to snap up any straggler. Not until the Company had learnt how essential it was to keep ships for fighting purposes only and not, as hitherto, make the same vessel fight and carry cargo, was any degree of safety attained.

The English were by no means the only sufferers from the pirates of Malabar. The Portuguese and Dutch lost increasingly large numbers of their merchant vessels every year, and the Dutch suffered the severest loss of all in 1754 when a ship loaded with ammunition was taken and two others were blown up after a furious fight in which Tulaji had two large grabs sunk and a great number of men killed.

With the extension of the English power over the whole of India following the defeat of the French, many of the lesser pirate chiefs were glad to make terms with the Bombay government. Even the proud Tulaji sent an agent to propose peace. The conditions he offered would have been readily accepted in his father's time, but now the Council was in a far stronger position, so that in answer to Tulaji's proposal to grant passes to the Company's ships it sent back the answer: "Can you imagine that the English will ever submit to take passes from any Indian nation? This we cannot do. We grant passes, but would take none from anybody."

Instead, an agreement was entered into between the Council and the Mahrattas not under Tulaji's sway to attack him simultaneously by land and sea. The naval force was to be under the command of Commodore William James, who, since his arrival in 1751, had rendered good service against the Malabar pirates and was now to win himself enduring glory.

On March 22nd 1755 Commodore James sailed in the *Protector,* forty guns, in company with the *Swallow,* 16 guns, and the *Viper,* a bomb-ketch, and a prahu, the *Triumph.* Two days out he was joined by the fleet of the allies, which consisted of some fifty craft, large and small. On the 29th Severndroog, Tulaji's chief stronghold, was sighted, with the pirates' fleet coming out. The signal to chase was at once made, but the Mahratta vessels, which were faster sailors than James's, hung back and by evening his allies were hull down astern.

The Angrians were far from wanting to fight, even with James's small squadron, and could be seen hanging out their turbans and clothing to catch every breath of wind. All the following day the chase continued, the *Protector* gradually outsailing her consorts, while the Mahratta fleet had long ago dropped out of sight. Finding that further pursuit was useless, the Commodore altered his course and stood for Severndroog. This town stood on a rocky inlet at the end of a peninsula and was protected by "the Golden Fortress," a bastion with walls fifty feet in height. To the landward side was another strong fort, armed with forty-five guns, while to the south were two smaller forts.

The remarkable action which followed is well described in "The Pirates of Malabar":

James at once saw that the reduction of the different forts by the Mahratta troops would be a matter of months, even if he was able to keep out succour from the sea, which the monsoon would render impossible, so, in spite of the Council's order, he resolved on taking matters into his own hands. He had been brought up in a good school, and knew that, to match a ship against a fort with success, it was necessary to get as close as possible and overpower it with weight of metal. After taking the necessary soundings, on the 21st of April he stood in to four fathom water, taking with him the *Viper* and *Triumph,* and bombarded Severndroog fort. The Mahratta fleet gave no assistance so the *Swallow* was detached to guard the Southern entrance.

All day long the cannonade continued, till a heavy swell setting into the harbour in the evening obliged a cessation of fire. The fort fired briskly in return, but did little damage, while the Mahratta fleet lay off out of range, idle spectators of the conflict. At night there came on board the *Protector* a deserter from the fort, who reported that the Governor had been killed and a good deal of damage done. He told them that it was impossible to breach the site on which the *Protector's* fire was directed as it was all solid rock.

In the morning the *Protector* weighed and ran in again, James placing his ships between Severndroog and Gova. The flagship engaged Severndroog so closely that, by the small-arm fire of the men in the tops, and by firing two or three upper deck guns at a time instead of in broadsides, the Severndroog gunners were hardly able to return a shot. With her lower deck guns on the other side the *Protector* cannonaded the mainland forts, which also received the attention of the *Viper* and the *Triumph.* It would be difficult to find a parallel to this instance of a single ship and two bomb-ketches successfully engaging four forts at once, that far out-numbered them in guns; but so good were James' arrangements that neither his ships nor his men suffered harm. Soon after mid-day a magazine exploded in Severndroog, the conflagration spread and before long, men, women and children were seen taking to their boats and escaping to the mainland. Numbers of them were intercepted and taken by the *Swallow* and the Mahratta gallivats. The bombardment of the mainland forts was continued till night, and resumed the following morning, till about 10 o'clock, when all three hauled down their colours. Thus, in forty eight hours, did James, by his vigorous action reduce this Angrian stronghold, which was second only to Gheriah in strength, and without losing a single man.

At Shooters Hill on Woolwich Common there still stands a tall monument, Severndroog Tower, built by Commodore James's widow to the memory of her illustrious husband's feat, and known as "Lady James's Folly."

This far seen monumental tow'r
Records the achievements of the brave,
And Angria's subjugated pow'r,
*Who plundered on the Eastern wave.**

Emboldened by their surprising success at Severndroog the Bombay Council decided to make a similar attempt on the even stronger pirate fortress at Gheriah. On February 11th there assembled off Gheriah the most powerful naval force that had ever left Bombay. In addition to the Company's fleet of eighteen vessels, under the command of Commodore James, there was a squadron of six men of war under Rear-Admiral Watson, four of which were line-of-battle ships. For the land fighting, eight hundred European and six hundred native troops were carried, who were under the command of the immortal Robert Clive.

Part of the instructions of the Council to the naval and military commanders are of interest; they run as follows:

It is probable that Torlajee Angria may offer to capitulate, and possibly offer a sum of money, but you are to consider that this fellow is not on a footing with any prince in the known world, he being a pirate in whom no confidence can be put, not only taking, burning, and destroying ships of all nations, but even the vessels belonging to the natives, which have his own passes, and for which he has annually collected large sums of money. Should he offer any sum of money it must be a very great one that will pay us for the many rich ships he has taken (which we can't enumerate), besides the innumerable other smaller vessels.

Above all the Council wished to get Tulaji, dead or alive, into their own hands, for as long as he was alive and free he was certain to cause mischief.

On reaching Gheriah the allied Mahratta army was found encamped opposite it and a messenger came off to report that with a little patience the fort would surrender without a shot being fired, as Tulaji was in the camp and ready to treat. This did not at all suit the English, who knew that the Mahrat-

* Robert Bloomfield, poet and maker of Æolian harps.

tas were only concerned with the booty, which would be divided if the fort surrendered peaceably, whereas if it were taken by arms the spoils would go to the victorious English. Despite the tender of a bribe Admiral Watson declined to treat and summoned the fort to surrender without conditions. At half past one in the afternoon a refusal was sent back and the signal was given for the fleet to stand into the harbour, across whose mouth Tulaji's grabs were drawn up. Amongst his fleet of fifty-eight warships of all sizes was the *Restoration,* which had been captured six years before.

A terrific bombardment was opened by the English fleet, the shells falling so heavily into the fort that it was impossible for the pirates to work their guns. "In that February afternoon many a cruel outrage was expiated under the hail of iron. After two hours' firing a shell set the *Restoration* on fire; it spread to the grabs and before long Angria's fleet, which had been the terror of the coast for half a century, was in a blaze."

Late in the afternoon Clive landed at the head of his troops and took up a position a mile and a half from the fort, where he was joined by the Mahrattas. All through the night the bomb-ketches continued their deadly work, but still the fort held out. The burning ships of the pirate fleet set fire to the bazaars and warehouses, and provided the English gunners with perfect illumination.

Early next morning Admiral Watson sent another flag of truce, but the defenders still refused to yield, so the line-of-battle ships were warped in and the bombardment was reopened while Clive attacked on the land side. At four o'clock in the afternoon a great explosion took place within the fort, followed by the hoisting of a white flag. An officer was sent ashore but Tulaji still refused unconditional surrender. The fire was reopened once more and twenty minutes later the pirate flag was hauled down for good.

One hundred and thirty thousand pounds worth of gold, silver and jewels was secured in the fort and divided between the land and sea forces, much to the chagrin of the Mahrattas, who, although they had done nothing to deserve it, considered that they should have had a share of the spoils. But Tulaji himself surrendered to them and not to the English and was held a prisoner for the rest of his life, so that he never had another chance of doing harm to native or foreign sailors. With his fall and the capture of Gheriah ended for all practical purposes the reign of the Malabar pirates.

CHAPTER III

THE PIRATE COAST

THE country of Arabia ends towards the east with the great peninsula of Oman. It is bounded on the north by the Gulf of Persia, which is entered from the Arabian Sea through the narrow straits of Ormuz. As the sailor approaches these straits from the Gulf of Oman he sees on his left hand a low indented shore known to sailors for hundreds of years as the dreaded Pirate Coast. It extends approximately a hundred and fifty miles.

These waters were probably the cradle of navigation and, as a natural consequence, of piracy. From their geographical position they became the first link in the commerce between the East and the West. When the merchandise of the East began to be carried to the West, it was the Arabs of the Oman who brought it to Arabia from India. This intercourse is already mentioned in the monumental records of Nineveh, Babylon and Egypt which take us back to about 5000 B.C. The Arabs of this coast, originally fishermen, gradually rowed or sailed their small craft further and further along the Arabian shores. As they became more skilled in shipbuilding and navigation, they dared sail out of sight of land and ultimately make for distant countries.

By the ninth century the Muscat Arabs were trading with Canton in China and had their merchants settled at such remote places as Siam, Java and Sumatra. The goods they brought back to the Gulf of Persia were the spices, incense, silks and other luxuries of the Far East. It was the Omanis who supplied the Egyptians with myrrh and spices for the embalming of their dead.

The merchandise brought from India was reshipped at Omani, up the Persian Gulf, and then taken up the Euphrates to Babylon, whence it was carried by caravans across the desert to the Mediterranean. The latter part of the carriage and trade was in the hands of the Phœnicians who, although amongst the earliest of navigators, were preceded by thousands of years by the Arabs.

It was not until much later, perhaps somewhere about 500 B.C., that the Red Sea began to compete seriously with the Persian Gulf as a channel for the carriage of Eastern goods to Europe.

There were several ocean sailing tribes on the Pirate Coast, but the most powerful and the one which played the biggest part in piracy were the fierce Joasmees, who first became known to Europeans when the Portuguese merchant ships began to penetrate the Straits of Ormuz into the Persian Gulf during the sixteenth century.

It was not unnatural that this coast, indented from end to end with creeks, lagoons and breakwaters, and inhabited by a race with strong predatory instincts, should have become a nest of sea robbers as soon as there were foreign vessels to be preyed upon. The chief town of the Joasmees was Ras-al-Khyma, which lingered on until late in the nineteenth century as one of the last centres of the slave trade.

The activities of the Joasmees began to assume a more than local importance in December 1778, when six of their dhows attacked an English vessel bearing official despatches in the Gulf of Persia and, after a stubborn fight lasting three days, captured and took her to Ras-al-Khyma. Emboldened by this success they repeated the feat on two English ships in the following year.

By October 1797 their contempt for the European was shown in a surprising attack, not on a defenceless merchantman but on an English cruiser, the *Viper,* which was lying in the harbour of Bushire. She had anchored close to a fleet of Joasmee dhows, whereupon the Joasmee admiral promptly called upon the agent of the East India Company in the town, and after many protestations of friendship asked for a supply of powder and shot which, with incredible stupidity, the agent ordered Captain Carruthers of the *Viper* to supply.

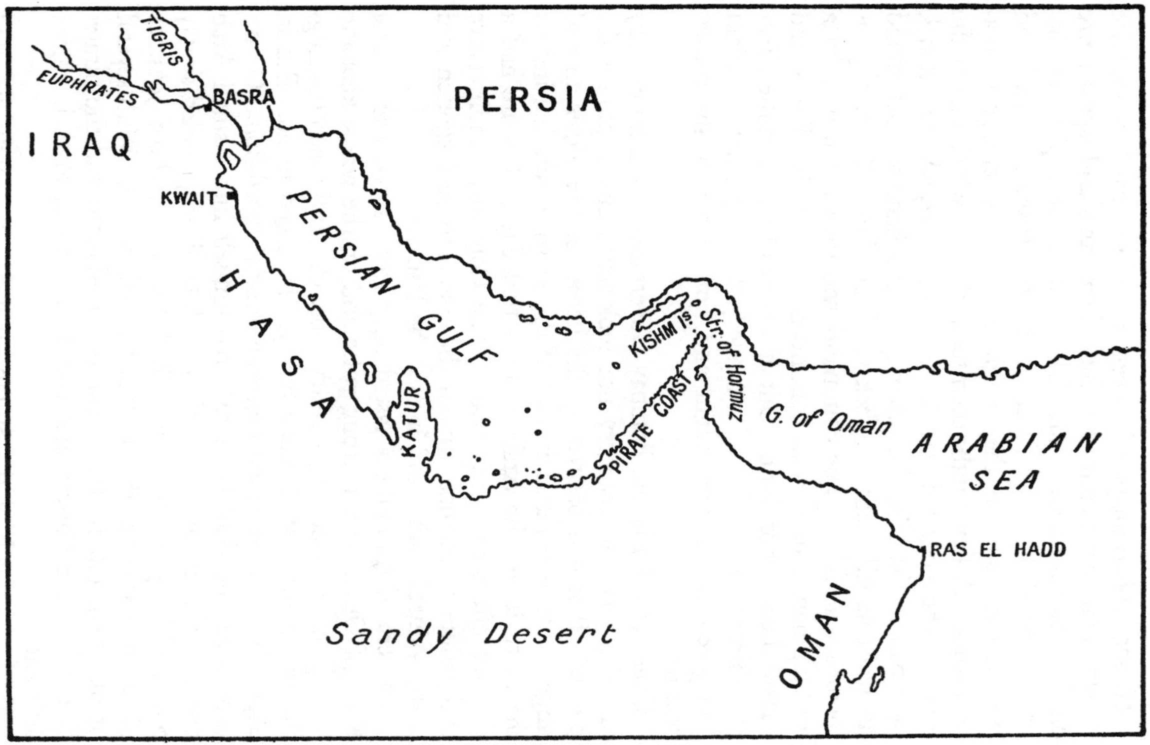

THE PIRATE COAST AND THE PERSIAN GULF

No sooner had the powder been carried on board the Joasmee dhows than they rammed it into their guns and opened fire on the English man-of-war. The crew of the *Viper* were below at breakfast at the time, but at once rushed on deck and cut the cable so that they might have an advantage in manœuvring. A fierce fight then took place in which one of the earliest to be wounded was Captain Carruthers, who was struck by a ball in the loin "but after girding a handkerchief round his waist he still kept the deck until, another ball entering his forehead, he fell." The command was then taken over by a midshipman, Salter, who continued to fight the dhows and chased them out of sight. Out of a crew of sixty-five the *Viper* lost thirty-two killed and wounded, showing what a gallant and severe action she fought and how narrowly she missed capture.

Characteristically the Bombay Government held no enquiry into this piece of treachery nor took any steps to punish the pirates. If it had backed up the heroes of the *Viper* an end might have been made at once of the Joasmee corsairs; indeed the sharp lesson the Arabs learned that day at Bushire had a salutary effect for some years. The Company's indifference and failure to retaliate caused the lesson to be forgotten and many valuable ships and lives to be lost.

The era of tranquillity lasted only about seven years. The King of Oman was a strong ruler and on the whole kept the lawless coastal tribes from piracy more efficiently than the English government at Bombay had yet managed to do. But in September of 1804 he left home on a naval expedition. On his way down the Gulf he transferred himself into a small Arab boat in order to land at Bassidore while his ships sailed slowly on. Suddenly, as he approached the shore, three Joasmee dhows darted out of the creek and attacked him. With several of his attendants he fell at the first onslaught and the pirates fled before the Muscat fleet could turn about to their ruler's assistance.

With the death of the Sultan all order and safety departed from the Gulf, and the Joasmees, no longer held in check, became more audacious than ever. A whole series of outrages followed, involving the destruction of a large number of English ships, until Captain David Seton, the Resident at Muscat, persuaded the Muscat Government to send a force to punish the Joasmees. Captain Seton himself led the Arab fleet, which blockaded the pirates at the island of Kishm and forced it to surrender. After long negotiations between Bombay and the Joasmees a treaty was drawn up in 1806 under which the pirates promised not to molest British shipping in return for permission to trade at English ports between Surat and Bengal.

The futility of such a treaty was seen very shortly afterwards when a Company's ship was attacked by four pirate dhows. Three of them were soon run down at Surat, their crews seized and sent to Bombay. There, although found guilty, they were unaccountably released. The Joasmee answer to the incredible weakness of the Bombay Government was to capture at once twenty native craft, which were carried away to the Gulf and later used as part of a fleet of fifty dhows for a fresh invasion of the Indian coast.

The pirates had by this time forgotten their fear of the Company's warships, which they attacked freely. Occasionally they were repulsed; in April 1808 they tried to board the *Fury* of six guns, commanded by Lieutenant Gowan, under the impression that she was an easy prey because of her size, but she lived up to her name by driving them off against overwhelming odds. One might have thought that Lieutenant Gowan and his gallant little crew would have been rewarded by the Government but the commander received, on the contrary, a sharp censure on his return to Bombay.

The result of this policy was only too obvious. In the same year the *Sylph,* a vessel of seventy-eight tons, was sailing to Bushire in company with two cruisers which were taking Sir H. I. Brydges as ambassador to Persia. The *Sylph,* having dropped behind the other cruisers, was approached by several dhows but the commanding officer, Lieutenant Graham, in obedience to his strict orders from the Bombay Government, refrained from firing until the Arab craft had come alongside. Then, when it was too late to act, the dhows poured in a volley of shots and made the *Sylph* an easy prize without her having fired a single shot in her own defence. The Joasmees as usual murdered the entire crew, twenty-two in number, by cutting their throats over the side of the ship in the name of God. Lieutenant Graham escaped, having fallen severely wounded down the fore hatchway in the general mêlée of boarding; he managed to drag himself into a storeroom where he remained hidden. The pirates then sailed in triumph for Ras-al-Khyma but on the way were overtaken by the frigate *La Néréide* and Graham and his ship were rescued.

It was also in the same year, 1808, that there occurred one of the most unusual and exciting experiences that ever befell a company of Englishmen in contact with the Joasmees. The brig *Fly*, of fourteen guns, belonging to the East India Company and under the command of Lieutenant Mainwaring, was captured off Kais by a famous French privateer, Captain Lemême of *La Fortune*. Before the enemy boarded, the English officer threw overboard his despatches and treasure, marking the spot on his map in case an opportunity came for recovering them. Mainwaring and two of his officers were carried to Mauritius, while the other officers and the crew were taken to Bushire and liberated. Since they knew that the despatches from England were of great importance, the officers at Bushire bought a native dhow amongst themselves, fitted her out and began their voyage down the Gulf, bound for Bombay.

On their way they stopped at Kais and after great difficulty salvaged the despatches. With these on board they set off once more, but near the mouth of the Gulf were captured by a fleet of Joasmee dhows after a stout resistance in which several of the Englishmen were wounded.

The pirates carried their captives to Ras-al-Khyma. Here they were held for ransom and

During their stay were shown to the people of the town as curiosities, no similar beings having been before seen within the memory of man. The Joasmee ladies were so minute in their enquiries, indeed, that they were not satisfied without determining in what respect an uncircumcised infidel differed from a true believer.

When these unfortunate Englishmen had remained for several

months in the possession of the Arabs, and no hope of their ransom appeared, it was determined to put them to death and thus rid themselves of unprofitable enemies. An anxiety to preserve life, however, induced the suggestion, on their part, of a plan for the temporary prolongation of it, at least. With this view they communicated to the chief of the pirates the fact of their having sunk a quantity of treasure near the island of Kais, and of their knowing the marks of the spot, by the bearings of objects on shore, with sufficient accuracy to recover it, if furnished with good divers. They offered therefore to purchase their own liberty by a recovery of this money from their captors; and on the fulfilment of their engagement it was solemnly promised to be granted to them.

They soon sailed to the spot, accompanied by divers accustomed to that occupation on the pearl banks of Bahrain, and on their anchoring at the precise points of bearing taken, they commenced their labours. The first divers who went down were so successful that all the crew followed in their turns, so that the vessel was at one time almost abandoned at anchor. As the men too were all so busily occupied in their golden harvest, the moment appeared favourable for escape, and the captive Englishmen were already at their stations to overpower the few on board, cut the cable and make sail. Their motions were either seen or suspected as the divers repaired on board in haste and the scheme was thus frustrated.*

In spite of this attempt at escape the Joasmees kept their pledge and freed the Englishmen, who set out on foot towards Bushire, following the coast line. They suffered terrible hardships and privations of every kind. None of them knew a word of the language of the country, and as all their money and most of their clothes were taken from them, they gradually became exhausted by hunger and exposure. The first to die were the Indian sailors and native servants. Then, one by one, the Europeans fell by the roadside and had to be left to the mercies of the inhabitants. Through all their troubles the gallant men managed to keep the despatches, but by the time they reached Bushire only two of the original party were left alive, a merchant officer called Jowl, and an English sailor named Pennel.

* "Pirates' Own Book."

These two at last got to Bombay with the precious despatches, where instead of being thanked and rewarded for their heroism and sufferings, "Governor Duncan showed great ingratitude and cold-heartedness."

The strangest story of an Englishman amongst the Joasmees is undoubtedly that of Thomas Horton, which first appeared in Colburn's *United Service Magazine* in 1868 under the title of "A Renegade's Career." *

In the year 1818 the Honourable East India Company sent their sloop-of-war *Hope* to cruise in the Persian Gulf to protect English shipping from pirates, and ordered the captain to call on his way to pay the annual tribute to the powerful Sheik of Kishmah. This so-called tribute was ostensibly paid for the Sheik's services in suppressing pirates, but in reality it was blackmail paid to him to keep his own piratical hands off the Company's craft.

Unfortunately the *Hope* ran on to a sunken rock off the island and was considerably damaged. The vessel had scarcely struck before a company of Arab soldiers marched down to the beach and sent a message to the captain of the *Hope* that no one was to attempt to land without the written permission of the Sheik. There being no alternative, a letter was despatched and at the end of three days a favourable reply came back from the Sheik, with a cordial message inviting the captain and his officers to come to his capital and be his guests while their ship was being repaired. This invitation they dared not refuse, but arriving at the capital they found themselves graciously received by the august personage and lodged in his palace.

As none of the officers spoke Arabic, all conversation with the Sheik was carried on through an interpreter, so that naturally they were surprised when they learnt that their host was himself an Englishman. As long as his guests made no attempt to address him in English, the Sheik was cordiality itself.

Everything was done to make the officers comfortable, and when the Sheik heard that the crew of the *Hope* numbered a hundred and twenty officers and men, he graciously forwarded

* This story was brought to my notice by Mr. H. E. Wilson.

an equal number of female slaves on board as a present. "These girls were naturally delighted at being released from their bondage, but not so the captain, who knowing the mischief one woman often caused in a ship, wondered whatever he should do with a hundred and twenty on board." However, he dared not refuse the royal gift, so, after offering grateful thanks, he had the ladies conveyed to Bombay "where he got rid of the ebony angels."

By careful enquiry the story of the Sheik of Kishmah was gradually unfolded; when pieced together it proved that he was Thomas Horton — late thief, embezzler, pirate and murderer.

Born at Newcastle-on-Tyne in 1759, young Tom was twelve years old when he was apprenticed to a tailor and breeches maker at Sandgate. After spending five years cutting and stitching, he found a quicker and easier method of making money. One day his master sent Tom to the bank to cash a cheque for six pounds. Tom added an o after the 6, wrote "ty" after the six, cashed the cheque, and very honestly returned the six pounds to his master before taking the fifty-four pounds change and a passage on a collier to Stockholm.

The money was soon spent, so Tom enlisted in the Swedish army where "though a private soldier, his youth and good looks got him to be a favourite of the wife of his captain." The captain dying suddenly, his widow married Horton who was shortly afterwards appointed a lieutenant in the same regiment. But rumours as to the cause of the sudden death of the captain became so persistent that Horton resigned his commission and went with Mrs. Horton to South Russia, where he opened a tavern on the banks of the river Volga. This venture proved most profitable for, what with supplying refreshment to passing travellers and a brisk trade in smuggling, Horton was soon a rich man.

But before long Mrs. Horton had cause to remonstrate with her husband over certain infidelities on his part, which led to high words between them, and it ended by the wife threatening that if he did not mend his ways she would denounce him as the murderer of her former husband. That very night Mrs.

Horton disappeared and her husband, to explain her sudden absence, gave out that she had returned to visit some friends in Sweden. Unfortunately for Horton, a sack was found by some fishermen three days later which contained the murdered body of his wife. He was arrested and, the evidence at his trial being conclusive, condemned to death.

By heavily bribing his jailer Horton managed to escape, and fled to the Crimea where he joined a band of Tartar bandits. After various adventures he thought it best to leave Russia and, with thirty thousand roubles in his pocket, turned up at Basra at the head of the Persian Gulf in the guise of an exemplary Mussulman merchant. A previous pilgrimage to Mecca had entitled him to wear the turban of the Hadjii and so gave him great claim to respect.

In the end he murdered the Governor of Basra and had to fly for his life to the protection of the Sheik of Kishmah. Here Horton settled down, bought land and slaves and built ships, being soon afterwards appointed Admiral of the Sheik's navy. With this and his own seven vessels Horton found himself in command of a useful little fleet with which he went pirating up and down the gulf. On one occasion he attacked and captured an armed brig belonging to the Honourable East India Company, and murdered the whole crew.

As Horton grew in wealth and influence he began to aspire after further pomp. Finally he headed a revolution, defeated the ruling Sheik who had befriended him, and strangled him with his own hands. Then, as before, he married the widow of the man he had murdered and ordered the Diwan to proclaim him Sheik, which was at once done. The embezzler had now raised himself to sovereign power. But though he had been an unsatisfactory breeches maker he turned out to be an excellent ruler. He amended the laws of the country and enforced them with severity, yet contrived to make himself popular with the people he governed. When the *Hope* was driven on to his territory he had been king for twenty years and was acknowledged to be respected and beloved by his subjects for his mercy and justice.

By this time he had acquired four wives and ten concubines,

but no children. He lived the life of an austere Mohammedan, having completely renounced his native country and religion, never having been known to utter a word of his own language. His end is unknown, so he probably passed away amidst his possessions in the bosom of his family and with all the consolations of his adopted religion.

THE scandal of the Joasmees finally became so great and the complaints so many that the superior government at Calcutta was forced to take a hand. Lord Minto was the Governor-General at the time and he directed the Bombay Government to prepare an expedition for service in the Gulf. The force prepared, in September 1809, under Colonel Lionel Smith, was a strong one consisting of two frigates, nine cruisers, a regiment and a half of regulars and about a thousand native troops. It sailed first of all to Muscat, where Colonel Smith obtained the co-operation of the two rulers of Oman, then to the Joasmee capital, Ras-al-Khyma, where it arrived on November 11th. The troops were landed and drove the pirates before them at the point of the bayonet. They soon had possession of the town, which they were allowed to plunder before it was burnt to the ground. Some sixty pirate craft in the harbour were destroyed, and one captured ship retrieved for her lawful owners. The fleet then sailed to another pirate stronghold, Shinas, which was treated in the same manner.

The expedition had met with unqualified success but was now forced to go home owing to "the wavering and infatuated policy of the Bombay Government in tying the hands of its naval officers and in regarding the pirates as *innocent and unoffending* Arabs — to quote the Governor's own words." * Of course in less than a year the Joasmees had reorganised their fleets and soon again reigned supreme from one end of the Gulf to the other.

Even this did not now satisfy them. They next turned their attention to the Red Sea and began to intercept trade between India and Mocha. In 1816 they took four Surat ships, with cargoes valued at twelve lacs of rupees, and slaughtered the

* Mills.

native crews. An expedition was sent from Bombay to demand satisfaction for the loss of the Surat vessels, but the sheik Hassan of Ras-al-Khyma after long negotiations not only refused redress but claimed the privilege of plundering Indian vessels as a natural right, pleading that if the English were going to protect these there would be nothing left for the Arabs to rob.

By the following year the Joasmees were methodically ravaging the Indian coast and intercepting the coastal trading vessels, some of them within seventy miles of Bombay itself. The days of the Angria had returned. In this year they captured more prizes than ever before. Their fleet had grown to great size — sixty-four war dhows, as well as vast numbers of small craft, with crews aggregating seven thousand men. The bigger dhows had become formidable fighters, with high sterns which reached above the bulwarks of a frigate and so enabled the pirates to capture large vessels by their favourite method of boarding. Most of the dhows were armed with a long gun on the upper deck, with which they could sweep the decks of their enemies.

The final conquest of the Joasmees occurred in 1819. Sir W. Grant Keir was placed in command of a squadron which included the *Liverpool,* fifty guns, the *Eden,* of twenty-six, and half a dozen or so of the Company's cruisers. The land forces consisted of one thousand six hundred Europeans and one thousand four hundred native troops. The fleet was joined by Seyyid Saed, King of Oman, who contributed three Muscat ships and four thousand Arabs.

The expedition was brief and altogether successful. The despatch with which Keir razed the strongholds and demolished the ships of the Pirate Coast was a testimony to the criminal inefficiency which had allowed the Pirate Coast to last so long. Occasional outrages occurred after this, but principally as incidents of the Joasmee slave trade from Africa to Asia rather than as systematic attacks on English ships, and were invariably followed by severe reprisals from the strengthened hand of the government in India.

CHAPTER IV

JAPAN AND CHINA

LIKE the Red Sea Arabs and the Phœnicians the Chinese were practising piracy before history began to be written; the records of the Celestial Empire, however, go back further than those of other countries. There exist in the archives of Pekin accounts, written many centuries ago, of sea robbers who infested the creeks and rivers of the Chinese coast. Few of these have yet been translated, and there is a mine of information waiting for the scholar with the knowledge and patience to explore it. It is contained in the last three of the sixty books of the "Memoirs Concerning the South of the Meihling Mountains" and carries the story up to the end of the Chow dynasty.

In the intermediate period between this early history and modern times most of the pirates in the China Sea were Japanese and Europeans rather than Chinese. In the Middle Ages China was a far richer country than her neighbour across the Yellow Sea and offered tempting opportunities to adventurous seafaring Japanese. The Japanese pirates worked in large fleets, and wore standardised uniforms of red coats and yellow caps. They conducted their principal raids on the coasts of China, often marching many miles inland to plunder towns. In battle they carried two swords, one in each hand, and the Chinese were no match for them at hand to hand fighting. In return, however, whenever the Chinese caught a Japanese pirate they promptly threw him into a cauldron of boiling water, which probably stimulated the pugnacity of the invaders, as death in battle was preferable to surrender.* These Japanese pirates did not limit their operations to the coast of China but worked as far south as the Straits of Malacca. It

* "Pirates of the China Seas," by S. Charles Hill; *Asia,* April 1924.

was not until the middle of the sixteenth century that they were effectively checked.

One of these Japanese corsairs, Yajiro, was a pioneer of the Church in the Far East. He turned pirate in the way that many good men have become outlaws, after accidentally killing a man and being forced to flee the country. In the course of his career he turned up at Malacca while St. Francis Xavier was preaching there, and was converted to Christianity. In 1549 he accompanied the saint back to Japan as pilot on a ship known as the "Thief's Junk." When Xavier left Japan he installed Yajiro as head of the Church he had founded there, but the Portuguese priests were so jealous of the Japanese convert placed over them that Yajiro resigned his charge in disgust and returned to piracy. He was eventually killed in a raid in China.

By the time the Japanese had been suppressed the Europeans had begun to reach the China coast and from the very first gave the Chinese the impression that they were worse barbarians than any Orientals. The first to reach the China Sea, Simon de Andrada, a Portuguese who tried to establish himself as a merchant in 1521, committed every known act of violence, including the capture of Chinese boys and girls for sale into slavery. A Portuguese commander, Antonio da Faria, fought off a Gujerat pirate in 1540, but promptly imitated his antagonist and went off to try his luck amongst the Chinese, not only robbing merchant ships but even attempting to plunder the sacred tombs of the Emperors near Pekin.

By far the most famous of the Europeans in the China Sea was Mendez Pinto, a sixteenth-century Portuguese, who attained deserved celebrity as explorer, traveller, author and pirate.*

His most famous exploit was his union with a Chinese pirate to suppress a rival from Malabar. He was cruising about with his Portuguese crew when "it pleased God to make us encounter a junk of Patana, which was commanded by a Chinese

* Cf. "The Voyages and Adventures of Ferdinand Mendez Pinto, the Portuguese," Fisher Unwin, 1891. There is also an edition of his adventures in the publications of the Hakluyt Society.

Pyrat, named Guiay Panian, a great friend of the Portugal nation and much addicted to our fashions and manner of life, with him there were thirty Portugals, choice and proper men, whom he kept in pay, they were all very rich."

This meeting between the pirates almost ended in tragedy, for "this pyrat had no sooner discovered us," writes Pinto, "but he resolved to attack us, thinking nothing less than that we were Portugals, so that endeavouring to invest us, like an old soldier that he was, and verst in the trade of pyrats, he got the wind of us, and saluted us with fifteen pieces of ordnance, wherewith we were much affrighted."

Fortunately Pinto's party was able in time to make known to Panian who they were, and while the two crews fraternised, the Captains agreed to terms of partnership. After sailing together for a few days, they met with an open boat, containing thirteen dying men. These were lifted on board Pinto's ship and proved to be eight Portuguese with their servants, who had escaped after a sanguinary fight with a Malabar pirate, Coia Acem, who had killed the rest of the crew of over one hundred and fifty men and stolen their ship and valuable cargo, these few survivors escaping at night.

This news greatly excited Pinto and his fellow-countrymen, who, "with marvellous ardour and great acclamations" set sail in quest of the pirate Coia Acem, who boasted of the title of "Shedder and Drinker of the Blood of Portugals."

Within a few days Pinto arrived at night off the mouth of a river where the Malabar pirates were reported to be and sent spies out to make enquiries. They returned with the news that the quarry was lying at anchor about two leagues higher up. The next night the Portuguese pirates sailed silently up the river until close to the Malabars, who, when they saw them, rang an alarum bell, "the sound whereof caused such a rumour and disorder, as well amongst them that were ashore as those aboard, that one could hardly hear one another by reason of the great noise they made."

Without further ado, the Portuguese ships let fly with every gun they had, quickly drew alongside and boarded. A bloody hand to hand fight ensued, which was made all the more terrifying because of the "most dreadful noise of drums, basins, and bells, accompanied with the report of the great ordnance wherewith the valleys and rocks thereabouts resounded again."

In a quarter of an hour two of the enemy junks were sunk, another was in flames, and hundreds of the pirates killed or drowned. Just when the battle seemed over Coia Acem appeared, lit up by the flames of the blazing junk, exhorting his men to further efforts. "He had on a coat of mail lined with crimson sattin, edged with gold fringe, that had formerly belonged to some Portugal; and crying out with a large voice that every one might hear him," he called upon his followers as "Mussulmans and true believers in the holy law of Mahomet" not to suffer themselves to be vanquished by such "feeble slaves as these Christian dogs, who have no more heart than pullets, or bearded women."

"These cursed words of the devil so encouraged them," writes Pinto, "that rallying all in one body, they reinforced the fight, and so valiantly made head against us as it was a dreadful thing to see how desperately they ran amongst our weapons."

The two leaders now met face to face and the Portuguese with his two-handed sword struck a great blow on the head of Coia Acem which cut through the cap of mail he wore and split his head in two, when with a reverse stroke he cut off both his legs.

With the death of Coia Acem the fight ended and only five of the pirates were left alive. These were bound and thrown into the hold, "to the end that they might afterwards be forced by torments to confess certain matters that should be demanded of them, but they fairly tore out one another's throats with their teeth for fear of the death they expected."

The total casualties in this encounter were, on the enemy side three hundred and twenty killed or drowned while the Portuguese had forty-two men killed.

When the victorious pirates went on shore they found

In a very pleasant valley, by a delicate river of fresh water, wherein were a number of mullets and trouts a very fair house, or Pagoda that was full of sick and hurt persons, whom Coia Acem had put there to be cured; amongst these were divers Mahometans of his kindred, and others of his best soldiers, to the number of ninety six, who as soon as they perceived the Portuguese afar off cried out for mercy and forgiveness, but they would by no means hearken to them, alleging that they could not spare those that had killed so many Christians; saying which they caused the house to be fired in six or seven places, which in regard it was of wood bepitched and covered with dry palm leaves, burned in such sort as it was dreadful to behold; in the meantime it would have moved any man to pity, to hear the lamentable cries made by these wretches within, and to see them cast themselves headlong out of the windows, where our men provoked with a desire for revenge, received them upon their pikes and halberds.

The most illustrious European victim of the Japanese pirates was John Davis, the Arctic explorer and one of the greatest of the race of English sixteenth century sailors. Davis sailed from Cowes for the East Indies in December 1604 as senior pilot in the *Tiger,* commanded by Sir Edward Michelborne. After a long and tedious voyage the *Tiger* reached Bintang, to the east of Singapore. Off this island was seen a small junk, disabled and barely seaworthy but crowded with Japanese who had been wrecked on the coast of Borneo after pillaging in China and had seized the crazy vessel they were now in. The English befriended the castaways and supplied them with their immediate needs.

For two days the English and Japanese vessels lay at anchor together and the two crews fraternised. Then, without warning, the pirates suddenly attacked the twenty Englishmen on board their junk, killing or driving them overboard. At the same moment twenty-five Japanese who were on the *Tiger* hurled themselves on their unsuspecting hosts. With their swords they hacked and slashed at Davis, who fell into the waist of the ship and expired almost immediately.

The Englishmen, however, recovered themselves, killed the twenty-five desperadoes after a terrific hand to hand fight and escaped with the *Tiger,* though very few of the survivors of her crew remained unwounded.

The most celebrated of all the pirates who ever infested the China Sea was Koxinga, the second of a long dynasty—it is curious to remark how a talent for piracy, like a talent for the stage, seems to be transmissible from generation to generation.

Koxinga's father, Cheng-Chi-Ling, had been a poor boy who had been driven by necessity to find work in the Portuguese factory at Macao, where he made a fortune. He then went on a visit to an uncle in Japan where he married a Japanese lady called Tagawa, by whom he had one son, Koxinga, born in 1623. After leaving Japan Cheng invested his money in a pirate fleet, and in a few years controlled practically the whole trade of the south-east coast of China. He plundered not only Chinese towns and junks, but those of the Dutch East India Company as well.

Many years before this China had been overrun and in large part conquered by the Manchus; the Ming dynasty was making a last stand against the invaders in the extreme south of China. As a measure of desperation the Ming ruler turned for help to Cheng and invited him to become admiral of the Ming fleet. The result of this alliance was that the Manchus were driven back. Cheng asked as his reward that the Emperor should adopt his son and make him a prince. When the request was refused Cheng got into communication with the Manchus and was invited by them to attend an audience at Pekin to discuss the possibility of his becoming the Emperor of the southern provinces. On his arrival at Pekin in 1640 he was immediately thrown into prison, tortured and finally executed.

Koxinga now took command of his father's fleet. Vowing to be revenged on the Manchus he joined wholeheartedly with the Mings. For twenty years he sailed up and down the coast, burning and plundering towns and villages until the Manchu government had to resort to the extraordinary expedient of ordering the inhabitants of eighty seaboard townships to destroy their homes and migrate inland. Koxinga then turned his attention to his father's old enemies, the Dutch in the island of Formosa.*

* M. Paske-Smith, "Western Barbarians in Japan and Formosa," Kobe, 1930. For much information about the early Chinese pirates I am indebted to Mr. S. Charles Hill.

In May 1661, at the head of a fleet of six hundred vessels, he attacked the Dutch forces in Fort Zelandia. For nine months the gallant Dutch commander held out, but at last capitulated, terrified lest, if the fort was taken by storm, the women and children might be exposed to the horrible tortures that Koxinga was known to inflict on his prisoners. After this the whole of Formosa passed under the rule of Koxinga. He did not, however, live long to enjoy his triumph, but died the next year, to be succeeded by his son Cheng-Ching.

Koxinga had the distinction of being one of the small but select band of pirate princes who, after reaching the highest step on the ladder to fame, managed to remain there. His deeds had a profound influence on the history of the Far East, and it was through him that Formosa became a part of the Chinese Empire. In the eyes of the Chinese his acts of patriotism so far outweighed his piratical means of achievement that after his death he received official canonisation and founded a dynasty which continued until quite recently, when one of his direct descendants was among the very few hereditary nobles in the whole of the Chinese Empire.

It is not until the beginning of the nineteenth century that we get any very minute account of the activities of the Chinese pirates. In 1831 Charles Neumann translated a contemporary Chinese work written by Yuentsze-yung-lun, which covers the period between 1807 and 1810.* The original, published at Canton in 1830, is chiefly devoted to the exploits of one pirate, and that a woman.

This lady was the widow of one Ching, who, as admiral of all the pirate fleets, had become such a thorn in the flesh of the government that in 1802 the Emperor appointed him Master of the Royal Stables. The duties of that exalted post seem to have been only nominal, for shortly Admiral Ching was to be found ravaging the coasts of Annam and Cochin China, until at length the inhabitants rose and after a fierce battle on land routed the pirates and slaughtered the terrible Ching.

The survivors escaped to their ships and sailed away to fight another day, under the command of the bereaved widow.

* "History of the Pirates Who Infested the China Sea," London, 1831.

That lady (who must be referred to as Mrs. Ching, since no other name is given her) assumed complete command of the six large squadrons which composed the pirate fleet. Each of these flew a flag of different colour, red, yellow, green, black, blue or white. They were led by lieutenants who, like the buccaneers, were known by various fancy noms de guerre: "Bird and Stone," "Scourge of the Eastern Sea," "Jewel of the Whole Crew" and "Frogs' Meal." Previous to her husband's death Mrs. Ching had commanded the senior squadron, which flew the red flag.

Under their new admiral the pirates soon became more powerful than ever before so that "peace and quietness was not known by the inhabitants of the sea coast for ten years."

The lady commander was a strict disciplinarian. She drew up a code of rules for her crews which somewhat resembled those subscribed to by earlier European pirates. Three of the articles were:

1. If any man goes privately on shore, or what is called transgressing the bars, he shall be taken and his ears perforated in the presence of the whole fleet; repeating the same, he shall suffer death.

2. Not the least thing shall be taken privately from the stolen and plundered goods. All shall be registered, and the pirate receive for himself out of ten parts, only two: eight parts belong to the storehouse, called the general fund; taking anything out of this general fund, without permission shall be death.

3. No person shall debauch at his pleasure captive women taken in the villages and open spaces, and brought on board a ship, he must first request the ship's purser for permission and then go aside in the ship's hold. To use violence against any woman without permission of the purser shall be punished with death.

Mrs. Ching was also an excellent business woman. All plunder taken had to be correctly entered in a register kept for the purpose at the warehouse. She apparently entertained nicer views about her trade than the world at large: amongst her instructions was one that forbade the use of the ugly word "plunder" and ordered it to be referred to in future as "Transhipped Goods."

MRS. CHING IN ACTION

The enlightened efficiency of the lady led to happy results, not the least of which was a friendly relationship between her pirates and the country people, which was fostered by her command that all wine, rice and other goods should be paid for, and that any spoliation of villagers was to be visited with capital punishment. As a result her fleet was always well supplied with provisions and gunpowder, while the discipline of the crew was little short of exemplary.

Her strategical gifts were illustrated in a battle which took place in 1808 between her ships and those of a government fleet sent to attack her. When the Imperial vessels approached she sent against them only a few of her own, hiding the rest behind a headland. When her decoys had joined battle, she brought out her main squadrons and attacked the enemy suddenly in the rear. The fight continued from early morning until late evening: "the bodies of the dead floated on all sides of the vessel and there perished an immense number of pirates." But at length the government forces were defeated and compelled to surrender. The admiral of the Imperial fleet, however, preferring death to the disgrace of capture "seized hold of Paou by the hair and grinned at him," hoping that at this insult the pirate would kill him. But instead Mrs. Ching's lieutenant, who admired old Admiral Kwo-lang's bravery, "spoke kindly to him and tried to soothe him." Kwo-lang, finding insults fail, thereupon committed suicide and expired on the deck of his ship at the feet of Mrs. Ching.

Lieutenant Paou was considerably moved by this tragic end of his brave opponent and was stirred to make the following oration on the deck of the vanquished flagship, amidst all the dead and dying Chinamen. Addressing himself to Mrs. Ching and the piratic crew he declared,

We others are like vapours dispersed by the wind, we are like the waves of the sea roused up by a whirlwind; like broken bamboo-sticks on the sea, we are floating and sinking alternately, without enjoying any rest. Our success in the fierce battle will, after a short time, bring the united strength of government on our neck. If they pursue us in the different windings and bays of the sea —

they have maps of them — should we not get plenty to do? Who will believe that it happened not by my command, and that I am innocent of the death of this officer? Every man will charge me with the wanton murder of a commander, after he had been vanquished and his ships taken? And they who have escaped will magnify my cruelty. If I am charged with the murder of this officer, how could I venture, if I should wish in future times, to submit myself? Would I not be treated according to the supposed cruel death of Kwo-lang?

In revenge for the disaster to the fleet and the death of Admiral Kwo-lang, the Chinese government ordered General Lin-fa to attack the pirates. When he came in sight of the enemy's fleet, however, he lost heart and tried to retire, but the pirates pursued him and overtook his fleet at Olang-pae. Just at the moment when the attack was to begin, the wind dropped and the two opposing fleets were left lying opposite each other, neither able to move. The savage pirates were so eager to get at the throats of their fellow countrymen that they jumped overboard and swam towards the opposing ships, up whose sides they clambered with their daggers between their teeth. Falling upon the crews they quickly captured all the ships and slew the faint-hearted general himself.

The following year the government sent a fleet of a hundred warships under the command of Admiral Tsuen-mow-sun to retrieve Lin-fa's disaster. In the ensuing battle the long ropes and matting sails of the pirate ships caught fire and Mrs. Ching gave the order to retire. To prevent this Tsuen instructed his gunners to fire at the rudders so that the enemy could not steer. The battle ended with the utter defeat of Mrs. Ching's forces, an immense number of the pirates being killed, drowned or captured. The heroine of the engagement, however, was on the losing side, the wife of one of the pirates who stuck to the helm of her ship and refused to quit her post. Armed with a cutlass in either hand she fought on furiously and wounded several soldiers before she was struck down by a musket ball, fell into the hold and was taken prisoner.

Before the government even had time to welcome the victors home Mrs. Ching had retrieved her position. Quickly collecting her scattered followers and summoning two other pirate chiefs to her aid she sailed in search of the government fleet. When she found it she fell upon it with the result described by one of the regular sailors: "Our squadron was scattered, thrown into disorder, and consequently cut to pieces. There was a noise that rent the sky, every man fought in his own defence and scarcely a hundred remained together."

Unable to subdue Mrs. Ching's united organisation, the government attempted to break it up piecemeal. Not long afterwards a convoy of Chinese merchant vessels guarded by several warships sighted "Jewel of the Whole Crew's" squadron while passing Tang-pae-keo. As the rest of the pirate fleet was absent it was decided to attack and destroy the single squadron. The fight lasted till sundown and began early again next morning. During the night the opposing ships were so close to one another that the pirates and their enemies were able to exchange insulting remarks. When the battle was resumed the exhausted pirates, according to observers on the merchant ships, began mixing gunpowder with their liquor, which made their faces and eyes go a bright red colour and apparently screwed up their determination to an even greater pitch. The battle raged for three whole days, until both sides were so weary and their ships so damaged that they were both glad to separate without insisting on a victory.

"Jewel of the Whole Crew" was not long in recovering from his punishment and was soon back at his business of burning towns and stealing women. The Chinese government sent out a fleet under Admiral Ting-kwei-heu to catch him. The Admiral took his time: it had been raining heavily for several days, which he thought would prevent the pirates from leaving their harbour, so he took the opportunity of rearranging his ballast. While so engaged Mrs. Ching appeared at the head of a line of two hundred pirate junks, and Ting-kwei found himself caught with his anchors down and his sails furled. His officers, never thirsty either for blood or glory, "being afraid of the large number of the enemy, stood pale with apprehension near the flagstaff unwilling to fight." To hearten them the admiral implored them by their fathers and mothers, their wives and children, and the hope of immense rewards from their country to do their duty. Stirred by this more than Roman exhortation the timorous officers became quite eager for the fight, and a ferocious engagement began in which "Jewel of the Whole Crew" himself was killed by a cannon ball. For a moment the pirates were on the point of breaking but reinforcements arrived opportunely under Lieutenant Paou, who boarded the government flagship, whereupon Admiral Ting-kwei committed suicide and all twenty-five government ships surrendered.

After this Mrs. Ching was left severely alone, and with her fleet bigger and stronger than ever, swept up and down the China Sea at her own sweet will. On the eighteenth day of the Eighth Moon she attacked the town of Shaon-ting at the head of a fleet of five hundred junks, and carried away four hundred men and women prisoners. During the remainder of this year, 1809, she devoted her attention to the Chinese rivers, up which she sailed, robbing and murdering left and right, capturing hundreds of men and women, particularly the latter, and plundering the villages and towns on the river banks. Such was the terror she inspired that the peasants fled and hid themselves on news of her approach.

Sometimes the villagers defended themselves, as at Kan-shin, where the inhabitants entrenched themselves and put up a desperate resistance. One hero, Kei-tang-chow, the village boxing master, after killing ten pirates himself, fought valiantly shoulder to shoulder with his wife until surrounded. Mrs. Kei-tang's father also flung himself on the pirates, killing several of them, before the brave trio fell dead at the feet of the assassins.

In the end the village was taken. The pirates entered it in four divisions and proceeded to plunder the place, carrying away immense quantities of clothes and other goods, and one thousand one hundred and forty captives of both sexes. The village was then burnt to the ground and left desolate so that in the whole of it "you could not hear the cry of a dog or a hen."

About a hundred women had fled and hidden themselves

in the neighbouring paddy fields but a crying baby led to their discovery by the pirates, who carried them off. Amongst these women was the beautiful Mei-ying, wife of Ke-choo-yang. One of the pirates seized her by the hair and she abused him roundly, so when he got her aboard his ship he bound her to the yard-arm, but she abused him yet more, "so the pirate dragged her down and broke two of her teeth, which filled her mouth with blood." The pirate then sprang up again to bind her. Mei-ying allowed him to approach, but as soon as he came near her "she laid hold of his garments with her bleeding mouth and threw him and herself into the river where they were both drowned."

The Chinese Emperor, like many a European monarch, tried pardon when suppression proved impossible. So it happened that O-po-tae, the leader of the Black Squadron, deserted Mrs. Ching and submitted himself and his pirates to the Emperor. His force consisted of eight thousand men, one hundred and sixty vessels, five hundred large guns and five thousand six hundred various military weapons. The Chinese Government allotted him and his men two towns to live and settle in. O-po-tae himself was given a lucrative government appointment and changed his name to Heo-been, which in English means "Lustre of Instruction."

Mrs. Ching was very naturally annoyed at this act of treachery on the part of one of her lieutenants, but at the same time reflected that it might pay her to do the same. "I am," she observed, "ten times stronger than O-po-tae, and the government would perhaps, if I submit, act towards me as they did with O-po-tae." But it was rather a delicate business to arrange the details of the submission of Mrs. Ching and her bloodstained crew, until an emissary appeared: a Dr. Chang, physician in practice at the Portuguese settlement of Macao.

After much discussion and bargaining, it was agreed that Mrs. Ching and her crews should be pardoned and, on surrendering, each man was to be given pork and wine as well as a sum of money.

Hereafter the Chinese Government was now strong enough to deal with the few pirate squadrons who had not surrendered, and very soon "Scourge of the Eastern Ocean" gave himself up, while "Frogs' Meal" fled with his squadron to Manila. More than five hundred pirates, men and women, were captured, while nearly four thousand made their submission, with eighty-six vessels. Several of the leaders were executed, as were a hundred and fifty of the crews. Thus for a while peace reigned in the eastern and the western seas. The widow Ching ended her days in comfortable obscurity as the head of a big smuggling combine.

"From this period," writes the Chinese historian lyrically in conclusion, "ships began to pass and repass in tranquillity. All became quiet on the rivers and tranquil on the four seas. People lived in peace and plenty. Men sold their arms and bought oxen to plough their fields. They buried sacrifices, said prayers on the tops of hills, and rejoiced themselves by singing behind screens during the day-time." The Governor of the province, in consideration of his valuable services in the pacification of the pirates, was allowed by an edict of "The Son of Heaven" to wear peacock feathers with two eyes.

It is interesting to hear something of Mrs. Ching's pirates from another side, that of an English captive. This was a Mr. Glasspoole, an officer in the East India Company's ship *Marquis of Ely,* who had the misfortune to be captured by the pirates in September of 1809, only a few miles away from Macao. Glasspoole, with seven British seamen, was returning to his ship from the Portuguese settlement in an open cutter, but in consequence of thick and squally weather missed the ship and for three days he and his men were at sea in an open boat without provisions or compass before being captured by a boatful of "Ladrones" or Chinese pirates.

About twenty savage-looking villains [says Glasspoole *] who were stowed at the bottom of the boat, leapt on board us. They were armed with a short sword in either hand, one of which they laid upon our necks, and pointed the other to our breasts, keeping their eyes fixed on their officer, awaiting his signal to cut or desist. Seeing we were incapable of making any resistance, the officer

* Richard Glasspoole's "Narrative of the capture and treatment amongst the Ladrones": Wilkinson, "Travels to China."

sheathed his sword, and the others immediately followed his example. They then dragged us into their boat and carried us on board one of their junks, with the most savage demonstrations of joy, and, as we supposed, to torture and put us to a cruel death.

Once on board, the pirates rifled the Englishmen and chained them down to the deck. After a long interrogation it was decided that Glasspoole should be given his liberty if a sum of seventy thousand dollars was sent for his ransom, and a letter to this effect was despatched by boat to Macao. Before any answer came the pirate fleet, numbering about five hundred sail, weighed and proceeded on their intended cruise up the rivers to levy contribution on the towns and villages. For several weeks the same procedure took place each day: the fleet would anchor opposite a village or town and, unless paid handsomely to spare it, would rob the place and burn down the houses.

Sometimes the inhabitants dared to fire at the pirate fleet in resistance, which did little harm to the pirates, but a great deal to themselves.

The Ladrones were much exasperated, [wrote Mr. Glasspoole] and determined to revenge themselves; they dropped out of reach of the shot and anchored. Every junk sent about a hundred men each on shore to cut paddy and destroy their orange groves, which was most effectually performed for several miles down the river. During our stay there they received information of nine boats lying up a creek laden with paddy; boats were immediately despatched after them. Next morning these boats were brought to the fleet; ten or twelve men were taken in them. As these had made no resistance the chief said he would allow them to become Ladrones if they agreed to take the usual oaths before Joss. Three or four of them refused to comply, for which they were punished in the following cruel manner: their hands were tied behind their backs, a rope from the mast head rove through their arms, and hoisted three or four feet from the deck, and five or six men flogged them with their rattans twisted together till they were apparently dead; then hoisted them up to the mast head, and left them hanging nearly an hour, then lowered them down and repeated the punishment till they died or complied with the oath.

On October 28th Mr. Glasspoole at last received a letter from Captain May of the *Marquis of Ely* to say that he was offering three thousand dollars for his release, but was prepared to offer more if need be. In the meanwhile the English prisoners, under threats of torture and cruel death, had been forced to carry arms and fight on the side of the pirates, Glasspoole and his quartermaster being put in charge of one of the great guns.

In one battle against a government fleet, which was fought fiercely though intermittently, Glasspoole had two narrow escapes, the first when a twelve pounder shot fell within three feet of him and another when a cannon ball struck a small brass swivel on which he was standing. During this fight he served on the pirate flagship and recounts how during the thickest fighting Mrs. Ching, the Ladrone admiral, frequently sprinkled him with garlic water which was considered by the pirates a certain charm against shot.

At length after many hardships and dangers the protracted bargaining over the captives' ransoms was finally settled and the Englishmen conveyed down the river and handed over to their countrymen, lucky to escape after a captivity of three months.

The horrors of life aboard one of these Chinese pirate junks are vividly set forth by Mr. Glasspoole:

> The Ladrones have no settled residence on shore but live constantly in their vessels. The afterpart is appropriated to the captain and his wives; he generally has five or six. Every man is allowed a small berth about four feet square, where he stows his wife and family. From the number of souls crowded in so small a space, it must naturally be supposed they are horribly dirty, which is evidently the case, and their vessels swarm with all kinds of vermin; rats in particular which they encourage to breed and eat as great delicacies, in fact there are very few creatures they will not eat. During our captivity we lived three weeks on caterpillars boiled with rice! They are much addicted to gambling and spend all their leisure hours at cards and smoking opium.

Although no other woman pirate in all history reached so high a pitch of glory and renown as the widow Ching it would be unfair to the memory of another, more recent, widow, Mrs. Hon-cho-lo, to pass her by in silence.

Mrs. Lo, like Mrs. Ching, was married to a pirate and on his death, as recently as 1921, took over command of his fleet. She soon struck terror into the countryside round about Pakhoi, where she carried on the best traditions of the craft as admiral of some sixty ocean-going junks. Although both young and pretty, she won a reputation for being a thoroughgoing murderess and pirate.

During the late revolution Mrs. Lo joined forces with General Wong-min-tong and received the rank of full colonel. After the war she resumed her piracies, occasionally for the sake of vanity surprising and plundering a village or two, from which she usually carried away some fifty or sixty girls to sell.

Her short but brilliant career ended quite suddenly in October 1922.

THE war between England and China over the opium trade ended in 1842 with the cession of Hong-Kong to the victors. That island was then and always had been one of the principal hotbeds of Chinese piracy, and the planting of a foreign power there merely drove the bandits to settle in other suitable hiding places in the neighbourhood.

Although the pirates were now scattered they were by no means disheartened or less powerful. On the contrary, under the capable leadership of two rascals, Shap-ng-tsai and Chuiapoo, they did enormous damage not only to Chinese shipping and villages but particularly to British trade. In the summer of 1849 the British China squadron alone destroyed fifty-seven pirate junks and killed more than nine hundred pirates.

This China squadron, which ranged over a thousand miles of perilous and unknown waters, was commanded by Captain, afterwards Admiral, Sir John Dalrymple Hay, who on Trafalgar Day 1849 led his little fleet into the dangerous and narrow creek where Shap-ng-tsai had drawn up his well-armed vessels. After a fierce bombardment every one of the junks was destroyed and the pirate admiral's vessel blown up.

Shap-ng-tsai and a large number of his men managed to escape to the shore and the pirate chief soon afterwards surrendered to the Chinese authorities who, in their usual obliging way, gave him a free pardon and a well paid official post.

As to Chui-apoo, he held out for another year, when his fleet met with a disastrous defeat though he himself escaped to China. The British Government had put a high price on his head, which induced some Chinamen to seize him on Chinese territory and take him to Hong-Kong, where he was tried and sentenced to transportation for life, a punishment which he considered such an insult that he hanged himself in jail in March 1851.

There were some very odd characters amongst the pirates at this time, including a number of Europeans. Not the least bizarre was an American, Mr. Eli Boggs, whose appearance was scarcely in harmony with his name. The *Times* correspondent, who was present at his trial for piracy in July 1857, wrote of him that: "It was almost impossible to believe the handsome boy, with carefully brushed hair, girlish face, charming smile and delicate hands, could be the pirate whose name had for three years been associated with the boldest and bloodiest acts of piracy."

When Boggs stood up in court to make his defence he spoke for two hours "without a tremor and made no plea for mercy." During the trial it was proved conclusively that the prisoner had been seen in company with the pirates, had acted as their commander on several occasions and had been observed to fire on the men in the ships that were attacked. However, since no witness could swear to have actually seen Boggs kill a man, a merciful jury acquitted him of murder, but pronounced him guilty of piracy and he was sentenced to transportation for life.

Once the steamship had become common in the China Sea piracy on any extensive scale was too dangerous a practice to serve as a profitable investment to shipowners, and the business fell into the hands of small and isolated individuals. But though the days of the great commanders like Cheng-Chiling, Koxinga, Ching-Yih and Shap-ng-tsai were over, the tradition of piracy in the Celestial Empire never died out entirely and there have been frequent revivals, especially during the troubles of recent years. The reader curious to see how the business was run under modern conditions will find a detailed account in The *Times* of December 12th, 1929.*

* See Appendix VII.

CHAPTER V

THE MALAY ARCHIPELAGO

THE pirates who infested the great group of islands which lie between China and Australia were drawn from two races, the Malay and the Dyak. The Malays, when they invaded and settled in Borneo and the neighbouring islands, were already experienced practitioners of piracy, but the indigenous Dyak population were as yet merely headhunters, a practice peculiar to themselves. Every active male Dyak collected human heads as eagerly as certain members of our civilization collect postage stamps or birds' eggs, and like true collectors each strove to outstrip his neighbour in the number and variety of his specimens. But the advantage of wholesale piracy at once became apparent to the Dyaks, since it combined profit with the opportunity to collect still more heads.

Although the bulk of these pirates resided in Borneo many of them were scattered about in the Sulu Islands, which lie between North Borneo and the Philippines and the Straits of Malacca. It is evident from the journal of William Dampier that piracy was a fairly late development amongst these people, since he makes no reference to it when describing his six months residence amongst the Illanun tribe of the Sulu Islands in 1687. Dampier specifically described them as a very peaceable people; yet a hundred years later these same Illanuns were perhaps the most bloodthirsty rogues in the whole archipelago. Their only rivals in ferocity were the Balanini, who also inhabited certain of the Sulu Islands. Both these tribes were Mohammedans and did not fear to attack European ships. It was their policy never to give quarter to a white man because, it is believed, of the treatment they had received from the Spaniards.*

* "Pirate Wind," Owen Rutter.

These tribes sailed in vessels known as prahus, which exceeded ninety feet in length and were propelled by a double tier of oars pulled by a hundred or more slaves. At the bow and stern were long brass guns, while along the sides were numerous swivel guns. Along the entire length of the vessel, above the rowers, ran a platform on which the fighting men stood during an engagement. These warriors were dressed in scarlet tunics, with coats of mail and feather headdresses. They carried besides firearms a long spear and wore a heavy two-handed sword and a kris or short sword. A cruising fleet often consisted of over a hundred war-prahus under the command of a single chief.

The form of plunder at which they particularly aimed was prisoners, as being the easiest to acquire and dispose of. The woolly haired Papuans of New Guinea were always a popular "line" and great numbers of them (particularly women and children) were captured from time to time. There were certain chosen markets for different kinds of slaves. Thus Papuans found a ready buyer in the Rajah of Achin, while captives from the south of Borneo were sold in Brunei; but the chief slave market of all was the island of Sarangani, to the south of Mindanau. All good looking girls of any race were reserved for the Batavian market, to be bought by the Chinese settlers who were not allowed by the laws of their country to take women out of China.

The first outstanding pirate prince was one Raga, who for seventeen years dominated the Straits of Macassa, between Borneo and the Celebes, and was known all over the Malayas as the "Prince of Pirates." He was remarkable for his cunning, intelligence and barbarity, the extent and daring of his enterprises, and his disregard for human life. His organisation was vast and he had his spies everywhere.

It was in 1813 that Raga began operations on a big scale. In that year he captured three English ships and beheaded their captains with his own sword. England sent out two sloops of war to track him down, receiving some assistance from the Dutch, upon whose settlement at Batavia Raga had committed systematic depredations.

The expedition did not work out exactly according to plan. The trackers became for a time the tracked. At three o'clock on a misty morning, with torrents of rain falling, the captain of one of the prahus caught sight of one of the British sloops, the *Elk*, which he took to be a merchant ship and at once determined to capture.

When within about two hundred yards of the *Elk* the pirates fired a broadside, gave a loud shout and with their long oars pulled rapidly towards their prey. When too late they saw their mistake. A drum rolled out the call to quarters, the ports opened and the pirates received the full benefit of a broadside accompanied by three British cheers. A few more broadsides were sufficient to sink the prahu, all but five of whose crew were killed or drowned. These few survivors were picked up by a native craft after floating on some spars for four days, and through them the story of the disaster reached Raga.

The pirate chief swore in his anger to destroy every European who should ever fall into his clutches, and kept his oath to the letter. During the years that followed until his downfall he captured more than forty European ships, whose crews he murdered to a man, in each case reserving the captain for death at his own hands. He held sway all along the two hundred and fifty miles of the Celebes coast, fifty to a hundred of his prahus always ready to sally forth from creek or harbour at the word of command. On the summits of the neighbouring mountains were stationed look-outs who on sighting a ship signalled the news by means of white flags by day and by fires by night.

An intrepid traveller, Mr. Dalton, had the audacity in 1830 to visit Raga in his headquarters, at the mouth of the Pergottan river. He had little opportunity to see all he wished, but was permitted to wander about the bazaar where Raga sold the plunder stolen from European and native craft. Amongst other odds and ends exposed for sale Mr. Dalton noticed four Bibles in English, Dutch and Portuguese, many articles of European wearing apparel, such as jackets, trousers and shirts, several broken quadrants, telescopes and binoculars, with pieces of ships' sails and bolts, and a considerable variety of gunners' and carpenters' tools and stores.

The inquisitive visitor also observed several pairs of women's stockings, some of which were marked with the initials "S. W.," two chemises similarly marked, and two red flannel petticoats, surely unsuitable garments for the tropics. When Mr. Dalton enquired to whom these articles had belonged he was given a broad hint that it would be better for him to mind his own business. Once, on suddenly coming round a corner behind the Rajah's compound, he caught sight of a European woman, who on perceiving him turned her head away and ran into the house, evidently wishing not to be observed.

Retribution overtook Raga the following year at the hands of the American Government. The Salem schooner *Friendship* was lying at anchor at Kuala Batu on the west coast of Sumatra in September 1831, taking in a cargo of pepper with no proper watch being kept and numbers of apparently peaceable natives coming aboard, when there was a rush and scuffle and the unarmed crew was cut down with the exception of half a dozen, including Captain Endicott, who escaped in a boat.

When news of the outrage reached the United States the Government immediately sent out Commodore Downes in the frigate *Potomac* to punish the murderers.

On arrival at Kuala Batu the warship, disguised as a merchantman, anchored in the outer roads. Every boat which visited her was detained in order that her true character might not be revealed to those on shore, and the natives were imprisoned in the hold, where they lay in momentary expectation of death.

The same night three hundred men, under guidance of the former second officer of the *Friendship,* landed to the westward of the place in order to surprise the forts in the town. At dawn the landing party captured the forts by storm after some hard fighting and then set fire to the town, which was burnt to ashes. The natives including the women fought with great desperation; many of them refused to yield and had to be shot down or sabred.*

When James Brooke became Rajah of Sarawak in 1842 he saw that there was no hope of order in Borneo as long as piracy remained rampant there, so the first task he set himself was to exterminate the pests who were making all honest trade, including agriculture, impossible.

The homes of the two principal pirate tribes were on the banks of the Sarebas and Sakarran rivers. It was to the Sarebas pirates, fine men and well armed, made up of several thousand Malays and Dyaks, that Brooke first turned his attention. In 1843, in company with Captain the Hon. Henry Keppel, commanding H.M.S. *Dido,* and with a mixed squadron of Europeans and Malays following, he sailed up the river, attacking and destroying every pirate fort or settlement he found. The ruling chief of the Sarebas put up a stubborn fight, which caused some casualties amongst the English crews, but most of the local chiefs surrendered and swore great oaths of reform.

A year later Captain Keppel was brought back from China at the urgent request of Rajah Brooke and ordered to assist in an expedition against the Sakarrans, who were out on the war path. The Sakarrans were more formidable than the Sarebas; their war-fleet consisted of a hundred and fifty prahus, and their chief, Seriff Sahib, was equally noted for his abilities and his atrocities.

It was on August 5th 1844 that the avenging fleet set off from Sarawak, amidst the fire of cannons and the cheers of the assembled natives who lined the river banks. The armada was composed of an odd assemblage of craft. In the place of honour was the armed paddle-steamer *Phlegethon,* followed by H.M.S. *Dido,* accompanied by her cutters manned by bluejackets, while the rearguard consisted of a large contingent of sampans and prahus, filled with wild and yelling Sarawaks, to whom the prospect of plunder and possible heads was irresistible.

* A full account of the taking of the *Friendship* is to be found in R. D. Paine's "Ships & Sailors of old Salem," Lauriat & Co., Boston, 1923.

THE ATTACK ON PADDI BY THE BOATS OF H.M.S. *DIDO*

The next day the fleet swept up the Batang Lupar river with the flood tide and anchored off the town of Patusen, the fortified stronghold of the Sakarrans. This place fell almost immediately and the town, a large one, was plundered before being burnt to the ground. The fleet then proceeded higher up the river and did the same thing to another but smaller town, the home of the pirate rajah Seriff Sahib. Evening was now drawing near so "at the close of a successful day we returned to our boats and the evening meals fatigued but pleased with our day's work." *

During these few hours the habitations of five thousand pirates had been burnt to the ground; four strong forts destroyed, together with several hundred boats; upwards of sixty brass cannons captured, besides vast quantities of other arms and ammunition "and the powerful Seriff Sahib, the great pirate-patron for the last twenty years, ruined past recovery, and driven to hide his diminished head in the jungle."

As long as a firm hand was kept on these unruly tribes there was little to complain of, but in 1848 Rajah Brooke was in England and the orgy of murder and pillage broke out again. On March 1st, 1849 a formidable fleet of between sixty and a hundred Sarebas prahus dashed up the Sadong river under the leadership of a notorious chief, the Kaksimana of Paku, attacking every detached farmhouse they met. It was the time of year when the harvest was being gathered and the peasants were widely scattered, leaving the unfortunate women and children an easy prey to the invaders.

How extremely cowardly these savages were is illustrated by their conduct when any sort of defence was put up. At one farm where the hands had just begun work as the prahus came sweeping round a bend in the river, the owner and twenty-seven of his men managed to get back to the house in time. Pulling up the ladders after them — all Malay houses are built on piles — they shot down the first three pirates who landed, upon which the rest ran away.

Their cunning was greater than their courage and they preferred attacking women whenever possible. Thus, on the

* "Expedition to Borneo of H.M.S. *Dido,*" by Captain Keppel, 1846.

above expedition, a few of the pirates lingered behind after the main body had quitted the river, and dressing themselves in the clothes of their victims, with the broad brimmed hats worn by the labourers, stealthily dropped down the river in small canoes which they had found on the banks. Wherever they thought any women might be hiding they would call out to them in the Sadong dialect to come out and be carried to a place of safety. In many cases the ruse succeeded and the frightened women came running down to the canoes with their infants in their arms, only to have their heads chopped off.

Amongst these Sarebas was one ferocious old ruffian, Dung-dong, a Malay by birth, who had adopted the Dyak costume and custom of head hunting. While his crew were engaged in plundering a farmhouse, Dung-dong was captivated by the appearance of a young girl who was endeavouring to make her escape into the jungle. Dung-dong pursued her, but being encumbered by his heavy iron-headed spear, he stuck it into the ground purposing to pick it up on his return. The pirate soon overtook and seized the girl in a paddy field, and returned carrying her shrieking in his arms to the place where he had left his spear, but it was gone. He then hurried on with his prize towards the boat, but coming round a corner, was pierced through the neck by his own spear, hurled by the hand of his victim's father.

On Brooke's return he promptly collected a fleet, which was ready by July 24th, 1849. The force included H.M.S. brig *Royalist,* the Honourable East India Company's steamer *Nemesis,* with the gig, pinnace and cutter of H.M.S. *Albatross.* In addition there were several cutters and a steam-tender, the *Ranee,* as well as three boats from the *Nemesis.* The Rajah of Sarawak himself went in the largest of his Malay prahus, the *Sing Rajah* or Lion King, which carried a crew of seventy fighting men and rowers. Seventeen other smaller prahus made up the fleet, which was afterwards joined by several local chiefs with their followers, so that the total native force amounted to about seventy fighting prahus and three thousand five hundred men. The steamer *Nemesis* towed all the European boats to the mouth of the Batang river, whither the native craft followed.

From information procured from a captive it was learned that a large Sarebas fleet had slipped out to sea only a few hours before Rajah Brooke's force appeared, and plans were at once made to waylay the enemy on their return.

For three days the Sarawak force waited for their victims. In the meantime further particulars were gathered of the enemy, for it was learned that their fleet consisted of one hundred and fifty prahus, each armed with muskets, while some carried brass guns in addition. Few of the prahus carried fewer than thirty fighting men, while some had as many as seventy. News kept coming in from spies that the enemy were making a plundering raid up the rivers to the north; among their prizes were two Singapore trading vessels, which the pirates robbed and then burnt.

Then came news that the pirates had heard that the White Rajah was out after them, and were hurrying homewards, ignorant of the fact that he was waiting for them there. Towards evening of July 31st, a scout-boat arrived with the intelligence, so welcome after three days of watching, that the Sarebas fleet was approaching in two divisions. Half an hour later a rocket announced the near approach of the enemy flotilla and the splashing of their paddles could be distinctly heard, although it was impossible to see the prahus in the darkness.

Eventually the leading prahu sighted the steamer, and the pirates, seeing their danger, sounded a gong, their method of calling together a council of the chiefs. With the booming of the gong a profound silence fell, and not a sound was to be heard in the, by now, pitch-black tropic night. Then, all of a sudden, a yell of defiance broke out, which signified to friend and foe alike that the enemy chiefs had made their decision to fight.

But it was too late. Rajah Brooke and the English naval commander, Captain Farquhar, had caught the enemy in their well and widely spread net. Their fleet of ships' cutters and Malay prows had been drawn up in a large semi-circle, the extremities of which were eight miles apart. Behind the centre of the half-circle lay the mouth of the Sarebas river, for which the enemy were making.

All at once a rattle of musketry rang out as the leading pirate prahus came in contact with the men-of-war's boats, but the pirates were so panic-stricken that their marksmanship was wild. Eighty of their vessels were speedily run ashore, while the rest made for the open sea. Seventeen of the larger prahus attempted to pass close by the steamer, but every one was destroyed.

> The excitement caused by the reports of fire-arms — by the bright flashes of the guns — by the blue lights burnt by the man-of-war boats to distinguish friend from foe — the glare of the rockets, while passing through the air — the yells of defiance from both sides — was increased by the obscurity, and by the extended nature of the operations, for the combatants were spread at one time over a space of not less than ten miles.*

When at last dawn broke the full disaster to the pirates was apparent. On the beach lay some sixty deserted prahus, and the débris of the large pirate fleet, while boats that had been swamped were being carried backwards and forwards by the tide. Another eighty prahus were soon captured, many of them from sixty to eighty feet in length.

The total pirate casualties were never known but it was calculated that altogether more than eight hundred pirates were killed or drowned that night. Of prisoners there were but few, although this was not the fault of the victors. Mercy was not understood by the head hunters. When they took to the water, they did so with sword in one hand and shield in the other, and any attempt made to save them from drowning was met by armed resistance, which accounted for most of the wounds received by the Rajah's troops.

Had the victors been content with this success and returned home, no doubt the pirates would before long have recovered and been up to their old mischief. But this time Brooke meant

* Captain H. Keppel, "A Visit to the Indian Archipelago," 1853.

to stamp out piracy in his realms once and for all. After spending two days securing prisoners in the jungle, and destroying such captured prahus as were not required for use, the expedition proceeded up the Sarebas river on August 2nd. The small steamer *Ranee,* attended by the man-of-war's boats, led the way, followed by several hundred native boats. The crews of these were so eager for plunder that it was with the greatest difficulty they were kept back. Every mile or two the advance was checked by freshly felled trees which had been thrown across the stream and tied together by rattans, which had to be cut and the trees removed to allow the boats to pass. Every native who resisted was killed, and the houses of those who ran away were burnt down. In most of these houses were found trophies of human heads, many being obviously quite recently procured.

The ascent of the river soon took on the appearance of a triumphal progress, as from the jungle on either bank the local rajahs and head men of the different towns and villages came down to the bank to make their surrender to Rajah Brooke and give well-sounding assurances as to their good intentions for the future.

Many of the pirates who surrendered were fine specimens of Dyak manhood, with long black hair, and a number of brass rings in their ears as well as round their arms and legs, which bore out the well-known caution of the Borneo coast to "beware of a Dyak with a profusion of rings, he is sure to be one of a pirate band."

By August 19th the fleet was back again at the mouth of the river, and went off to pay a visit to the Kanowit Dyaks, who were the great receivers of plundered property. These wealthy traffickers in stolen goods lived in two large houses, built on piles forty feet high, which were big enough to house one thousand five hundred people as well as great quantities of goods.

As a punishment for their misdeeds, the Kanowit Dyaks were ordered to pay as fines brass guns and jars; these were afterwards sold by Rajah Brooke by public auction at Sarawak and the proceeds given to the captors of prisoners taken without hurt, an act of the Rajah to encourage a more human system of warfare amongst his savage troops, and particularly to check head hunting.

On August 24th, 1849 the conquerors arrived back at Sarawak, having once and for all stamped out wholesale piracy on the northern coasts of Borneo.

EPILOGUE

THE END OF THE PIRATES

THE Malay Archipelago was the last stronghold of piracy on a large scale. The break up of its gangs finished, probably for ever, piracy as it had existed for many thousands of years.

However, here and there amongst the out of the way islands and atolls of the Pacific Ocean, a few white men carried on a precarious sort of piracy for some years longer. These men were the very offscourings of civilisation, escaped Australian convicts, run away whaling men or mutinous sailors. These individuals shared with the missionaries the task of instructing the simple natives of the South Seas in the ways of white civilisation.

Several of these degenerate heirs of a great tradition enjoyed picturesque names worthy of their earlier prototypes or even of a Chicago gangster: Paunchy Bill, Joachim Ganga, Paddy Coney and Joe Bird; but the biggest man of them all wore only the plain title of Bully Hayes.

Hayes's first appearance in the South Seas was on another stage than that of piracy, for he first turned up as a member of a small travelling concert party in New Zealand.* This enterprise came to an end with the breaking out of the Maori war, and Hayes gave up music for traffic in arms and gunpowder with the rebellious islanders.

After this he turned "blackbirder," which meant that he would visit some out of the way island, inveigle on board his vessel, the *Lenore,* a number of unsuspecting natives, and carry them off to Samoa or some other island for sale to planters in need of labour. Before long his name was famous from Australia to San Francisco and he was wanted by several governments. But he was a hard bird to catch and being a tee-

* Basil Lubbock, "Bully Hayes."

totaller the usual bait to catch men of his stamp failed. But at length, in 1875, the Spaniards caught him and clapped him into prison at Manila to await trial. Hayes passed the time of his confinement in theological studies with the result that he became a devout Catholic. The Bishop of Manila, delighted with the return of a fallen sinner, used his influence to have him released. Hayes thereupon promptly set out to take up his old trade, to which he now added the theft of ships on a large scale.

He was again arrested by the British consul at Samoa for an act of piracy and held prisoner to await the arrival of the next British man-of-war to take him to Australia for trial. In the meantime he was allowed to go about the island as he liked and became popular as the leading spirit in organising picnics.

During this interval there arrived on the island one Captain Ben Pease, another bad man of the South Seas. Hayes and Pease were old colleagues in crime but almost at once on their encounter plunged into a violent quarrel. The consul was pleased with this turn of affairs, as Pease's ship was the only one by which Hayes could possibly have attempted to escape.

Then one morning Captain Pease said farewell to his friends and sailed away. Several hours later Hayes was missed, and only then did it dawn on the consul that the quarrel was an elaborate bit of acting arranged for his deception.

The law did not touch Hayes again; he met his death at the hand of his Scandinavian mate, who struck him on the head with an iron boom and flung him overboard.

Almost the last of the pirates were the American slavers. As early as 1808 a law had been passed in the United States making the importation of negro slaves illegal and trade in them piracy, but the law was a dead letter from the beginning and it was more than forty years before anything was done to enforce it. By the middle of the century the business had reached its greatest dimensions and it was computed that in 1859 no fewer than fifteen thousand negroes were brought into the country, the largest number of any single year. The trade paid so well that if but one slaving voyage out of three was successful the profits were immense. Most of the dealers in "black ivory" were Northerners.

With the accession of President Lincoln and the outbreak of the Civil War in 1861, strong measures were at once taken to put an end to the traffic.

The scapegoat to be caught and punished was one Captain Nathaniel Gordon, a native of Portland, Maine, who commanded his own vessel, the *Erie*, of five hundred tons. Gordon had made four voyages altogether, on the last of which he was overhauled and captured off the west coast of Africa by the American ship *Mohican;* nine hundred and sixty-seven negroes were found on board the *Erie* and carried back to Monrovia, but so overcrowded was the slave ship that more than three hundred of the poor blacks died on the short voyage. Gordon was taken to New York and put up for trial on the charge of piracy, which rendered him liable to capital punishment.

The case created tremendous excitement. Every possible opposition was raised to the trial, both legally and by public opinion, but the prisoner was found guilty and sentenced to death. Large numbers of posters then appeared everywhere in the city with such appeals as:

> Citizens of New York, come to the rescue! Shall a judicial murder be committed in your midst and no protesting voice raised against it? Captain Nathaniel Gordon is sentenced to be executed for a crime which has virtually been a dead letter for forty years.

Yet in spite of appeals and threats Gordon was duly hanged on March 8th 1862 in the Tombs prison, whose every entrance was strongly guarded against the mob by armed marines. He was the last white man to die on the gallows for the crime of piracy on the high seas.

THE modern age seems to have done away with piracy, save in an occasional and bastard form, as it has done away with many more attractive expressions of human activity. What with thirty-five knot cruisers, aeroplanes, wireless and above all the police power of the modern state, there seems very little chance for the enterprising individual to gain a living in this fashion and still less for capital so invested to earn a satisfactory return for the risk involved.

Though the passing of the pirate has taken some of the colour out of the world, yet it is difficult to deplore his disappearance. For he was not on the whole an attractive individual: and the more we learn about him the less attractive does he become. The picturesque swashbuckler, with pistols stuck in his belt and curses pouring from his mouth, makes a very good subject for a story, but in actual life he must have been an exceedingly unpleasant character. The romantic and the eccentric pirate is the one we usually meet in books, including this one; but the genuine article was on the whole a coward and a cut-throat who made away with his victims because dead men tell no tales.

It is likely that the disappearance is permanent. It is hard to conceive that, even if our civilisation is overturned and lawlessness again becomes law, the pirate will emerge again. It seems fantastic to think of great powers fighting one another in a Holy Crusade, as did the Turks and the Christians, with outlaws and renegades, or of peaceful steamer lanes haunted by buccaneers from little island republics of their own creation whither the fleets of the nations dare not penetrate.

Yet it is possible. The spirit in man that produced pirates is probably as strong as it ever was, and the occasional outbursts in China, the existence of the hijacker off the northern coasts of America, indicate that it is ready to take advantage of any favourable condition. There is no doubt that the type of man who once turned to piracy still exists, but is compelled to find other channels for his talents.

I was one day talking to a young man in a cell of Wandsworth Gaol, where he was serving his third sentence of imprisonment for a "smash-and-grab" raid. Feeling it my duty as a prison visitor to point out the folly of his ways I rashly asked him why he preferred the risk of imprisonment to a safe and honest life. "Well, sir," said my young friend, "you see I *must* have money and I *must* have excitement."

Then he went on to tell me, as a friend, of an exploit of which he had never been suspected. At four o'clock one afternoon he had, at the head of his gang in three motor cars, drawn up opposite the windows of a famous jewellers' shop at the corner of Grafton Street and New Bond Street. There he had jumped out, smashed the plate glass window of the shop, grabbed a tray of diamond brooches, leapt back into his car and got away. His eyes shining with enthusiasm he concluded, "if you want *excitement,* sir, you smash . . .'s window at four o'clock in the afternoon and you'll get all you want." Had that young man lived two hundred years ago I have no doubt that he would have been a pirate; could the conditions of two hundred years ago be repeated I have no doubt that he would be a pirate today.

Piracy may be a blot on civilization and its practitioners criminals whom it is a duty to extirpate. Yet there will always be a sympathetic response in the human heart to the appeal of the adventurer who dares go to far and dangerous places and in defiance of all organized respectability take his courage in both hands to carve out his fortune.

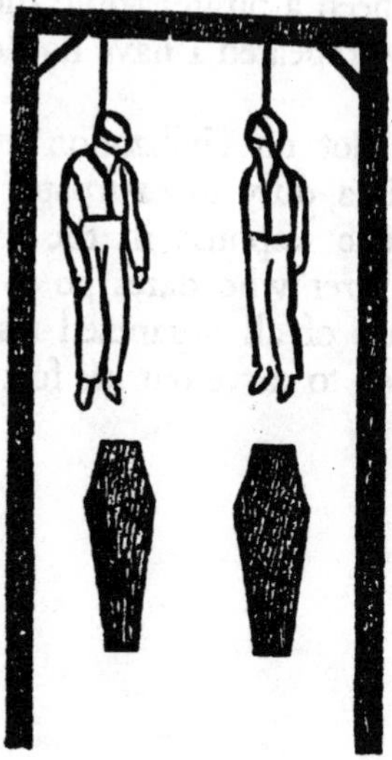

FINIS

APPENDIX I

THE CLASSICAL PIRATES

THE early literary references to Mediterranean piracy indicate that it had already attained to a certain degree of respectability. One of Homer's characters greets a sailor landing on his shore with a casual enquiry as to whether he sailed for some merchant or as a pirate. The hero of his first epic, Achilles, was by any definition a pirate before he enlisted for the war against Troy; and the second has for its hero a man who would receive short shrift in a modern Admiralty Court. Herodotus begins his First Book with an account of the exploits of a corsair and describes without reprobation his success when waylaying merchant ships carrying goods from Syria to Egypt. In fact to most of the Greek writers piracy was a recognised profession like any other, pirate being virtually synonymous with navigator, and odium only attaching to the name if the possessor was in the service of an enemy.

From these early writings it is fairly easy to reconstruct the methods of these primitive corsairs. Their craft were light, shallow and flat-bottomed. Speed was essential for attack and escape, and shallow draught equally so, as it allowed the crew when hard pressed by enemy ships to escape by rowing into water where their heavier pursuers were unable to follow. The places chosen for attack were the well-known trade routes. In the early days of navigation these routes were easy to predetermine. The sailor steered by sight only, picking his way along the coast and taking his bearings by well-known landmarks, such as mountains, headlands and islands, never daring to lose sight of land for many hours together. Of course this primitive method of reckoning made sailing by night impossible, and no early Mediterranean sailor ever thought of attempting it. At sunset he dropped anchor and lay until sunrise made it safe to continue his journey.

Such methods of navigation rendered the tactics of the pirate as simple as those of the highwayman, and his escape rather easier. He had but to lie quiet in a rocky cove until he spotted his prey and then stalk him. If the prey were too fast it ran away; if it were too strong the pursuer ran away, but the merchantman too elusive or too powerful to be boarded by day was helpless by dark, for the pirates simply watched to see where it dropped anchor at night, came alongside in the darkness for a swift rush when most of the crew were asleep, and with terrifying shouts swarmed over the side and made their capture before the victims were fully awake. The vessel was then rowed by her own crew under the captors' lash to the pirates' lair and the division of the spoils completed.

But sea-going vessels were not the only objectives of these early pirates. Not infrequently they collected in force and conducted swift raids on the sea-coast towns. To this day there are to be seen on many of the Ægean islands ruins of high towers of great antiquity which were built as places of refuge to which the islanders could flee from the corsairs' raids. These towers were also used to give warning of the presence of pirate ships off the coast, signals of smoke being sent out to the inhabitants of the neighbouring country by day and of fire by night. In this type of raid unexpectedness was consequently essential — a quick swoop before the victims had time to prepare a defence, the hasty collection of as much plunder and as many prisoners as could be got together in a few minutes, and then a lightning dash to sea before the countryside could be aroused.

A raid of this sort is vividly described in the Ninth Book of the *Odyssey*. It contains an impressive moral which the wiser pirates heeded but the more stupid ignored to their cost:

The wind that bare me from Ilius brought me nigh to the Cicones, even to Ismarus, whereupon I sacked their city and slew the people. And from out the city we took their wives and much substance, and divided them amongst us, that none through me might go lacking his proper share. Howbeit, thereafter I commanded that we should flee with a swift foot but my men in their great folly hearkened not. There was much wine still a drinking and still they slew many flocks of sheep by the seashore and kine with trailing feet and shambling gait. Meanwhile the Cicones went and raised a cry to other Cicones their neighbours dwelling inland, who were more in number than they and braver withal; skilled they were to fight with men from chariots and when need was on foot. So they gathered in the early morning as thick as leaves and flowers in Spring. They set their battle in array by the swift ships and the hosts cast at one another with their bronze-shod spears. So long as it was morn we abode their assault and beat them off, albeit they outnumbered us. But when the sun was wending to the time of loosing the cattle, then at last the Cicones drave in the Achæans and overcame them, and six of my goodly-greaved company perished from each ship, but the remnant of us escaped death and destiny.

Thence we sailed onward stricken at heart, yet glad as men saved from death, albeit we had lost our dear companions.*

Time and time again in the annals of piracy the forces of order were able to take their revenge because the thieves had either not sufficient patience or confidence in one another to put a safe distance between themselves and their pursuers before falling to a division of the spoils.

The quotation from Homer also indicates the nature of the plunder which the pirates carried away. By far the most valuable portion of the spoils was in the form of human beings. The traffic in slaves is the outstanding feature of Mediterranean piracy, the one appalling fact that distinguishes it from the activities of the Atlantic buccaneers in the sixteenth and seventeenth centuries. The latter were, it is true, not altogether above making a profit out of blacks, but by far the largest part of their effort was directed to the acquisition of inanimate cargo.

It was the revenue derived from the sale or ransom of slaves that built up the great pirate organisations and made them so powerful that proud states were compelled to bribe them for protection. The business became so extensive that at its height there were recognised clearing centres, such as the island of Delos in the Ægean, to which captives from all the coasts of the Mediterranean were brought as to a legitimate market.

The first struggle between a merchant state and organised pirates of which there is any authentic tradition had as protagonists the Phœnicians and the Greeks.

The Phœnicians of Homeric times had a virtual monopoly of the carrying trade of the Mediterranean. It was they who brought the jewels, spices and silks of the East, carried across the deserts and unloaded at their ports, to the city states of the Ægean and of both sides of the Western Mediterranean. They were not only the first navigators and first merchants of the age, but the colonisers of Southern France and Spain and of North Africa; Carthage and Marseilles were amongst their offspring. Like true Imperalists they colonised for the purpose of creating markets for themselves, and as their enterprise went further and further afield, extending ultimately through the Pillars of Hercules to the west coast of Africa, their trade grew richer and the hazards that accompanied

* "Odyssey," II, 39–52. Ormerod.

the longer voyages it entailed proportionately greater. Their enterprise ultimately carried them to the stormy and mysterious north in search of the precious amber of the Baltic or to Britain for tin to carry back to Tyre and Sidon in exchange for the wares of the East. It is even believed that they circumnavigated Africa in a voyage of three years.

The Greeks of this era, far poorer and with no great aptitude for the sea, were the natural enemies of their rich oriental neighbours. A restless, turbulent, hardy people, they were excellently situated to cut across nearly all the ordinary Phœnician trade routes, spy on and intercept the merchant vessels and effect quick escapes into the countless little rocky bays that indent the long coastline of Hellas. Montescue may have exaggerated when he called all the early Greeks pirates; but at one time it was probably the principal and certainly the most lucrative activity of the maritime portion of the peninsula. It is more than likely that the end of the Trojan War found many besides Odysseus to pass the time and get a living in this way; it was a recurrent phenomenon of great wars that the returning sailors, finding no other employment open to them, joined an old or formed a new team of corsairs.

During most of this time the Phœnicians possessed no fighting navy adequate to cope with these enemies. The heavy inroads of the pirates was the normal tribute they had to pay for their seaborne wealth. Occasionally, being a resourceful people and no more unanimously honest than most, they got their own back. Sailing into a Greek harbour in the guise of ordinary merchants, the Phœnician would spread his wares out on board and invite the natives to inspect, admire and buy. The customers were of course principally women. When a sufficient number were collected the anchor would be weighed abruptly and the Greek ladies would find themselves merchandise instead of customers.

It was a Phœnician however, one of the Minoan kings of Crete, who made the first determined and successful attempt to clear the Mediterranean of pirates. Beginning as pirates, this mighty line established on the island the most formidable military power of its time during the century preceding the Trojan War.

Their power once established and resting largely on commerce, one of them (his name is unknown) constructed from the thick forests of their island kingdom the strongest fleet known to antiquity and proceeded ruthlessly to hunt out and destroy his former rivals. The geographical situation of Crete, almost in the centre of the shipping lanes of the Mediterranean, enabled him to keep an eye on all that was going on in the adjacent Greek waters and soon his relentless energy brought the Hellenic tribes to heel. They were compelled to accept an agreement to own no vessel manned by a crew of more than five, with a single exception, the *Argos,* which they were permitted to retain as a defence against other pirates.

During the lifetime of this Minos Mediterranean commerce was comparatively secure. After his death the naval power of Crete quickly declined, the corsairs again flourished and it was nearly a thousand years before another power rose strong enough to check them.

The prince of pirates in post-Homeric times was Polycrates, the Tyrant of Samos, who flourished in the sixth century B.C. At the height of his power he owned more than a hundred vessels of war and reigned supreme over the waters of the Ægean. Ultimately, by defeating the rival pirate fleets of Melita and Lesbos, he became the absolute ruler of the whole coast of Asia Minor, whence he could both guide the waning power of Phœnicia and damp the efforts of the terrible sea brigands of the Cilician coast. But even in his day of authority, enjoying the position of legal ruler, he was unable to cure himself of the habit whereby he had grown great. Ships of other states sailed only by his permission and after payment of tribute, or ran the normal risk of seizure. On one occasion he even interrupted the ceremonial intercourse between several of his fellow sovereigns, seizing a vessel of state which Amasis, the king of Egypt, was sending to Lacedæmonia with a present of a linen corselet embroidered with tissue of golden cotton, and a magnificent bowl profusely ornamented with precious stones on its way to that noted hoarder of gold, Crœsus the King of Lydia.

Like many another gentleman gifted with the power of acquisition, Polycrates was a connoisseur in spending. While making Samos the first city of its age in riches, he made it the first in the arts as well. The palace he built for himself was included amongst the wonders of the world. Like the Renaissance pirates he tempted contemporary artists to come and remain in residence at Samos, and paid them vast sums to decorate the city with statues and buildings. Democedes, the foremost physician of his time, was seduced from Athens at a fabulous salary, and the poet Anacreon, whose verses are filled with references to the Tyrant, was his intimate friend.

Polycrates finally succumbed to the kind of treachery which he himself had frequently practised with notable success. Orœtes, the governor whom the conquering Cyrus had placed over Lydia, besieged Samos in 515 B.C. but the Tyrant held out until by attractive promises of a profitable bargain the Persian lured him on a visit to the mainland, where the versatile prince, pirate and patron of the arts was seized and crucified.*

With the Roman defeat of the Greeks and the final extermination of Carthage after the Third Punic War there was a sudden revival of piracy on the greatest scale known to antiquity. Both the defeated races possessed a certain maritime experience and a substantial tradition of naval aggression. The coming of the Romans had reduced them in importance, swelled their unemployment and for the time being at least made a living hard to get. Great numbers naturally turned to the ancient art of their tribes.

The line between piracy and war was for almost the first time clearly drawn. Rome was an organised state, a dominant power; she represented the law. Any violence done to her subjects by land or sea could no longer be regarded as a contest between equals, but as an act of defiance by the outlaw against the law-abiding. Rome's pride, as well as her interest and her sense of order, demanded that her merchants should be able to carry on their trade overseas as safely as overland, but it was a long time before her effectiveness equalled her desire. A passion for the sea had been omitted from the Roman temperament. Her magnificent soldiers could fight effectively as a boarding party, but there were few Romans who had been trained as professional sailors — most of the carrying was done by foreigners who had come under Roman dominion — and anything in the sense of a Republican navy had not yet been born. In consequence, during the eighty years from the fall of Greece to the punitive expedition under Pompey, there were constant famines and panics in the markets of Rome due to supplies being shut off by a more than usually sustained activity on the part of the corsairs, and once or twice the very life of the haughty Republic seemed in grave jeopardy.

During the long Civil War, when all the energies of Rome were absorbed in the internecine struggle between Marius and Sulla, the pirates grew constantly more aggressive and more numerous, until at length they had achieved a practical blockade of the Italian ports. Rome soon began to feel the pinch. The most serious shortage was in corn, a commodity imported in great quantities from Egypt and Africa. The price of this necessity soon rose to such a height that only the wealthy could afford it and the ordinary folk in the great capital were starving; food riots were hourly incidents. The seas were no longer even nominally policed, the pirates went where they

* Sestier: "Piraterie dans l'antique."

would unmolested, and Rome could no longer speak with pride of *Mare Nostrum*. The Ægean, "The Gulf of Gold," was entirely in the hands of the corsairs.

The danger reached its height when the pirates found a protector in Mithridates, King of Pontus, the most redoubtable of the Republic's foes. As in later times a potentate of the East made use of the outlaws in his struggle with the West, so Mithridates took the worst of the robbers, the Cilicians, under his wing and gave them entry to his ports and even the use of his war galleys, on at least one occasion accompanying the arch-pirate Selencus on one of his expeditions. His allies were no longer an aggregate of furtive cut-throats; they had grown into the semblance of a naval organisation, attacking according to a considered strategy instead of, as hitherto, without order or unity of command. This, from the point of view of the lawyers at least, begins to resemble war more nearly than piracy, but a similar confusion was to prevail for some seventeen hundred years more at the top of each piratical cycle. In practice the thing was still piracy — the crews were not subject to the law of the country under which they fought, they took no wages, being content with the plunder, for which they made their own accounting, treating captives not as prisoners of war but as victims of piracy (though this distinction was not so great as it became in later times) and realising perfectly well that in the event of their own capture they had nothing to hope for save summary execution or sale at the option of their captors.

Finally, when the plight of Rome was so desperate as even to lull the hatreds of the rival parties, the Senate resumed the function of a national legislature and in 67 B.C. prepared an expedition to save the State from extinction. The commander they selected was Pompey, who had emerged from the civil wars as the first man of the Republic. He was clothed with dictatorial powers and all the resources of Rome were put at his disposal. He himself considered the task so formidable that he demanded and received three years of authority in which to accomplish it. The confidence which the dictator enjoyed was indicated by an abrupt fall in the price of corn on the news of his appointment.

The immediate business was to clear the Western Mediterranean of the pests, so as to re-open the Italian ports and restore the vanishing trade. To this end Pompey divided the area into thirteen districts, each under the command of a lieutenant who had orders to make a thorough search along every coastline for the marauders, who were to be captured or sunk at sight. Pompey himself sailed at the head of the Rhodes fleet, whose duty it was to sweep the coasts of Africa, Sicily and Sardinia, while his lieutenants operated off Spain and Gaul. In forty days the commander was able to report that the whole of the Western basin was free of corsairs.

Pompey then headed eastwards with sixty vessels to rout out the pirates from their native strongholds. They had already been thoroughly intimidated by his successes in the east, and at his coming fled from the open seas to the creeks and concealed harbours of their own rugged coast. The only ones who made any show of resistance were the Cilician sea barons who were easily defeated off Coracesium. Mithridates' towns and ships submitted readily, a fact largely due to the conqueror's reputation for leniency at a time when the common practice was to nail this kind of enemy to the cross. Instead of slaughtering his prisoners Pompey settled them in the desolated cities of Cilicia, which henceforth became a Roman province.

In forty days after his arrival off the coast of Asia Minor the pirates were completely crushed, every fortified stronghold taken and the whole of the Mediterranean again open to Roman commerce. The booty was enormous: four hundred ships had been captured, thirteen hundred destroyed, all arsenals burnt, and all forts razed. More than ten thousand pirates were computed to have been drowned and twenty thousand captured. Amongst the Roman prisoners released was the admiral of the Roman fleet previously stationed at Cilicia.

Thus in three months, in place of the three years he had demanded, Pompey was able to lay down his commission. Nearly two thousand years were to elapse before the pirates of the Mediterranean encountered so swift and so complete a retribution.

For the next twenty years the merchants carried on their trade in comparative peace in the latter portion of it, secure in the protection of the stern and efficient government of Julius Cæsar. But on his death in 44 B.C. anarchy broke loose on land and sea. The discontented factions fled abroad and harassed the Republic either on their own or in the service of an enemy. Amongst those who took to the sea was, rather ironically, Sextus Pompey, son of the great Pompey, who after his banishment collected a fleet manned chiefly by other banished compatriots and slaves. Establishing his headquarters in Sicily, he ravaged the coasts of Italy so thoroughly that in a few years he nearly restored the state of affairs his father had ended.

But Rome was not strong enough at the moment to cope with

him, and entered into a treaty whereby he was granted Sicily, Sardinia and Achaia in return for free passage to Italian vessels. But Sextus had too much of the pirate in him to keep any such agreement and soon he was again pillaging and harrying, until eventually Octavius sent Agrippa to deal with him. Agrippa triumphed in a sea fight off the coast of Sicily and henceforward, until the Empire began to break up, Rome was able to keep her sea roads clear. With the eclipse of the Roman civilisation even piracy itself declined almost into oblivion: for a long time, until Europe awoke again, there was very little that travelled by sea that was worth the plundering.

APPENDIX II

THE STORY OF MRS. JONES

THE Rev. Thomas Bolton, chaplain to the Consulate at Algiers vouches for the following story of the Hibernian regiment:

On August 16th, 1747, a detachment of this regiment then in the service of Spain, was overtaken by Algerian corsairs on its way from Majorca to the mainland. They resisted the first xebeque that came up until all their powder was expended, whereupon they boarded the enemy and drove the Turks overboard. Another larger vessel now bore down upon them and they had no alternative but to surrender. One of the Turks cried out, "You are no Spaniards; if you are not English you are devils." The party consisted of a lieutenant colonel, six captains, ten subaltern officers, and about sixty privates; the poor shattered remains of the campaigns in Italy. On arrival at Algiers, the three colours of the regiment, a cross on a white field, and the arms of Ireland with the Inscription "Reggimento di Hibernia" were flying on the xebeque. Amongst the ladies were Mrs. Jones, with her two young children; her daughter Nancy by her first marriage, a lady of only nineteen years old, but much esteemed for her virtue and good sense as admired for her beauty; and a maid-servant."

After describing the hardships these ladies underwent and how the little child, not eight years old, was made to fetch water and sweep and carry away the dirt, with nothing but a ragged old Turkish coat to cover her, Mr. Bolton continues:

One day Mrs. Jones was sitting with her youngest child in her arms at the door of the home where she resided, when a Turk came up and began to importune her, giving her the choice of compliance or death. She retreated to an inner room and thence into a loft accessible only by a ladder, which she pulled up after her. The Turk brought the child, and having upbraided, threatened and entreated her by turns, he drew his sword and wounded the infant in one arm. She shrieked, he wounded it in the other; at last he cut off one hand and threw it at her, upon which she seized half a broken millstone that lay in the loft, threw it down upon the Turk and broke his leg. He then murdered the child, cut off its head, and discharged his pistols at the woman without effect. The latter watched her opportunity, and with the other half of the millstone crushed him in such a manner as to render him insensible. She then descended and despatched him with his own sword, put her child in a basket, and went and delivered herself to the Dey.

Sir Lambert Playfair, when he was Consul-General at Algiers was unable to trace the sequel of this story, but was led to believe that a cruel death was the only fate reserved for a slave who dared to kill or even to strike a Turk.

APPENDIX III

Jachimosky's Escape

An exciting escape of galley slaves from a Turkish warship, is contained in a very rare Spanish newsletter, whose translation runs as follows:

ACCOUNT

of the hold-up and seizure of the Admiral's Galley of Alexandria, in the port of Metellin, due to the efforts of Captain Marco Jachimosky, a slave on the said galley, and of the liberation of two hundred and twenty Christian slaves on the 18th July, 1628.

Printed in Rome
Translated from Italian into Spanish by
Miguel de Santa Cruz

The fortunate and successful seizure and capture of a Flagship of Alexandria and the liberation of two hundred and twenty Christians which happened on the 18th July, 1628, took place in the following manner: —

Mehemet, younger brother of Rassimbech, Governor of Damiata, and Rossero, a captain of four galleys set apart to navigate and guard the waters about Alexandria, whose flagship was manned by two hundred and twenty Christians, three of whom were Greeks two English and one only Italian—the remainder being Russians (commonly called Muscovites) set out from Constantinople taking Ysuf Cadi, a Turk, who had been appointed Judge of Alexandria by the Court of Turkey and by them called a Diwan, with his wife and family. They made for the Port of Metellin where, being rather unsafe, the Admiral's ship became separated from the three guard ships by about a mile, owing to rough sea, the weather being very stormy. Captain Mehemet disembarked on the 18th July to take refreshment together with a troop of about sixty Turks, more or less. There were a hundred and fifty passengers with soldiers and officers. Among the Christian slaves was one Marco Jachimosky, a vassal of the King of Poland and a native of Baro. He was a man of good birth and trained in all military exercises before he was made prisoner by the Turks in their raid on Poland. Seeing that the Captain was ashore with many of the Turks, he recommended himself to God and resolved to gain liberty for himself and his companions and consulted, concerning the situation, with two others — Stephen Satanowsky and Stolcina — who with him were chained, each to the other but loosened from their seat in the rowlocks and free to walk about the ship. These two, thinking the venture could never be successful, tried to dissuade him. Briefly, he set to work (he was never without courage in the face of Divine Providence) talking over the project and making preparations. Destitute of arms he set about making a club from a log which he got from the ship's cook, who, having offered some resistance, was struck on the head, whereupon he fell dead. Then the daring Marco rolled himself towards the poop where there were plenty of arms stored and, when a renegade Greek soldier opposed him he felled him with a cutlass which he had picked up by the cook-stove, thereby killing the Greek. Marco then took command of the poop, distributed the weapons among his companions and, with irons, logs and anything they could lay hands on, they attacked their enemies. They then made for the prow where the boatswain was, who, being under an awning had not seen what happened and thought the noise to be only the usual noise among the slaves. Seeing Marco and the rest nearly upon him he seized two cutlasses, one in each hand, but he was not quick enough, for Marco struck him in the ribs with his cutlass and he fell dead into the sea. The Turks had cut the cords of the awning in order to overpower the slaves, the greater part of whom were now armed by Marco's orders, and threw the awning over all. The slaves fought without intermission and having killed killed the majority of the Turks and flinging the remainder into the sea, they then cut the ropes by which the anchors were fastened to the galley, they dipped oars into the water and got clear of the port under a cannonade from the city and from other vessels which were in port, but they escaped unharmed and the galley ran to open sea, the Turks shouting and tearing their beards. The Christians were then followed by the three guard ships from three o'clock in the afternoon, during the whole night and well on into the following day, when a most fearful state of weather overtook them, fog, wind and rain, which forced the Turks to go back to Metellin and let the Christians escape.

Liberated from the attack of the Pagans and after many adventures in the storm, they arrived, after fifteen days, at Messina, and the weather now being more favourable, they went on to Palermo without wasting many days. This was by order of the Viceroy of Sicily. Having attained their beloved liberty without losing even one Christian they took the irons off twenty-two Turks whom they had chained to the rowlocks and sent them away with a God-speed, doing the same with the Ramer Cadenna, wife of the Judge Ysuf, who was in Metellin, though they could have sold her for much money. In her service were four young Christian girl slaves, two were named Anna, and one Catherine and the other Margaret. Besides these there was another slave who was to have been sold at Constantinople — she was a Christian and very beautiful and graceful in the extreme. Her name also was Catherine.

The said noble and brave Marco, elected Captain by his companions, married her, and of the other four, three were married to the three chief companions.

Lastly, leaving the Galley to the Viceroy of Sicily, the now famous and valiant Marco, not wishing to accept the one thousand five hundred escudos which the Viceroy offered him, received a gift of a brig and also the loan of a carriage to take him to Rome where he went with the five ladies and thirty of his companions on the 25th August.

The next day, as a sign of his thanks to God for so great a benefit as also in gratitude to the Vicar of Christ, they placed at the feet of His Holiness the Royal Standard of the Flagship which was made of white silk, embroidered and richly worked with four half-moons and covered with Arabic letters. They also offered a brass lantern of Moorish design, covered with gold and wonderfully engraved. They hung in the churches many other flags — especially in the church of St. Stanislaus of the Poles, and at St. Susanna, with the condition that when the building of the church of St. Cayo, Pope and Martyr, should be completed it must be transferred thither.

And in St. Geronimo of Ripera they were liberally entertained by the kindness of Cardinal Barrino; all having made confession and received Holy Communion as a termination to so fortunate an affair.

PRAISE GOD.

Licensed in Barcelona: By Stephen Liberos
in Santo Domingo Street. 1628

APPENDIX IV

PIRACY AND THE LAW

UNTIL the fourteen century cases of piracy in England were tried before the civil courts, but after 1340 when King Edward III destroyed the French fleet at Sluys, and claimed to be "Sovereign of the Narrow Seas," Admiralty courts were instituted. These courts were authorised to try all cases of piracy or any other crime committed below the high water mark.

Later on King Henry VIII and Louis XII made a treaty by which both monarchs agreed to take measures to suppress piracy amongst their own subjects and along their own coasts.

In 1536 Henry VIII passed the first Act of Piracy, which brought into being a new type of official, the Vice-Admiral of the coast, who was to "proceed in matters of piracy . . . according to the order of the laws" although many of these vice-admirals, like some members of the Cornish family of Killigrew, were little better than pirates themselves.

The earliest Vice-Admiralty Court to be set up outside the realm was in Newfoundland in 1615, when one was sent out to try the innumerable cases of piracy and other crimes committed by the rough unruly sailors who went in thousands to fish off the banks each summer; but this was only to meet an emergency and was not a permanent court.

The second and most important Act of Piracy in English law was that of 1699, which authorised Courts of Admiralty to try cases of piracy in the colonies and plantations of North America and the West Indies.

By the 1699 Act, all persons arrested and charged with piracy in the colonies could be tried and, if found guilty, punished on the spot. This was a great improvement on the old system, by which accused persons, with the necessary witnesses, had to be sent home to England to stand their trial, a costly and tedious process which more often than not resulted in the accused being allowed to go scot free to save trouble and expense.

Amongst the more important clauses of the 1699 Act were the following:

> . . . especially of late years it hath been found by experience that persons committing piracies robberies and felonies on the Seas in or near the East and West Indies and in places very remote cannot be brought unto condign punishment without great trouble and charges in sending them into England to be tried . . . insomuch that many idle and profligate persons have been thereby encouraged to turn Pirate and betake themselves to that sort of wicked life trusting that they shall not . . . be questioned for such their piracies and robberies by reason of the great trouble and expense that will necessarily fall upon such as shall attempt to apprehend and persecute them. . .

It was ordered therefore that piracies committed where the admirals had jurisdiction should be tried by the nearest Court of Admiralty, and that any authorized servant of the state could apprehend and try a person who was alleged to have committed an act of piracy on any sea, river, creek etc.

In 1721 another Piracy Act was passed which greatly added to the scope of that of 1699.

Amongst other things it observed:

> Whereas the number of persons committing piracies upon the seas is of late much increased; and notwithstanding the laws already made . . . have turned pirate and betaken themselves to that wicked course of life whereby the trade and navigation into remote parts will greatly suffer. . .

There follows a list of the punishments for

> All commanders or masters of ship who shall trade with, by truck, barter or exchange, with any pirate . . . if found guilty such persons will be esteemed pirates.

Amongst other penalties those found guilty were to be denied the benefit of clergy.

To encourage sailors to resist attacks by pirates it was ordered that all seamen wounded while fighting against pirates were to be rewarded and admitted into Greenwich Hospital with right of preferment to any other seaman or mariner. But those who did not defend themselves against pirates were to forfeit their wages and undergo six months' imprisonment.

The 1721 Acts also ordained that:

> A master of a ship, or any other person who trades with any pirate or furnishes him with ammunition or provisions or stores, or who fits out a ship for so trading or who consults combines or corresponds with a pirate knowing him to be such is by state a pirate felon and robber.

Two other Acts were passed for the suppression of piracy, one in 1744 and the other in 1837.

The punishment for those convicted of piracy was death, and is so still, in cases where violence has been used; otherwise the condemned is liable to a maximum punishment of penal servitude for life or some less punishment.

The Privy Council in 1873 (in A. G. for Hong-Kong *v.* Kwok-a-Sing) approved the definition of Piracy given in Rex *v.* Dawson 1696, as:

> Piracy is only the sea term for robbery within the jurisdiction of the Admiralty. . . If the mariner of any ship shall violently dispossess the master and afterwards carry away the ship itself or any of the goods with a felonious intention in any place where the Lord Admiral hath jurisdiction this is robbery and piracy.

In 1824 an Act was passed which declared any British subject guilty of piracy "who upon the high seas . . . carries away any person as a slave . . ." The punishment was death, but the 1837 Act changed this to transportation for life. This Act included "all those who deal in slaves or fit out a slave-ship, lends money to fit one out, or one who acts as surgeon or supercargo to a slave-ship, or insures slaves."

The ensign of authority to arrest both ships and vessels by the High Court of Admiralty of England, was, and still is, a silver oar. This is carried by the Marshal of the High Court and placed upon the table in front of the Judge.

The origin of the silver oar is unknown, but is of great antiquity, and can be traced to the early Tudor period. The most ancient existing silver oar is that of the Cinque Ports. The one belonging to the Duchy of Cornwall formerly belonged to Dartmouth, for the jurisdiction "of the water of Dartmouth" and most of the important sea-port towns in England had their silver oar.

Other places in the British Empire have their silver oars, such as Bermuda, Cape Town and Sydney. The one belonging to Ireland was stolen from the Marshal's Deputy in 1842 when he was executing his office in the West of Ireland and has never been recovered.

At all executions of pirates the procession to the gallows was headed by the Marshal, who walked or rode, with the silver oar over his shoulder.

APPENDIX V

THE LOG OF EDWARD BARLOW *

BARLOW sailed for England as chief mate of the *Septer* East Indiaman, but on the voyage the captain died and the command was taken by Barlow.

Aug. 15, 1697.

Being got past the small Bab Island † in the morning betimes we espid a ship more than our Compeney, all most gotten into the midell of oure fleet, for being a littell parted there was a vahensey in the midell that a ship might pass all most out of shot reach of any of oure fleet. He showed no colers but comjoging on with his courses hald up under two topsails, having more sails furled than usely shipes carrey, namely a mizon top galonsail and a spritsail topgalonsail, which made us jug (judge) presently what he was; he coming prety nere us but scarse within shot we perseved what like ship hee was, a prety frigat built ship, as we understood after ward built at Dedford called The Adventur Galley, she carrying about 28 or 30 gunns, having on her lower gunn deck a teire of ports for owers (oars) to rowe withall in calm wether; she showing noe colers nether had but only a Reed (red) broad pendent out without any Cros on it.

And thinking he might tak us for one of the Moores ships, having our shipp in a redeyness, we were willing to let him com as nere to us as he would, for the Duck Convoy was a long way astarne and we had very littell wind and he could not com nere us, but seeing the pirat as nere as hee intended to com, being all most a brest of us we presently huisted our Colers and let fly two or three gunns at him well shotted and presently got both our boats a head, having very litell wind, towing towards him. Hee having fired fore or five times at on of the Mores shipes, striking him in the hull and throu his sailes. But hee seeing us make what we could towards him presently mad what saile hee could from us, geting out his orres and rowing and sailing, we firing what we could at him, our men shoating which I believe hee heared and jug he tuck us for one of the Kings Shipes. We fired at him as long as hee was anything here and jug did hit him with som of our shot.

But he sailed far beter than we did, and being got out of shot of us, he

* Extracted from the original log-book of Edward Barlow, the property of Dr. Basil Lubbock.

† In the Red Sea.

touk in his owres and his small saile haling up his lower sailes in the Brales staying for us.

But having no wind to ingage, as we drue nere him, mad sail againe from us, doing so twis: and seeing us still folow him, at last set all his sails and away he went.

Som of the Mores ships having a great deal of money on bord, and sartainly the Fleet being a litell parted, had not our ship hapned to have been in ther company hee had sartanly plundred all the headmost shipes of all welth which he might very well have don and the Duch ship could not have helpen them being a heeifey sailor and littel or no wind, which proved to be a good sarveis don for the Compeney's (East India Company) intreast at Surrat, for had any of the ships miskried (? miscarried or been massacred) or robed (robbed) by the pirates, all the Eingles (English) would have beene confined againe at Surrat close prisoners. The pirat being frustrated in his desins and then seeing a good convoy along with the Mores ships, mad saile for the coast of India.

The Mores shipes seming verey thank full for being secured at that time from ye pirrat, whose comander being called William Kid, as we heard after.

And the next morning, being the 16 of August he was gon out of our sight.

After this exciting affair the *Septer* put into Karwar where they heard more news of Kidd and how that the

pirat had bene there in the Bay demanding wood and water, and that he had taken a Country Boat belonging to Bumbay with one or two English men in her, the rest Blacks: having taken all that was fit for his use out of her with all there money which was about three or four hundred rupes, and was gon further downe upon the coast, and that two or three of his men had left him, one of them a Jew which the Compeney Kech (Ketch) had carried to Bumbay.

At Calicut Edward Barlow heard that Kidd had already called there:

And sent ashore to demand wood and water and told Mr. Penning the Cheef there, that he was sent out by the King of England and had his comishon to tack pirates or French. But hee turned pirat him self. He had got a comishon with the Kings hand to it, how hee cum by it is best known to them that proquired it for him and he was desired to dwo mischeif and nogood with it. But the Cheif would not send him aney thing abord, taking him to be no other than what he was: yet Kid could send him word ashore that for deniiing him that small Request he would make it knowne at Whithalle when he arived in England.

APPENDIX VI

A DISCOURS ABOUT PYRATES, WITH PROPER REMEDIES TO SUPPRESS THEM

ABOUT 20 Years ago, King Charles the Second was pleased to send me to New England to Enquire into their Trade & Commerce. I observed that they fitted out Vessells of 60 or 70 Tuns a peece, very well mand whom they calld privateers, & Sent them without Comission to the Spanish West Indies, where they comitted all Acts of violence upon the Inhabitants, & brought home great quantities of Silver in Coins & Bullion, with Rich Copes, Church plate & other Riches, insomuch that the Spanish Embassadour complaind therof to his Majesty & It was at last agreed upon that his Majesty Should fit out 5 or 7 ffrigotts — well mand, but the whole charge to be defrayd by the King of Spain with intent to take & destroy the pyrates. The Execution wherof was comitted to Sir Robert Holmes, who had power by himself or his deputies, to procure Pardons (a duplicate wherof is anexd) to all such who came in upon his Majesties Proclamation (then issued) and gave Sufficient Security for their living peaceably &c. But the King of Spain not making good his payments, that designe faild. I have heard of no Pyracies done these Severall Years in those places for the Pyrates have found out, a more profitable & less hazardous Voyage to the Red Sea, where they take from the Moors all they have, without Resistance, & bring it to Some one of the Plantations on the Continent of America or Islands adjacent where they are received & harbourd and from whence allso they fit out their Vessells to the Same Place.

Upon my last Arrivall in England, I represented to the Courts of his Majesties Customs (among other things) that the Govrs. of Plantations, permitting pyrates of all Nations to be Masters & Owners of all Vessells, was a great Encouragement to the Illegall Trade, and then I proposed as one Remedy, that no privateer be admitted by the Govr. to Injoy any Liberty or priviledge in the Plantations, unless he have given Sufficient Surety, (not less than £1,000) to be taken & aprovd of by Such person as his Majesty shall pleas to apoint &c.

The chief places where Pyrates Resort & are Harbourd, are, as follows: *Bahama Islands:* About 8 Years ago, John Hoadley, Master of a Vessell of 32 Guns, came to the Island of Providence from the Coast of Brazeel, having a great quantity of Sugar aboard, and after some time, burnt her in the Harbour. The Year before Thomas Wooley & Christopher

Gosse of New England, brought in a Dutch East India Ship, of 40 Guns, from the East Indies. Shee had abundance of all Sorts of coine aboard. They shard the money, burnt the Ship, att Andrew Island, having a great quantity of peper aboard.

South Carolina: Besides severall other Vessells which have com thither from the Spanish West Indies, 5 Years ago, a Vessell of Jamaica, came thither from the Red Sea, with 70 men, who Shard about £1000, apeece, in Gold & Silver coine, The Vessell was forfeited to the Proprietors as a Wreck. She was bought by som merchants and coming to Virginia was Seizd, but acquitted by the Jury.

Pensilvania: Severall of those pyrates which came to South Carolina, came from thence to the Horkill & other places in Pensilvania, and were, upon an acknowledgement of the Govrs. favour, permitted to settle & Trade there. A Sloop of ten Guns was lanchd there, being built for the Trade to the Red Sea. Severall pyrates were concernd in her, I Saw her upon the Stocks. About 4 Years ago, one Cross came in with a Spanish Vessell of about 24 Guns & 70 men, to the Horkill to Victuall, he had apprehension that the ffrigott in Virginia would Seize him, and went from thence to Bermudos, where he Stayd for his provisions, which were bought at Philadelphia & Sent after him.

Road Island: Has bin many Years, and still is the Chiefe Refuge for Pyrates. In Aprill 1694 Thomas Tew, in his Sloop from the Red Sea, brought in £100000 in Gold & Silver and a good parcell of Elephants Teeth, bought up by the Merchants of Boston. Hee Shard about £12000 for his Sloop & himself. Hee soon after went out to the Red Sea, and upon such Great Encouragement, three other Vessells were fitted out to Joyne with him. they were all expected to return this last Spring to some of the aforesd places. 'tis Suposd Tew will go to the Bahama Islands.

Boston, in N. England: There is every Year one or more Vessells fitted to the Red Sea, under pretence of going to the West India plantations. Sir William Phipps, the late Govr. Invited the privateers to come from Pensilvania to Boston, assuring them their liberty to Trade. Tew had £2000 in the hands one Merchant in Boston, Others have mony in Road Island, & Some of the Govrs. have Enrichd themselves by the Pyrates.

For Suppressing these Pyrates, and the Preventing the like Mischiefs for the future, 'tis humbly proposd—

1. That no person be made Govr. in any of the Proprieties, untill he be first Aprovd of by his Majesties Order in Councill, as by the Act for preventing ffrauds, and Regulating abuses in the Plantation Trade, It is Enacted.

2. That his Majesty be pleased to send a first Rate ffrigott under the Comand of a sober person, well aquainted with the Bahama Islands & other places, where the Pyrates usually resort, with a Comission to Grant pardons to all such, who will give Security to settle quietly in the Plantations. That his Majesty pleas to grant a Pardon to one of Tews

men, now in England, who can make great discoveries of all the Intreagues of the Pyrates. If this Undertaking be done with speed and privacy, I don't question but many of the Pyrates will be suprisd at the Bahama Islands & South Carolina. They will not venture themselves amongst the Spaniards nor the French, this Warr time.

3. That all Encouragement be given, to discover what mony or Jewells has at any time bin given to any of the Govrs. or their Confidents, in the Plantations, either by Pyrates or by their Agents, and that all such Money be forfeited to his Majesty, and the Govrs. proceeded against according to their Demerit, and that all persons, having in their possessions any Mony or other Estate, belonging to any Pyrate, discovering the Same, to have a Compensation for it, but upon their neglecting to do so, upon proofs made therof, that They allso be proceeded against, as abettors & Comforters of Pyrates.

All which is humbly Subscribed
by

[1696] E. RANDOLPH.

APPENDIX VII

MODERN CHINESE PIRATES

Extract from the *Times*, December 12th, 1929:

Staging a piracy on the China coast is not unlike the preliminaries of certain forms of company promoting. Capital is needed and is generally forthcoming. There is much bargaining and negotiating behind closed doors, and though prospectuses and lists of directors and share-holders are not published, they exist. When the necessary capital has been found, a capable managing director is appointed. To recruit a reliable gang, select a likely victim, gather the essential information, carry through the enterprise and plan a retreat with spoil and prisoners, requires no ordinary ability.

When the victim has been selected the chief and his principal subordinates make several preliminary voyages to learn the ship's geography, her routine, and the qualities of her officers. In consequence, Chinese frequenters of any vessel are at once suspected, but the saloon passenger of one voyage is a deck hand a month later, and is hard to identify. When the preliminary survey has been completed, the whole gang goes on board, some in the saloon, the majority in the steerage and one or two among the crew. They are not slinking, cowardly ruffians, but men who know their job and usually try to do it efficiently and humanely — provided that humanity is compatible with efficiency.

Their first task is to get arms and ammunition on board. At Shanghai, Hong-Kong and Singapore, Chinese passengers and their baggage are overhauled by the water police, but when over a thousand Chinese are swarming in a thick line up the gangway a search is difficult, and at ports such as Amoy, Foochow and Swatow precautions are of a desultory nature, giving the pirates the chance they need. But at a word from some passenger or seaman that "plenty piecee bad men com ship side," the anti-piracy grilles are locked, the guards become alert, and officers carry loaded revolvers at their waists. Guards are always carried — about four Sikhs or Annamites — on board ships in the South Chinese passenger trade. The grilles consist of stout iron bar doors shutting off the promenade deck and the bridge.

HOW THE PIRATES WORK

Imagine the scene at sundown on board one of these coasters wallowing in the heavy swell of the south-east monsoon. The holds forward and aft have been turned into whitewashed dormitories, where a huddled mass of humanity, men, women and children, bivouac on mats and bundles with the close economy of a Chinese crowd. Some are preparing chow, others are washing clothes, or squatting in groups gambling. Under the boats and on the beams are sleeping figures, half naked if the night is fine and warm. Amidships, on the raised promenade deck, there are a few saloon passengers, English and Chinese, the officers' quarters and the bridge. At dinner time, when the officers off duty and all the passengers are seated unarmed at the saloon tables, a signal is given — once it was the lighting of a cigarette — a sharp "Hands up!" is called, the startled diners find themselves staring down the muzzles of automatics held by coolies, merchants and seamen.

Weapons are demanded, every one is seized, searched and locked up either in the cabins or in the saloons; armed piratical guards are set who make it clear that death is the penalty of resistance. On the bridge, in the guards' quarters, in the wireless room, and on the engine room starting platform, the same story is told: a sudden order, a pistol and inevitable surrender. Then the polite instruction: "You will steer for Bias Bay, getting there at 7 A.M. No one will be hurt — unless you attempt to retake the ship." Routine will go on as usual, watches being relieved as if nothing were wrong. Meanwhile the cargo is ransacked and every jewel and valuable garment stripped off the terrified passengers.

Navigation and cabin lights are put out, and in complete darkness the ship sets course for Bias Bay, a place of sinister significance on the China coast. It is a big sheet of shallow water landlocked by the sandy scrub-covered hills of that part. There are a few Chinese villages, a few sampans fishing, a suggestion of peace, seclusion and beauty. But, as the pirated ship drops anchor, swarms of sampans push off from the shore; their crews hail the pirates with grim impassivity, and these weatherbeaten, tattered men of the coast set to with a will in the task of stripping the ship. Even chronometers, sextants and brass fittings are often taken. There are piteous scenes when families are divided, a father or mother being roughly urged at pistol point into a sampan to be carried off to the mountains, perhaps to be rescued, more probably to die of hunger and exposure during the endless haggling between intermediaries over the ransom. The distressed ship steams painfully back to Hong-Kong where the police take charge, inventories of the robbery are made, and public interest slowly fades.

AN AMAZING FIGHT

But it is not every piracy that works smoothly. Often the Indian guard on duty is shot dead by a treacherous volley, and when the Norwegian coaster *Solviken* was captured the master, Captain Jastoff, was murdered because he did not immediately open his cabin door. In another big piracy, that of the *Anking*, a volley at close range cleared the bridge, killing the chief officer and quartermaster and severely wounding the captain. The chief engineer was murdered from behind, while sitting in a deck chair, and the second officer was knocked on the head. The pirates were particularly careful of him, however, because they needed some one who could navigate the ship.

The *San Nam Hoi* piracy is also memorable. About 30 pirates rushed the ship when it was only 15 minutes out of the little West River port of Pekhai. A volley accounted for the Indian guard, and his comrades off duty were at once overpowered. The officer on watch, Mr. Hugh Conway, dashed down the bridge deck, but fell mortally wounded. Mr. Houghton, the chief engineer, had in the meantime braved a shower of bullets in closing the stout grille on the port side of the bridge deck. He had his revolver and was able to cover the starboard side of the deck until the master, Captain W. H. Sparke, had joined him on the bridge. The starboard grille was open and desperate measures were taken to close it. With an automatic in each hand, Captain Sparke squarely faced the pirates, and under cover of his fire, Mr. Houghton ran quickly aft and slammed the grille in their faces. An amazing fight followed, Captain Sparke dodging from side to side to fire at the ugly faces aft, and between whiles he had to navigate the ship, for at the first sound of danger the pilot and quartermaster had bolted and hidden themselves with the crew. At this stage of the battle, ammunition being short, Mr. Houghton, a less certain shot than the master, acted as loader and look-out.

The pirates were an amateur lot, several being members of a semi-Bolshevised crew sacked some weeks before for insubordination. A simple ruse finished their ebbing spirits. Captain Sparke suddenly blew four blasts on his siren and altered course. The pirates, thinking that a gunboat was sighted, jumped over by the stern. Captain Sparke put his ship about, and with his gallant engineer opened fire on the swimming heads. The noise having attracted the militia of a nearby village, some fifteen of the gang were captured and sent in chains to Canton, where they suffered the usual fate of pirates.

The first real blow to piracy on the China coast was a patrol of Bias Bay by British submarines. A darkened ship was seen to approach one evening in October 1927, and she failed to answer signals. A shot across her bows was followed by another into her engine room and the ship started to sink. It proved to be the Chinese-owned vessel *Irene*, packed with steerage passengers. The submarine took off 226 passengers and captured seven pirates who were hanged in Hong-Kong gaol. There was some bother with the Chinese authorities and the ship's owners, but the Admiralty stood squarely behind the captain of the *L4*, and commended his resource and excellent seamanship. Then Marshal Li Chaisum, the able and enterprising Kwangtung Dictator, took the matter in hand. A military post with wireless was built and a gunboat placed on patrol.

But piracy is not a paying game; the initial expenses are heavy and the returns uncertain. The *Sunning* and *Irene* piracies were failures, and the returns from the others were disappointing. The looting of the *San Nam Hoi* produced $10,000; out of the *Hsin Wah* they got $25,000; out of the *Tean* only $7,000. The *Hsin Chi* and the *Ankling* were good hauls, each being worth about $100,000, but there can have been very little profit in the others.

BIBLIOGRAPHY

PUBLISHED WORKS

L. J. A.: Memoria contra os Piratas Chinezes. Rio de Janeiro 1828.

Alexander VI, Pope: Bulla in Cena Domini. (Pronouncement of Excommunication on heretics and Pirates.) Rome 1499.

Algiers: A Bloody Fight between the *Sapphire* and the *Half Moon* of Algier. 1681.

———: The late Bloody Engagement between the *Adventure* and the *Two Lions and Crown* of Algier. 1681.

———: True and Perfect Relation of the Engagement between H.M.S. *King's Fisher* and the *Golden Rose* of Argiers. N.D.

———: A Relation of the whole proceedings concerning the Redemption of Captives in Algier and Tunis. London 1647.

———: The Case of many hundreds of Poor English Captives in Algier, together with some Remedies. N.D.

Allen, G. W.: Our Navy and the West Indian Pirates. Essex Institute, Salem, Mass. 1929.

Andrada, J. I.: Memoria dos Piratas da China. Lisboa 1824.

Angriar: Authentick and Faithful History of that Arch-Pyrate Tulagee Angria. London 1756.

Avery: The King of Pirates, Captain Avery, Mock King of Madagascar. In two letters. London 1720.

Baring-Gould, S.: Cornish Characters and Strange Events. London 1909.

———: Devonshire Characters and Strange Events. London 1908.

Besson, M.: Les Freres de la Coste. Paris 1928.

Biddulph, J.: The Pirates of Malabar. London 1907.

Bordini, J. F.: De Rebus Præclare Gestis a Sixto. v. Pon. Max. Rome 1588.

Bowen, F. C.: The Sea, its history and romance. London N.D.

Bradlee, F. B. C.: Piracy in the West Indies and its Suppression. Essex Institute. Salem. Mass. 1923.

Brantome, P. deB.: Hommes illustres. Œuvres. Paris 1822.

British Annual Register. 1772.

Burney, J.: History of the Buccaneers of America. London 1816.

Butcher and Lang: Odyssey of Homer. 1897.

Butler, N.: Boteler's Dialogues. Navy Records Society 1929.

Calendar of State Papers: Colonial Series.

Calendar of Home Office Papers: 1760–1765. 1878.
Campbell, Lord J.: Lives of the Chief Justices of England. London 1849.
Case-Horton, C.: A Brace of British Pirates. Journal of the R.U.S.I. Vol. LX. 1915.
Chapin, H. M.: Privateer Ships and Sailors. 1625–1725. Toulon 1926.
Chatterton, E. K.: Seamen All. 1924.
———: Romance of Piracy. London 1914.
———: Sailing Ships and their Story. London 1909.
Colvin, I. D.: The Germans in England. London 1915.
Complete History of Europe for 1707. London 1708.
Corbett, J. S.: England in the Mediterranean. 1603–1713. London 1904.
Cotton, R. W.: Expedition against pirates. (1612) Devon Association. 1886.
Cries of Blood: London 1767.
Crump, H.: Colonial Admiralty Jurisdiction in the 17th Century. London 1932.
Dan, Père F.: Histoire de Barbarie et de ses Corsaires. Paris 1637.
Dampier, W.: A New Voyage round the World. London 1729.
Dictionary of National Biography. London 1917.
Dow and Edwards: Pirates of the New England Coast. 1630–1730. Marine Research Society. Salem. Mass. 1924.
Downing, C.: History of the Indian Wars, with an Account of Angria the Pyrate. London 1737.
———: Edited with an introduction and notes by W. Foster. C.I.E. 1924.
Drake, S. A.: Nooks and Corners of the New England Coast. New York 1875.
Drury, R.: Madagascar: or, Robert Drury's Journal, during fifteen years Captivity on that Island. London 1729.
Dunton, J.: A True Journall of the Sally Fleet. London 1637.
(Ellms, C.): Pirates Own Book. Portland U.S.A. 1844.
Encyclopædia Britannica. 14th Edition 1929.
Esquemeling, J.: Bucaniers of America. London 1684.
Fanning. E.: Voyages and Discoveries in the South Seas. 1792–1832. Marine Research Society. Salem. Mass. 1924.
Faye, Père J. de la.: Voiage pour la redemption des Captifs de Maroc et D'Alger. Paris 1726.
Firth, C. H.: Naval Songs and Ballads. Navy Records Society. 1908.
Forster, J.: Life of Sir John Eliot. London 1864.
Fugger: News Letters. 1924. 1926.
Fontana, F.: I Pregi Della Toscana. Florence 1701.
General Treatise on Naval Trade and Commerce. London 1739.
Gibbon, E.: Decline and Fall of the Roman Empire. London 1846.
Gibbs, C.: Confession of the Pirate Charles Gibbs. New York 1831.
Gosse, P.: Sir John Hawkins. London 1930.

——: Pirates' Who's Who. London 1924.
Grammont, H.: Histoire d'Alger. 1887.
Hacke, W.: A Collection of Original Voyages. London 1699.
Hædo, D.: Topographia e Historia General de Argel. Valladolid 1612.
Hakluyt, R., Voyages and Discoveries. Glasgow 1903.
Hannay, D.: Short History of the Royal Navy. 1217–1688. London 1898.
——: Ships and Men. London 1910.
——: Sea Trader. London 1912.
Haring, C. H.: Buccaneers in the West Indies in the 17th Century. London 1910.
Hart, F. R.: Admirals of the Caribbean. London 1923.
Hay, J. D.: Suppression of Piracy in the China Sea. 1849. London 1889.
Holland, C.: From the North Foreland to Penzance. London 1908.
Hurd, A.: Reign of the Pirates. London 1925.
Innes, A. D.: Maritime and Colonial Expansion of England under the Stuarts. London 1932.
Jameson, J. F.: Privateering and Piracy in the Colonial Period. New York 1923.
Johnson, C.: A General History of the Pyrates. London 1724.
Journal of the Historical Association.
Keary, C. F.: Vikings in Western Christendom. London 1891.
Kendall, C. W.: Private Men-of-War. London 1931.
Keppel, H.: Expedition to Borneo. London 1846.
——: A Visit to the Indian Archipelago. London 1853.
Kidd: Full Account of the Actions of the late Famous Pyrate Capt. Kidd, by a Person of Quality. Dublin 1701.
Kingsford, C. L.: Beginnings of English Maritime Enterprise. "History" Vol. XIII. 1928.
Labat, Père: Nouveau Voyage aux Isles de L'Amérique. Paris 1743.
——: The Memoirs of Père Labat. 1693–1705. Translated and abridged by John Eaden. London 1931.
Lane-Poole, S.: The Barbary Corsairs. London 1890.
(Leslie, C.): New History of Jamaica. London 1740.
Lithgow, W.: Rare Adventures and painfull Peregrinations. London 1632.
Lives of the most Notorious Pirates. By an old seaman. (The Miniature Library) London N.D.
Lubbock, B.: The Blackwall Frigates. Glasgow 1922.
——: Bully Hayes, South Sea Pirate. London 1931.
Lurting, T.: The Fighting Sailor turned Peaceable Christian. (1709) Leeds 1816.
MacFarlane, C.: Lives and Exploits of Banditti and Robbers. London 1833.
Mariners Mirror: Journal of the Society for Nautical Research.

Malefactors' Register, or, the Newgate and Tyburn Calendar. London 1778.
Malzac, J.: Case of the Brig Carraboo. Saint Christopher 1828.
Manwaring, G. E.: Bibliography of British Naval History. London 1930.
———: Life and Works of Sir H. Mainwaring. Navy Records Society. 1920.
Mathew, D.: Cornish and Welsh Pirates in the Reign of Elizabeth. English Historical Review. Vol. XXXIX. 1924.
Miles, S. B.: Countries and Tribes of the Persian Gulf. London 1919.
Mireur, M.: Ligue des Ports de Provence, contre les Pirates Barbaresques. 1585–1586. N.D.
Monson, Sir W.: Naval Tracts. London 1703.
Moresby, J.: Discoveries in New Guinea. London 1876.
Moss, F. J.: Through Atolls and the Islands of the great South Sea. London 1889.
Morgan, J.: Complete History of Algiers. London 1731.
Moule, H. J.: Descriptive catalogue of the Charter, Minute Books and other documents of the Borough of Weymouth and Melcombe Regis. 1252–1800. Weymouth 1883.
Narbrough, Sir John: Narrative of the Burning of Tripoli. London 1676.
Neumann, C. F.: The History of the Pirates who infested the China Sea from 1807 to 1810. Translated from the Chinese by C. F. Neumann. London 1831.
Newgate, Ordinary of: London 1738.
Newgate Calendar or, Malefactors' Bloody Register. London N.D.
Nicholl, J.: Some Account of the Worshipful Company of Ironmongers. London 1866.
Nicollière-Teijeiro, S. de la: La Course et les Corsaires du Port de Nantes. Paris 1896.
Olan, E.: Sjörövarna på Medelhavet och Levantiska Compagniet. Stockholm 1921.
Okeley, W.: Ebenezer, or, a small Monument of Great Mercy. London 1675.
Oppenheim, M.: History of the Administration of the Royal Navy. London 1894.
Oriental Pirates: United Service Journal. Vol. 82. 1835.
Ormerod, H. A.: Piracy in the Ancient World. Liverpool 1924.
Paine, R. D.: The Ships and Sailors of Old Salem. Boston 1923.
Paske-Smith, M.: Western Barbarians in Japan and Formosa. Kobe 1930.
Pérez-Cabrero, A.: Ibiza. Barcelona 1909.
Playfair, R. L.: The Scourge of Christendom. London 1884.
Pinto, F. M.: The Voyages and Adventures of Ferdinand Mendez Pinto, the Portuguese. London 1891.

Pointis, De: Relation de Cartagene. Bruxells 1698.
Powell, D.: Bristol Privateers and Ships of War. Bristol 1930.
Prowse, D. W.: History of Newfoundland. London 1896.
Purchas, S.: Purchas his Pilgrimes. Glasgow 1905.
Raleigh, Walter: English Voyages in the 16th Century. Glasgow 1910.
Renegade's Career, A: Colburns' United Service Magazine. 1868.
Roberts, G.: Social History of the People of the Southern Counties of England. London 1856.
Rutter, O.: The Pirate Wind. London 1930.
St. John, H. C.: Notes and Sketches from the Wild Coasts of Nipon. London 1880.
Sanders, E. K.: Vincent de Paul. London 1913.
Santa Cruz. M. de: Relacion de la presa de la Galera de Alexandria. Rome 1628.
Scott, B.: Suppression of Piracy in the Chinese Seas. Gillingham, Kent. 1851.
Senior, W.: Naval History in the Law Courts. London 1927.
Seitz, Don C.: Under the Black Flag. London N.D.
Sestier, J. M.: Piraterie dans l'antiquité. Paris 1880.
Sharp, Capt. B.: The Voyages and adventures of Capt. Bartt. Sharp, and others, in the South Sea: being a journal of the same. Also Capt. Van Horn with his Buccanieres surprizing of la Vera Cruz. etc. etc. London 1684.
Shepard, A.: Sea Power in Ancient History. London 1925.
Sirr, H. C.: China and the Chinese. London 1849.
Smith, A.: The Atrocities of the Pirates. London 1824.
Smith, Capt. J.: The True Travels and Adventures of Captaine John Smith. Edited by Edward Arber. Birmingham 1884.
Snelgrave, W.: Account of Guinea and the Slave Trade. London 1734.
Spragge, Sir E.: A true and perfect relation of the happy Success and Victory obtained against the Turks of Argiers at Bugia, under the command of Sir Edward Spragge. London 1671.
Tassy, L. de: History of the Piratical States of Barbary. London 1750.
Tedder, A. W.: Navy of the Restoration. Cambridge 1916.
Teonge, H.: The Diary of Henry Teonge. Edited by G. E. Manwaring. London 1927.
Twiss, T.: Jurisdiction of the Silver Oar of the Admiralty. Nautical Magazine. Vol. XLVI. 1877.
Veale, Capt. R.: Barbarian Cruelty. Exeter 1787.
Verney Papers. London 1853.
Verrill, A. Hyatt: In the Wake of the Buccaneers. New York 1923.
———: The Real Story of the Pirates. New York 1923.
Vryman L. C.: Iets Uit de Geschiedenis van den Zeeroof en van de Vrybuiters in de Lage Landen. Ons Zeewezen 1930.
Wafer, L.: A New Voyage and Description of the Isthmus of America. London 1699.

Williams, G.: The Liverpool Privateers. Liverpool 1897.
Wilson, T. W.: Piratical Descents upon Cuba. Havana 1851.
Williamson, J. A.: Maritime Enterprise. London 1913.
———: John Hawkins. London 1927.

MANUSCRIPTS

In the possession of the author

Charles V.: Contemporary Spanish Manuscript, containing dispatch from Emperor Charles V. to the Duke of Calabria respecting his defeat of Barbarossa the pirate, at La Goletta. Tunis 24th July 1535.
Munster: Interrogations as to the Pirates of Munster. *c.* 1625.
Cox, John: His Travills Over the land into ye South Seas from thence Round ye South Parte of America to Borbados and Antigoo. *c.* 1682.
Lynch: Letter from Sir Thos. Lynch to M[r] Secretary Jenekins. 1682.
———: Letter from Sir Thomas Lynch to the Earle Sunderland. 1683.
Carlile: Journal of Capt. Charles Carlile in H.M.S. *Francis*. 1683.
———: Relation of Capt. Carlile's burning ye Trompense and other Pyratts. 1683.
Holmes: Docquet of grant to Sir Robert Holmes of all merchandizes taken by him out of pirate ships in America. 1687.
Randolph, E.: A discours about Pyrates, with proper Remedies to Suppress them. 1695.
Barbary: List of Sufring Captives in Barbary. 1697.
Persia: Memoranda connected with the Expedition against piratical tribes of the Persian Gulf. 1818.

INDEX

A

B

D

I

J

M

N

O

P

Q

R

S

X

Y